A HOME OF
THEIR OWN

A HOME OF
THEIR OWN

THE HEART-WARMING 150-YEAR HISTORY
OF BATTERSEA DOGS & CATS HOME

GARRY JENKINS

BANTAM PRESS

LONDON · TORONTO · SYDNEY · AUCKLAND · JOHANNESBURG

I cannot understand that morality which excludes
animals from human sympathy, or releases man from
the debt and obligation he owes to them.

SIR JOHN BOWRING

He prayeth best, who loveth best
All creatures great and small;
For the Great God who loveth us,
He made and loves them all.

COLERIDGE

THE DOG
With eye upraised, his master's look to scan,
The joy, the solace, and the aid of man;
The rich man's guardian, and the poor man's friend,
The only creature faithful to the end.

BYRON

*From the title page of the Annual Report of the
Temporary Home for Lost and Starving Dogs, 1865*

CONTENTS

FOREWORD

As Battersea Dogs & Cats Home marks its 150th anniversary in 2010, it is fitting that the Home's history should be acknowledged. *A Home of Their Own* charts that long, and at times challenging, journey, and in so doing it offers a fascinating snapshot of how society's approach to the care and welfare of domestic animals has changed at key times over this 150-year period.

Battersea Dogs & Cats Home would not be here today were it not for the courage and resilience of its founder. Mary Tealby was clearly a remarkable woman of her time who pricked the conscience and challenged the values of Victorian society in its fundamental approach to animal welfare. But she does not stand alone; over the years there have been other champions of Battersea's creed never to turn away a dog or cat in need of care – a claim still proudly made to this day. The book acknowledges some of those unsung heroes, past and present.

Today, the Home bears no physical similarity to the disused stable yard in Holloway where Mary Tealby first set up her Temporary Home for Lost and Starving Dogs. Battersea Dogs & Cats Home is one of Britain's leading animal welfare charities; across three sites in London and the Home Counties over twelve thousand dogs and cats are cared for every year by teams of trained staff and dedicated volunteers.

Regrettably, what does remain the same is that there are still, and possibly always will be, far too many stray or unwanted animals in need of Battersea's care. Fortunately many animal lovers continue to come to Battersea to find their perfect pet. I was able to do so myself and could not have wished for a better companion than my black Labrador, Shadow.

As a result of this care, and with the continued generosity of supporters through donations, legacies and gifts, the work of Battersea Dogs & Cats Home will continue to go from strength to strength and, for many dogs and cats, *a home of their own* becomes a reality.

HRH Prince Michael of Kent
President, Battersea Dogs & Cats Home

PROLOGUE

THE WINTER OF 1860 WAS ONE OF THE COLDEST in decades, reviving memories of the infamous freeze of 1814 when Britain had seen snow right up until Midsummer's Day and "ice was discovered in certain quarters six inches thick". In London, in particular, the bitter winds and deep frosts made life even less tolerable than usual for the capital's one million poor and homeless. In December 1860, the city's poorhouses were almost overwhelmed. "The cry of distress seemed so great 95,237 persons were in the receipt of relief," the *Morning Post* reported, adding that the conditions London's less fortunate citizens now lived in were "a national disgrace".

Not all of the metropolis's lost souls were enduring such severe hardships, however. That month, the London correspondent of the *Belfast News-Letter* braved the biting cold to travel to Hollingsworth Street, off St James's Road in Holloway, home to the capital's newest – and most novel – refuge. Finding it, tucked away in a mews off the side street, was something of a challenge. The reporter had to rely on an "urchin" who pointed him to "an open space where I found a building, half workshop, half stable, with a painted board on which was inscribed in large letters 'Home for Lost and Starving Dogs.'"

The reporter had penned a sympathetic piece when the "Home" had opened just a few weeks earlier. "There cannot certainly be any lady who has ever had a pet dog or who has observed the faithful, affectionate and devoted nature of the creature that would willingly allow one of the species to suffer death by starvation if the means of prevention were in her power," he had written in support.

His first impressions of the venture were positive. Arriving at the Home, the visitor was greeted by its keeper, James Pavitt, "a decent looking man with wooden shoes", who was "engaged in washing a cab". Pavitt ushered him in from the cold and led him "into a long coach-house, neatly tiled, with a bright coke fire burning in a stove at the upper end".

Pavitt's fondness for dogs was immediately apparent:

The only occupants of this apartment were a large black and white yard dog that looked as if he could have dined with pleasure off the calves of my legs (and indeed made several attempts to do so), a butcher's dog of very unprepossessing appearance (having one black eye and no tail), and a wiry Scotch terrier that threw himself into such exaggerated manifestations of satisfaction at his keeper's presence that I imagined he would have wagged his hinder parts clean off.

The Home's population of canine foundlings was housed in an adjoining apartment. "Here I found about forty unhappy little dogs, all of the class termed 'street curs'. They yelped and roared and pushed their noses through the bars of their cages as if a visit from a stranger was quite an event in their lives," the reporter wrote.

The layout was simple yet comfortable. "The room was divided into four square compartments, with a passage running the whole length of the building. Around two sides of each compartment was what in the East would be called a divan, covered with straw, while the beds of the dogs were underneath," the man from the *Belfast News-Letter* continued.

Despite the simplicity of the accommodation, the visitor was impressed by the standards of hygiene and organization. A money box was "nailed to the walls with 'donations for this charity' inscribed in letters of gold". There was also a list of "rules and regulations for the conduct of the establishment", written by "Rev Mr Yates". It was not the only error the reporter made in describing the Home's founders.

He was, understandably, intrigued by the local woman "Mrs Tealby" who had inspired the Home's foundation and had hoped to meet her, not least because he had "heard some curious anecdotes respecting this lady". Like everyone else, it seems, he believed she was "a widow lady of independence". He was also led to believe that the Home was funded by "the private resources of the founder". There was no sign of her at the Home that day.

James Pavitt failed to shine any revealing light on his enigmatic employer. Instead he enthused about the "wonderful number of applications for lost dogs" he was getting. There had been "fifteen ladies and gents … inquiring after them that very day". His job was to care for the dogs and oversee their rehoming; how they got to the Home was another matter. "Can't say as how they finds their own way – leastwise I never seen 'em," he said. "Parties as feels for the critters takes 'em to Mrs Tealby's, and leaves 'em at her door," he explained.

Pavitt was clearly as resourceful as he was protective of his employer. As the reporter's visit drew to a close, the keeper tried to persuade him to take a "savage mastiff" for "half a sovereign". The visitor declined, made his excuses and left.

During the course of his long, appreciative article – the first account on record of the Holloway home – the reporter voiced only one minor criticism of the enterprise: "I must, however, in common with many others, protest against the exclusive character of the asylum. Cats have surely claims of nearly equal urgency," he wrote, but he felt strongly enough about the Home's future to predict: "The name of the benevolent founder will no doubt be handed down to a remote posterity."

It proved an astute forecast. One hundred and fifty years later, Mary Tealby's name lives on, nowhere more so than at the Home that continues her work half a dozen miles from Holloway and under a different name. It even takes in cats. Today the Temporary Home for Lost and Starving Dogs is known as Battersea Dogs & Cats Home, the world's oldest and best-known animal sanctuary.

Since it first opened its doors in October 1860, millions of lost, abused and abandoned pets have benefited from its founder's promise that no dog or cat "in any condition be, on any pretence whatever, refused admittance". Hundreds of animal sanctuaries around the world have been built in its image. Today Battersea is a byword for compassion and hope. Yet there were times when it seemed inconceivable it would make it to its first, let alone its hundred and fiftieth anniversary.

The Home has always held up a revealing mirror to society and its attitude to pet ownership. Many in Victorian London had little time or patience for the canine waifs and strays that routinely wandered the city's grimy streets. In this climate, large sections of the press ridiculed the sanctuary as a sentimental folly – and worse. One writer called it a monument to the "imbecility of mankind". During its early years the Home was threatened by financial crises and unscrupulous staff members, threats of eviction and legal action by neighbours upset by the constant barking.

That the Home not only survived, but thrived was a minor miracle. Yet it did. It went on to survive other crises too – from rabies epidemics and depressions to the First World War and the London Blitz. Many other animal sanctuaries have come and gone. Battersea, the pioneer, remains.

This is the story of a remarkable institution. On one level it is about how our treatment of cats and dogs has evolved during the past century and a half, and not always for the better. On another, it charts the growth and development of what has become a national treasure, a charity supported by the humblest and the highest in the land. Most importantly, it is the story of the remarkable characters – canine, feline and human – who built Battersea, beginning with the visionary, if mysterious, lady still referred to as the Home's "Foundress and Unwearied Benefactress", Mrs Mary Tealby.

CHAPTER ONE

THE MYSTERIOUS 'MRS TRULBY'

T HE 1861 CENSUS RECORD FOR Islington in north London is a fascinating, if slightly misleading document. The entry for 20 Victoria Road, Finsbury, for instance, records that one of its five residents, Mary Tealby, was fifty-nine years old and married, which didn't really tell the whole story.

Her age was accurate enough – she would be sixty that December – but her marital status less so. Mary Tealby's husband Robert, a retired timber merchant whom she had married twenty-eight years earlier, lived alone two hundred miles away in Hull. Unusually for their morally upright times, they were separated.

Legal niceties aside, the census's most flagrant error was its description of Mary Tealby as having "no occupation". Nothing could have been further removed from the truth. By 1861 Mary Tealby was completely and utterly occupied by the mission that was to dominate the final years of her life. With her brother Edward and a small group of friends, she was working ceaselessly to establish Victorian London's first home for stray and abandoned dogs.

The history of late-nineteenth-century England is rich in stories of remarkable female campaigners, from nursing pioneers Florence Nightingale and Mary Seacole to Frances Powers Cobbe, founder of the world's first anti-vivisection organization, and Octavia Hill, the co-founder of the National Trust and a campaigner for parks and open spaces for the poor. Mary Tealby is, perhaps, the least known of them. She has certainly been the most mysterious, with even the *Oxford Dictionary of National Biography* describing her as "a figure about whose early life nothing is known". Yet, in terms of her lasting legacy, she is as significant as any of her more celebrated contemporaries. It is time to draw back the veil.

She was born Mary Bates in Huntingdon on 30 December 1801, the daughter of Edward and Mary Bates. According to census records, her father was a "druggist", dispensing medicines to the local populace. His chemist's shop, one of only two in Huntingdon, was based in Market Place on the town's main square, within view of the family's local church, All Saints' and St John's. Mary was the first of three children; her brother Edward followed in February 1804, and another brother, John, was born in October 1805. A fourth child, Henry, died in infancy in June 1807. The three Bates children were christened at All Saints' and St John's in March 1810 when Mary was eight.

Life in Huntingdon revolved around farming and the weekly Saturday market, fox-hunting and horse-racing. As the county town of Huntingdonshire, it had a mayor, an alderman and two Members of Parliament. The biggest event of the year was the annual Huntingdon Fair on 25 March. In other words, it was a typical provincial English town.

Of the Bates children, it was Edward who was the focus of the family's ambitions. He was educated at Uppingham School and Clare College, Cambridge, joining the clergy on graduation with an MA. In comparison, the young Mary seems to have led an uneventful early life. Until, that was, in her late twenties she met Robert Chapman Tealby, a twenty-eight-year-old timber merchant from Hull in Yorkshire.

Robert was, on the face of it, a highly eligible bachelor. His father was a timber merchant, and in 1800 had founded Tealby & Company. It imported wood from Russia and Scandinavia, supplying businesses as far afield as Lancashire, Lincolnshire and the Midlands. An only child, the younger Robert Tealby was his father's heir. As a local captain of industry he was a substantial figure in Hull and was in line to serve on the local assizes. Mary and Robert were married on 30 December 1829.

It's fair to assume that the ceremony, which took place at All Saints' and St John's, was a happy occasion. Not only did Mary marry on her twenty-eighth birthday, the minister at the ceremony was none other than her younger brother Edward. It was almost certainly the first marriage at which he'd officiated. He had only been ordained a chaplain, or deacon, in March that year and as priest by the Archbishop of Ely a few weeks earlier in November, perhaps especially for the occasion. Given the zeal she demonstrated later in her life, perhaps Mary had played her part in pushing Edward along.

The wedding certificate tells us that the witnesses were Edward Bates and a family friend, Elizabeth Smith. It also reveals that the unusual Yorkshire name proved beyond the parish registrar. He registered the newly married couple as Mr and Mrs Trulby.

Mary moved to Hull with Robert. They set up home in a house with two servants on Charles Street, near Garrisonside, the docks district where Tealby & Company had its main office and counting house.

If her courtship and engagement to Robert Tealby had been a romantic affair, Mary's arrival in Hull might have provided something of a rude awakening. Hull was a bustling seaport, its streets alive with the smell of tar and freshly cut timber, the sound of rattling carts and salty language. Life was also less straightforward than it had been in rural Huntingdon.

Mary had married into a family with a murky past. Her parents-in-law were divorced, Robert's father having ended his marriage to his wife Mary in 1812 in circumstances that had scandalized the tight-knit community. Robert Tealby Senior and Mary Cross, the daughter of a clergyman, had been married in Hull in 1785. Robert, their only child, had been born in 1801. In March 1812, at the age of sixty and after twenty-seven years of marriage, Robert Tealby sought an annulment on the grounds that, unknown to him, Mary had been a minor at the time of their wedding.

Ruling in Tealby's favour, the judge decided that because Mary Tealby had been "under the age of twenty-one years" and had married without her father's permission, the marriage was "pretended", and thus "absolutely null and void". In his damning statement, he effectively said that Mary Cross had been masquerading as Mary Tealby for the past quarter of a century. The grounds for divorce were so spurious, cruel and opportunistic, they must have been contrived by his lawyers to allow Robert Tealby to divorce his wife as quickly as possible. The reason for his haste soon became clear.

As if the annulment of her marriage as a "sham" was not humiliating enough for Mary, she could only stand by and watch as Robert Tealby married again within three weeks of the divorce in April 1812.

The new Mrs Robert Tealby was Elizabeth Dowson, a local woman, thirty years his junior. She had been born and raised in the same Sculcoates district of town as the Tealby family and seems to have been a formidable figure. She was soon playing a major role in the family business.

Integrating herself into the Tealby family must have been awkward for Mary Bates. Her husband remained close to his mother, who lived near them on West Street, yet worked with his stepmother.

If there were tensions, they would only have heightened as Mary's time in Hull continued.

In January 1838, Robert Tealby Senior died aged eighty-seven. Eight years later, in 1846, he was followed by his first wife, Mary. Intriguingly, on her death certificate she remained Mary Tealby, "widow of Robert Tealby". There was, however, no doubt about who had inherited his business interests. By now Elizabeth Tealby had taken control of the accounts side of the business, running the operation with a financial clerk called John Fisher. Along with Robert Tealby, they had to steer the company through difficult waters.

In the late 1840s Hull suffered a double blow. First, in 1848 as a result of a trade dispute with the Danish, the British Government introduced a blockade of the Baltic ports. The impact on the businessmen of Hull, who had built their success on trade with Scandinavia, was huge. It was made even worse when the following year the city was hit by one of the worst outbreaks of cholera in British history. The disease was first diagnosed in August 1849, and within three months, 1,860 people had died, one in forty-three of the city's population. At one point, mass graves were dug to cope with the piles of bodies. The outbreak hit

> By 1861 Mary Tealby was completely and utterly occupied by the mission that was to dominate the final years of her life ... to establish Victorian London's first home for stray and abandoned dogs

the docks and the Sculcoates area hard, and the Tealby firm undoubtedly suffered losses, both personal and financial. It was a sign of the hard times that in 1849 Tealby & Company had to go to court to recover a debt of more than £181 from Leicestershire wood sellers.

Somehow the firm survived but when, in 1850, the British Government once more threatened to blockade the Baltic ports, Robert Tealby feared the worst. Worried at the impact a blockade might have, he joined in signing a letter to the foreign secretary begging him not to go ahead as the "evil consequences to the labouring poor … could scarcely be exaggerated".

While her husband devoted himself to keeping the family business afloat, Mary's greatest interest seems to have lain in the burgeoning area of animal rights. She was an energetic supporter of the Royal Society for the Prevention of Cruelty to Animals, the nation's and the world's first animal welfare charity. The Society had been formed in 1824 by – among others – Hull's MP, William Wilberforce. Twenty-five years on, it was highly active on the streets of his constituency.

Mary's interest in animal rights in general and the RSPCA in particular might have been sparked by some of the gruesome court cases involving the Society's agent in the Hull and Yorkshire area, a former bootmaker called John Hardy Vallance. In November 1848, for instance, he brought a prosecution against a John Webster for beating his horse. Vallance told the court he had witnessed Webster as he "took his whip and thrashed it most unmercifully".

Vallance was particularly active in prosecuting those who abused dogs. During the 1840s and early 1850s, dogs were still being used to pull carts around the town. It was not until 1854 that the practice was banned, despite the efforts of

Vallance and other RSPCA sympathizers, perhaps including Mary Tealby. In 1851, a member of the RSPCA in the town, Dr Horner, asked the council if something could be done about "the great cruelty inflicted on dogs in this town, by yoking them in carts". The town clerk found it "impracticable" to bring in a bye-law to stop it.

Dog-fighting was also rife. In 1851 the twenty-fifth annual meeting of the RSPCA in London singled out the success Vallance had achieved in convictions for dog-fighting in Hull. But he hadn't succeeded in stamping it out altogether: in another case a few years later at Hull Police Court, a group of men were charged with organized dog-fighting. Vallance told the court how, when he discovered the animals after the fight, they "were covered with blood and one of them nearly torn to pieces". The owners were fined ten shillings each, a sign of how lightly crimes against animals were still taken in the courts. There were many who were unsympathetic – even antagonistic – towards the RSPCA and its cause.

Vallance lost several of the cases he brought to court and also suffered intimidation and attacks. In November 1851, his dog George, a King Charles Spaniel that was "a great favourite" with his family, was found with its throat cut. Despite his attempts to save it the dog died. Vallance was certain that "the cause of the fiendish deed" had been his membership of the RSPCA.

At least he was not alone in his support of the organization. A branch of the RSPCA had been active in the town since October 1851. As was usual, the original list of members was confined to men, but there is no doubt that Mary Tealby was among the Society's supporters. Ten years later she

OPPOSITE Victorian London's population of scavenging street cats faced "being hunted and maltreated".

was still sending money to the RSPCA in Hull: on 24 January 1862, the *Hull Packet and East Riding Times* listed her as donating ten shillings annually for "the appointment of an officer for the Hull District". By then, however, those donations were being sent from two hundred miles away. In its list of RSPCA donors the *Hull Packet* simply referred to her as "Mrs Tealby (London)".

The precise reasons for Mary's separation from Robert Tealby are unclear. What we do know is that her mother, Mary, died on 27 July 1854 at 20 Victoria Road, Holloway, north London, where the family had moved from Huntingdon some years earlier. On the death certificate, the cause of death was "natural decay and haematemesis", better known today as a gastric ulcer. She was seventy-six. Given that she had suffered a long and probably painful illness, it is fair to assume that her daughter had left Hull to nurse her. The younger Mary's father, Edward, now eighty, was also living at Victoria Street and she might have remained in London to care for him for a time. But why didn't she return to Hull eventually? Or, failing that, why didn't her husband join her, especially as, by 1860, he had effectively retired?

On Friday, 24 August 1860 the *Hull Packet and East Riding Times* carried a notice confirming that on 30 April that year Elizabeth Tealby and Robert Chapman Tealby had "dissolved by mutual consent" the partnership they had run "under the style and form of Tealby and Co". The business had, to all intents and purposes, been taken over by Elizabeth Tealby. The paper went on to report that "the said business … will be carried on under the said style

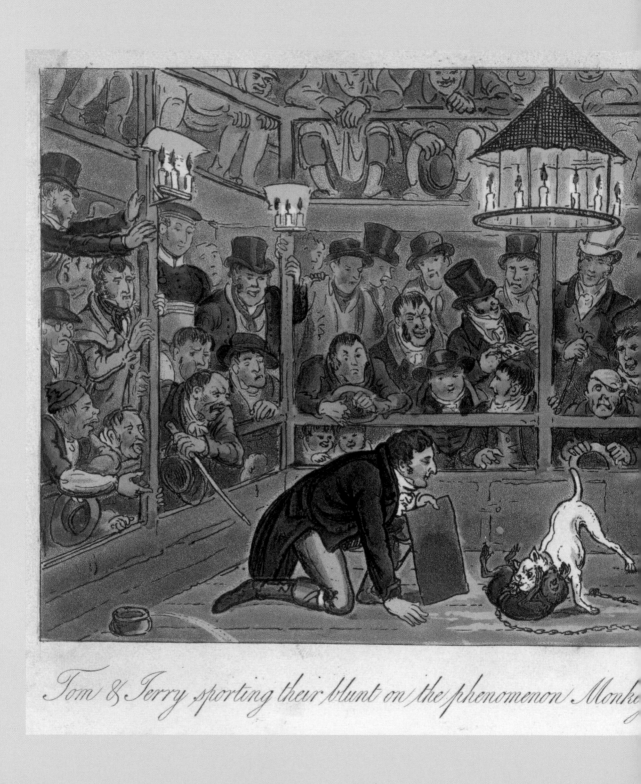

Tom & Jerry sporting their blunt on the phenomenon Monkey

Drawn & Engraved by I.R. & G. Cruikshank.

Macacco, at the Westminster Pit.

Dog-fighting was also rife. In 1851 the twenty-fifth annual meeting of the RSPCA in London singled out the success Vallance had achieved in convictions for dog-fighting in Hull

LEFT A grisly spectacle: an artist's impression of organized dog-fighting at the "Westminster Pit" in London, 1820.

or firm of Tealby and Co by me, the undersigned Elizabeth Tealby alone, by whom all Debts due to and owing by the said late firm of Tealby and Co will be received and paid".

Robert, then fifty-eight, might have expected to leave the firm with a healthy pay-off but it seems he retired to a life that was far from luxurious. In the census record of 1861 he is listed as living not at the old marital home on Charles Street but on Storey Street with a fifty-two-year-old unmarried housekeeper, Maria Kirton, whom, in July that year, he had made the sole beneficiary of his will. Was there more to that relationship than met the eye? We cannot know. But Mary and Robert's separation was clearly permanent: he would not otherwise have excluded her from his will.

In the wake of her marriage ending, Mary Tealby was supported by the two other men in her life – her father and, more significantly, her brother Edward. Following his ordination, Edward Bates had taken up respectable positions in Northamptonshire, first as a priest in Kelmarsh and Oxendon, then as chaplain at Clipston Grammar School. In 1856 he had successfully applied for a prestigious position as Master of the medical school at Clipston Hospital near Market Harborough on a salary of £100 a year. The job brought with it a pension and living quarters within the hospital. It was the kind of position a man might have kept for life.

In 1860, however, Edward left Clipston for London, to be with Mary and his father. The move left him jobless. According to the 1861 census records, Edward Bates was an "unmarried Clergyman, without care of souls". He no longer appeared in *Crockford's*, the official register of England's churchmen. He was fifty-seven, possibly too young to retire. The fact that he, too, relocated to London is puzzling. What drove him to join

his elder sister and father when his career was prospering? Had he come to help care for his elderly father?

Whatever the reasons for her separation, Mary's move to London must have required considerable courage. Divorce was extremely rare within Victorian society, although it appears Mary and Robert did not dissolve their marriage. Her decision to separate would have been made even more difficult by her brother's profession. Was her separation, perhaps, the cause of Edward's departure from his job? That Mary seems to have told people she was a widow suggests she was keen to keep secret her true marital status and was ashamed that her marriage had broken down.

Whatever her personal troubles, Mary Tealby did not spend her years in London hiding or feeling sorry for herself – quite the opposite. With her father and brother, she continued living at the modest townhouse at 20 Victoria Road. They must – between them – have had a reasonable income, perhaps from pensions due to her brother and father. The records show that the household included a cook and a housemaid.

In the years following her mother's death Mary gave in to her passion for the RSPCA and animal welfare. In particular, she began to take an interest in the capital's much-abused dogs – and found her vocation.

⁓

Dogs had roamed the streets of London since the earliest days of the city's history. Like the human inhabitants of the capital, the quality of their lives depended largely on their owners' social class. As far back as the twelfth century, royal edicts had warned ordinary dog owners that "if a greedy ravening dog shall bite … a Royal beast" then they and their pet would forfeit their lives. In 1387 it was ruled "that dogs shall not wander in the City at large", although there was an allowance for the household dogs of the wealthy and well-connected.

At the start of the Victorian era, the distinction was as pronounced as ever: "The proportion of wealth to poverty is about the same among dogs as men – a few hundreds nursed in the very lap of luxury and thousands brought up coarsely and hardly, and not a few, alas, not knowing where to turn for a meal or lodging," observed one Victorian journalist.

Yet as the second half of the nineteenth century got under way, the winds of change were blowing. The Victorian passion for animal rights was a natural extension of the humanitarian philosophy that had, at the start of the nineteenth century, inspired the abolition of slavery.

The Society for the Prevention of Cruelty to Animals had been formed in 1824 to support Martin's Act of 1822, brought in to protect farm animals, particularly cattle, from cruelty. It had become the RSPCA in 1840 when Queen Victoria, an avowed animal lover, had granted it royal status. Despite suffering widespread derision in its early days, the Society had gone from strength to strength, employing a team of inspectors, based in London but paid a guinea a week to travel the country investigating reports of animal abuse. The cases that men like John Hardy Vallance regularly brought to court had done much to open Victorian society's eyes to the cruelty routinely meted out to all animals and dogs in particular.

In London it wasn't uncommon for stray dogs to be shot on sight. In 1831 an MP complained to the House of Commons about an incident in which no less than seven dogs had been gunned down in a single day in Hyde Park. The deaths were part of an ongoing campaign by the park's keepers that had "spared no dogs whatever which they found straying or roaming in the Park, but shot them all indiscriminately, from the lady's lap dog up to the Newfoundland dog".

The cull had been a reaction to one of the capital's periodic rabies scares. In 1830 a particularly bad outbreak of the disease had resulted in four hundred cases and the death of several people. At the time of the outbreak the best remedy was agreed to be the "gradual reduction of all stray street dogs". For park keepers, however, this wasn't happening fast enough. While the House agreed with the MP that the practice was "cruel and disgusting", it was accepted that the park keepers could kill dogs if they were "chasing the deer". Twenty years on, for all the libertarian opinions on the streets of London, there was still a hard core of people who felt dogs were not deserving of any protection.

In 1854 Parliament finally debated the banning of dog carts. Yet there were some who argued passionately in favour of the practice. Dogs, they said, were "as well adapted as the horse" to the job of hauling carts through the muddy streets. Others pointed out that to ban the practice would be to harm the economy. Given that there were "16,000 to 18,000 of these carts in the district south of London alone", this would be "a very large part of the population to deprive of their bread", the Earl of Hardwicke thundered.

The voices of men like him would soon be turned against Mary Tealby.

'OUR LADY OF ISLINGTON'

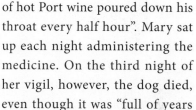

IT BEGAN OVER AN ENCOUNTER with a stray. The precise details are unclear, but it seems Mary Tealby met the dog during a visit to the home of a wealthy friend, Sarah Major, at Canonbury Square in Islington. She entered the hallway of the imposing townhouse to be ushered not into the drawing room, where she and Mrs Major usually took tea, but into the kitchen. There she saw her friend attending to a terribly emaciated dog, lying on a blanket next to the open range. She had found the forlorn creature while out walking in Islington earlier that day. Despite its unkempt appearance and terrible condition, Mary took the dog with her to Victoria Street in the hope of nursing it back to health.

According to the most contemporaneous account, written a few months later, she called in a vet who recommended the dog "had a teaspoonful of hot Port wine poured down his throat every half hour". Mary sat up each night administering the medicine. On the third night of her vigil, however, the dog died, even though it was "full of years and bones". According to the account, Mary "had the melancholy satisfaction of closing the eyes of the sufferer".

If the precise details of this historic encounter are unclear, the consequences are not. The dog's death had a profound effect on Mary. In the days and weeks afterwards she resolved to establish a "canine asylum".

At first that asylum seems to have been based in her scullery. The streets of Islington were no different from those of the rest of the metropolis in which stray and abandoned dogs roamed freely. Mary began taking them in to nurse them back to

PREVIOUS PAGE "An opportunity to alleviate so much misery": an early resident of the Temporary Home For Lost and Starving Dogs.

health. She succeeded. People were soon delivering stray and sickly dogs to her doorstep. It wasn't long before her collection had outgrown its new home, and neighbours began to complain about the noise. "I remember very well how impossible it was to find accommodation for even a small number of dogs without arousing the indignation of neighbours," recalled a friend who went on to play a key role in the Home, John Colam.

Rather than giving up, though, Mary began a search for an alternative place to keep her dogs. Close to her home in Victoria Street, she discovered unoccupied stables in a mews behind numbers 15 and 16 Hollingsworth Street. It wasn't the most salubrious of areas. A pub on the street, the Prince Albert, was "full of notoriously bad characters", the *London Daily News* had reported the previous August. The stables were also dark, damp and poorly insulated but Mary had few options. She approached the owner, Charles Marriott, who agreed to let her house dogs there. With the support of her brother and Sarah Major, she drew up plans to turn the building into a "Home for dogs".

It is hard to overstate what a daunting task Mary Tealby had set herself. She and her family were not wealthy, far from it. Transforming the stables into a home for large numbers of canines would be expensive, and she would need at least one permanent keeper to look after them. She would also face opposition. So how did she do it?

With the benefit of hindsight, it is clear that some important forces were working in her favour. First, Mary's venture chimed perfectly with the times in which she lived in two significant ways. To begin with, animal rights had, thanks largely to the work of the RSPCA, become a popular cause.

In recent times, Charles Darwin had done as much as anyone to promote the idea that animals deserved society's compassion. The author of *The Origin of Species* was convinced, for instance, that dogs had more intelligence than they were given credit for. Darwin cited as evidence the way his household pets recognized him after his five-year absence on the *Beagle*. More generally, he believed in the interdependence of species and argued that all animals were bound together. His views were winning wide support.

Mary's venture also coincided with an important shift in society's attitudes towards dogs. For the first time they were beginning to be viewed as genuine members of the family. This was fuelled by sentimental stories, poems and cartoons that had created the notion of a dog as "man's best friend". A popular poem, "Told to the Missionary", recounted the story of a poor man who tried to drown his beloved dog in a canal because he couldn't afford to keep it but was saved by it when he slipped and fell into the water. The tale of Greyfriars Bobby sanctified a Skye Terrier who apparently spent fourteen years guarding the grave of his master, John Gray, after he had died in Edinburgh in 1858. The world's first "conformation dog show", held in Newcastle upon Tyne the previous year in 1859, was another manifestation of this new attitude. Dogs were being treated as household pets in a way they had not been before.

Mary Tealby's new venture was timely in a third way. It coincided with a period when women were more active than they had ever been in humanitarian and charitable work. It wasn't hard to find their role model. Florence Nightingale's work in transforming the disorganized and unhygienic

OPPOSITE "Man's best friend": Greyfriars Bobby lies next to the grave of his master, John Gray, in Edinburgh, 1858.

THE LIVING MONUMENT TO GRAY.

military hospitals on the Crimean war front had earned her the admiration of the nation and the nickname "the Lady with the Lamp". A charity had been set up to further her work in England and by 1859 the Nightingale Fund had £45,000 at its disposal. That summer the Nightingale Training School was set up at St Thomas's Hospital and opened on 9 July 1860.

Nightingale's example sparked a wave of other charitable efforts. Fundraising bazaars and tea parties became *de rigueur* in polite society. New charities were formed almost weekly, dedicated to causes from providing cattle troughs on the streets of London to women's suffrage. In the summer of 1860 a group of women philanthropists had formed the Society for the Relief of Distress (later the Charity Organization Society), a London-based group that aimed to save those on the "recoverable verge of pauperism" and return them to a life of respectability. The Home for Lost and Starving Dogs, as Mary would call her asylum, became its animal equivalent. Her choice of the word "Home" helped to ensure that women were drawn to her appeals. Mary could have called it a refuge, a hospital or an asylum but, as the social historian Hilda Kean has pointed out, "Home" suggested "a domestic venue rather than a place of custody or imprisonment".

Perhaps Mary's greatest asset, however, was the influential and high-profile connections that she, her brother and her friend Sarah Major had within London society. One of the most useful was Lady Millicent Barber, from Huntingdon, whom Edward and Mary probably knew through her husband, the Reverend John Hurt Barber, formerly the rector of Little Stukeley, a village near Huntingdon. In London, they might have attended the same church, St George's, in Hanover Square, where both had strong connections: the Barbers had been married there in 1826 and Edward ordained in 1829.

The daughter of the 1st Earl of Gosford, Lady Millicent had a home in Montagu Square and was a prominent figure in the charitable world, supporting, among other good causes, the British and Foreign Bible Society. She also had a strong interest in London's less fortunate citizens and was a leading light at the London Hospital for Women in Soho Square, a charity that described itself as "the first Institution established in this or any other country exclusively for the treatment of those maladies which neither rank, wealth, nor character can avert from the female sex".

Lady Millicent undoubtedly opened many doors for Mary and Edward, but Sarah Major also introduced Mary to aristocrats, clergymen, retired military men and society ladies, all of whom seem to have been impressed by her blend of ambition and zeal. Between them they had soon offered around fifteen pounds in donations. Mary and Sarah Major had led the way by putting in a guinea each. A Mr and Mrs Phillipson, from Lyndhurst in Hampshire, put in four pounds. A Lady Duckett from Lincolnshire gave a pound. There were anonymous donors too. "A lover of dogs" sent a pound while someone else gave a 1*s* 6*d* on behalf of their old dog, Billy.

Mary, Sarah and a friend, Mrs Whaley, even took to the streets to raise funds: Sarah and Mrs Whaley collected half a crown each but, tellingly, Mary achieved twice that, 5*s*. She seems to have been a woman to whom it was hard to say "no".

Perhaps the most significant help Mary and her colleagues received, however, was from the RSPCA. Why the Society extended a helping hand is not clear, although Mary's support of the organization must have played its part. Whatever the reason,

OPPOSITE "Half workshop, half stable": the entrance to the original Home in Hollingsworth Street, Holloway.

in October 1860, Mr Middleton, then secretary of the RSPCA, agreed to receive subscriptions to the new Home at the Society's offices at 12 Pall Mall, London. He also agreed to let Mary and the Society she was planning to form to run the Home meet at the offices when necessary. It was to prove a crucial alliance.

Mary knew she needed to connect with a wide audience. With Edward's help, she wrote the Home's first "prospectus". It was published on 2 October 1860 and read:

Persons walking through the streets of London or of its suburbs, can hardly fail frequently to have seen lost dogs in a most emaciated and even dying state from starvation.

The lady who is endeavouring to organize this society has in one suburb only (Islington) found so many in the state that she cannot help feeling

convinced that the aggregate amount of suffering among those faithful creatures throughout London must be very dreadful indeed.

The object of this society is to give humane persons an opportunity to alleviate so much misery. Any valuable dog found and brought to the Home if applied for by the owner, will be given up to his master on payment of the expenses of its keep, but a dog of that description not owned will, after a reasonable time, be sold, and the money applied towards the support of the Home. Any dogs lost by the subscribers and brought to the Home will be given up free of all expenses.

Common-bred dogs will be given to any person who might require a useful dog, on promise of taking care of it. The plans for the reception of dogs will be made known by advertisements or some such means, in order

'The lady who is endeavouring to organize this society has in one suburb only (Islington) found so many in the state [of starvation] that she cannot help feeling convinced that the aggregate amount of suffering among those faithful creatures throughout London must be very dreadful indeed'

RIGHT Back Home: a century or so later, a Battersea van is parked in Hollingsworth Street, outside the original site of the Home.

that any well-disposed and humane persons may know where starving dogs will be received, and to prevent dog stealing no reward will be given to any persons bringing them.

The prospectus attracted a deal of publicity. Locally it appeared in the *Islington Gazette* but it was also reported on widely in provincial papers from London to Scotland and Ireland. Edward used his influence to get a piece into the *English Churchman* the same month.

Public reaction presented Mary with her first significant setback. Some papers were sympathetic but many were scornful. *Punch*, then the most influential and widely read magazine in the country, typified many. "A lady charitable to the canine species has established a 'Home for dogs' at Islington," it wrote. "Now a home for dogs may be a very admirable institution; but Islington is not by any means the best place for it. A more appropriate site for such an establishment would have been found in Kenilworth." Such sarcasm, though irritating, was bearable.

The tone of the most powerful newspaper in the country – and the world, at the time – was far harder to take. On 18 October *The Times* carried two items on the Home. One was a letter to the Editor, responding to the notice earlier in the month: "What are we to have next? Surely charity can be better bestowed by thinking of homes for starving and wandering children! Surely such nonsense should be exposed!" blustered "A.N.". But it was the full-length editorial devoted to what the headline called the "Home for Lost & Starving Dogs" that contained the most savage attack:

What a wonderful period of the world's history is this for all homeless persons! No matter what your calling or condition in life, if you have not a home of your own a number of benevolent persons will start up and form a society for the purpose of providing you with one.

One might, however, have expected that human benevolence would have its limits, and that those limits would be marked somewhere within the regions of humanity, as far as mere sentimental interference was concerned. It is, of course, right and proper that humane men should endeavour to stand between the brute creation and the infliction of unnecessary suffering. The exertions of the Society for the Prevention of Cruelty to Animals have been attended with the happiest effect.

In this great town which we inhabit it is well nigh impossible that a horse in the public streets be put to work for which he is manifestly unfit. There are thousands of eyes to notice, and thousands of tongues ready to denounce in any case in which a horse with a gall beneath his collar has been set to labour. Not so many years since you might have seen a hulking fellow in a little cart drawn by two dogs driving furiously about the streets of London, although the wretched animals were never intended by nature for this class of labour. Of this form of torture too there is an end. Every now and then in the reports of our Police Courts there is a mention of a parcel of wretches who skin cats alive for the sake of their skins. When they are detected they are punished, and in sufficient measures. Whatever may be our shortcomings as a nation in other respects we have little to blame ourselves with as far as animals are concerned. England is the first, perhaps even now the only nation, in which the rights of animals are recognized …

So far all is well, but from the sublime to the ridiculous – from the reasonable inspirations of humanity to the fantastic exhibitions of ridiculous sentimentalism – there is but a single step ... When we hear of a "Home for Dogs" we venture to doubt if the originators and supporters of such an institution have not taken leave of their sober senses. The thing, however, exists, and our only wonder must be that the Secretary for the Society for the Protection of Cruelty to Animals should have consented to receive subscriptions for such purpose. The programme of this new Society amounts to this –

There is a lady residing in Islington whose zeal we will venture to say outruns her discretion, who in her walks through the streets of London has noticed many dogs in a most emaciated condition, nay, it is to be feared that many are dying from starvation. The remedy suggested for this manifest and deplorable evil is the establishment of a "Dog Home" or "Home for Dogs". A Home for Dogs with its male side and female side, no doubt, for is it not founded by a Lady of Islington!

The paper's major objection to the Home seems to have been that it simply didn't believe valuable dogs would ever be found wandering the streets of London.

A valuable dog is worth something which varies between 1 shilling and 20 shillings. Now, this sum of money does not commonly run upon four legs about the streets of London for any considerable time without attention. There are plenty of gentlemen lounging about the streets of London with long coats and keen wits who will take ample care that no "valuable" dog shall undergo any kind of canine suffering. Such an animal is the nugget of the London streets. A valuable dog, indeed, found in a state of emaciation! You would as soon find a goose suffering from atrophy at Strasbourg or a lean bullock in Baker Street about Christmas time.

If it were possible to conceive that such an institution as this "Home for Dogs" could even find a place among the charitable arrangements of this metropolis what a wonderful concourse of dog-stealers – men in velveteen shooting jackets with immense pockets – would surround the place! The habitat of every "valuable" dog in London is carefully noted down in the *Dog-stealer's Manual* and these interesting animals are the objects of the most subtle schemes and contrivances to seduce them from their allegiances to the old dowagers and bachelors who seem to live for no other purpose than to protect them. One is therefore struck by the superfluity of these new institutions. Why not a "Home" for five-shilling notes dropped in the streets?

The Times even made light of the subscribers, whose names had been listed beside the notice announcing the Home.

As might be supposed, most of the subscribers are ladies. Among them, however, figures a certain Billy, no doubt a descendant of the famous dog of that name who was so great at rats. Rats! Are there no rats in Islington? Why should there not be a home for rats? The great and unmerited sufferings of those interesting members of the brute creation have not yet attracted the notice they deserve.

∼

With work already under way to prepare the mews in Hollingsworth Street, the article was a hammer blow to Mary, especially given that *The Times* seemed to have singled her out for opprobrium. Yet she had already shown herself to be a resilient character and didn't let it deter her. She went ahead with her plan to rent Mr Marriott's premises and even engaged a keeper. His name was James Pavitt, a local man, married with children and some experience of looking after dogs. He started work on 5 November 1860.

On 27 November 1860, with the Home open for business, Mary sat patiently in a Committee room at the RSPCA on Pall Mall and took the minutes at the very first meeting of the Society that would run the Home. Despite – or maybe because of – the editorial in *The Times*, she and Edward had managed to enlist the support of a prominent MP, Lord Raynham, who had agreed to chair the meeting.

Raynham, who would later inherit the title Marquess Townshend and the family seat in Norfolk, was MP for Tamworth in Warwickshire and a well-known animal lover. Stories were told of how he would buy dozens of maltreated creatures from street traders to nurse them back to health at his home in Norfolk. His views on animal cruelty were the most extreme in Parliament. If Raynham had had his way, *Punch* wrote, "all fish shops in Haymarket would have had to put up their shutters" and "it would not be safe for any man to open an oyster … Lord Raynham must have a heart as big as Noah's Ark. All things that bark, bray, bleat, grunt, crow, scream, whistle or cackle are allowed to take shelter in it."

The first meeting was a largely procedural affair to deal with the formalities of setting up an organization. Its primary resolutions were:

- That an institution be now established for the care of lost and starving dogs.

- That the following be the rules of the Institution:
    1. That the name of the Institution be the "Home for Lost and Starving Dogs".
    2. That an annual subscriber of five shillings or a donor of five pounds be a governor of the Institution.
    3. That the Institution be under the management of a Treasurer, Hon Secretary and a Committee.

The meeting also resolved to hold annual general meetings and resolved that one supporter, Captain Jesse, be asked to be treasurer, and that Edward Bates be secretary. Five prominent women, Lady Millicent Barber, Lady Wiseman, Lady Duckett, Mrs Phillipson and Lady Talfourd, were named as patronesses. Four men, F. H. Buckeridge, William Chambers, Captain Elliott and Captain Liveing, agreed to become Committee members, along with Mary, Sarah Major and five other ladies, Mrs Ratcliff Chambers, Mrs Hambleton, Mrs Jesse, Mrs Liveing and Miss Morgan. The Committee's first full meeting was held a week or so later, at the RPSCA in Pall Mall on 4 December 1860.

Not everyone could commit themselves to supporting the cause, it seems. The most glamorous – and infamous – members of Mary's fledgling committee were Emily and Captain Richard Jesse. Emily Jesse was the sister of the poet Alfred, Lord Tennyson, and had been engaged to marry his best friend, the brilliant poet Arthur Henry Hallam, when he died suddenly in 1833. Emily was heartbroken and the Hallam family had cared for her with an allowance of £300 a year. But then, in 1842 while still enjoying the Hallam family's support, she had

OPPOSITE Pastures new: an artist's impression of the Home, featuring what is believed to be the original keeper, James Pavitt, and his daughter.

shocked them and the rest of society by quietly marrying a newly commissioned young naval captain, Richard Jesse. The marriage had caused outrage, prompting Elizabeth Barrett Browning to call Emily "a disgrace to womanhood". For whatever reason, between the first and second meetings, Captain Jesse "declined to accept the position of Treasurer". His wife, however, remained a staunch supporter and Committee member. At Mary's request, Edward Bates agreed to step into the breach, doubling up as treasurer and secretary.

Whether Captain Jesse had been influenced by *The Times*'s article is unclear. What was obvious, however, was that the damage inflicted by the piece had to be limited. The minutes of the first Committee meeting recorded that it was agreed a letter, "in defence of the Home", should be written by the much-put-upon Reverend Edward Bates and sent to *The Times* for publication. Edward's well-chosen words fell on stony ground: the newspaper refused to print them.

As the Home took shape, Mary could take comfort from two things: people were bringing a steady stream of dogs to Holloway and her keeper was caring for the new arrivals admirably. Her choice of James Pavitt for the job may have been one of her best decisions. Within a few months of the Home opening its gates, Pavitt had become indispensable, so much so that the Committee had found him living accommodation in the yard. Funds didn't allow for the Home to pay his rent in full but in March 1861 he was given an extra shilling a week to cover the costs. With dozens of dogs in residence, and more arriving at all times of the day and night, he had to be close at hand.

By that spring, the Home had to face up to some tough decisions. With many dogs remaining unclaimed at the Home, space was now at a premium. The Home simply couldn't continue to accumulate inmates. There were already mutterings from neighbours about the noise the few dozen dogs were producing.

With a heavy heart, Mary Tealby, Sarah Major and the other female members of the Committee agreed to introduce new rules. In March, it was agreed that "Any dog brought to the Home not identified and claimed within fourteen days from the date of its admission will, by order of the Committee, be sold to pay expenses or be otherwise disposed of". The Committee recorded that it passed this motion "with the utmost reluctance on the part of the Ladies present". The rule was later amended to read that "the number of dogs that have been in the Home longer than a fortnight be kept down as nearly as possible to forty".

To cope with the growing numbers, the quality of the accommodation needed improvement. In April Mr Marriott was asked to renovate the flooring and ventilation in the two main kennels. To finance the works the Home issued a new appeal for funds. Again, some quarters of the press poured scorn. The *Spectator* had ignored the Home's first request for money when it opened in October 1860, "believing a project of this kind a little too absurd even for the large class of amiable gullible". As news of its latest appeal reached the magazine, it decided belatedly to offer its withering opinion: "We underestimated, however, the imbecility of mankind," it wrote. "We suppose the committee read their Bibles, or at least eat meat for dinner. If they do either they must know that the whole race of animals in existence are not worth one human life."

If ever Mary felt despondent, she only had to talk to friends like John Colam and others at the RSPCA to realize her troubles were minor compared to those that it had faced in its infancy. In 1826, two years after its formation, it had been so short of money it had been forced to leave its first office in Regent Street. For a time its meetings had taken place in coffee-houses. Even worse, its driving force, the Reverend Arthur Broome, was thrown into debtors' gaol, responsible for its £500-worth of unpaid bills. The Home wasn't in such a parlous state – far from it. In response to the latest appeal for funds, donations flowed in.

⁓

Eight months after she had opened the doors at Holloway, Mary Tealby faced having to close them – permanently. In the late summer of 1861, the landlord, Mr Marriott, gave the Committee notice to leave. It is unclear why he did this. Perhaps it was the continued ridicule. Perhaps it was that he wasn't being paid what he considered to be enough money for his yard. More likely he was reacting to the stream of complaints he was receiving from local residents, fed up with the twenty-four-hour barking. Whatever the reason, the Home faced a crisis.

With the notice to quit hanging over them, Mary persuaded Mr Marriott to attend a meeting at Pall Mall on 1 August 1861. It was an astute move. The impressive, mildly intimidating surroundings and the high-powered individuals she had gathered to plead her case softened the landlord's resolve. The Home was reprieved: Mr Marriott was persuaded to "withdraw the notice for the present".

For the Committee, however, the message was clear. Their Home was not their own. Within

OPPOSITE A faithful record: the hand-written minutes of the historic, inaugural meeting of the Home's Committee on 27 November 1860.

Home for Lost and starving dogs.

The first meeting of this Society was held in Pall Mall on the 27th of November 1860, when the following members were present,

Lord Raynham, in the chair.
Mrs Ractcliffe Chambers. Mrs Hambleton.
Mr Jesse. Mr Major. Miss Morgan.
Mrs Tealby. Mr Hopkinstall and the
Revd Edward Bates.

The following resolutions were proposed by the chairman and adopted unanimously,

1. That an Institution be now established for the care of Lost and starving dogs.
2. That the following be the rules of the Institution,

1.

That the name of the Institution be the "Home for Lost and starving dogs."

2.

That an annual subscriber of five shillings or a donor of five pounds be a Governor of the Institution

3.

That the Institution be under the management of a Treasurer, Hon: Secretary, & a Committee.

the month, it was agreed to send a letter to all subscribers stating the "absolute need of funds for the purchase of the property on which the Home stands". Raising money was hard work, especially when those charged with persuading the public to part with their cash were fleecing the Home.

The Committee meeting of 6 June hinted that things weren't quite as shipshape as they might have been with Mr East, who was in charge of collecting money from the Home's subscribers. There had been mutterings about his book-keeping. The Committee asked that Mr East "be requested to provide once a week the list of subscribers and the money". On the face of it this was because "the Committee are anxious that the accounts be made up quickly" and that "official receipts for money received be sent by the Secretary to the different subscribers". There was clearly more to it than that, though. It was the only resolution passed at the meeting so it must have occupied a large part of their time.

Evidently Mr East didn't provide what they wanted. On 4 July 1861 it was "resolved that Mr East be dismissed from the office of collector of subscriptions to the Home" and that he "be required to give up to the Hon. Secretary the money which he has already received as well as the book authorizing him to collect". Soon afterwards another man was hired to "dispose of prospectuses, receive donations etc for a remuneration of 10 per cent upon all money received by him".

The new fundraiser certainly marked a step in a new direction. Mr East was replaced by a man from Newgate Street called Mr West.

~

With the Home desperate to raise money for the purchase of the Hollingsworth Street property,

Mary Tealby and her colleagues had to consider every money-making possibility. It had been agreed earlier in 1861 that the Home should operate as boarding kennels, as well as a charity for strays, and a steady flow of dogs had begun to live there "during the absence of their Masters". The weekly charge varied according to the size of the dog. A note in the minutes from November 1861 recorded that the Home collected 4s for Newfoundland and Mastiff-type dogs, 3s for Greyhounds, Pointers and Setters, and just 2s for Terriers and Spaniels.

Charging for boarders was a more palatable option than some of the other, less savoury, money-making ideas that had come the Home's way. At one point some consideration had been given to selling dog skins. But as well as being offensive this possibility was also uneconomic: the "highest price which has been given for a large skin of a long curly coated dog capable of being converted into a foot mat has been sixpence", it was reported to the Committee.

Inevitably, there had been approaches from shadier characters, including scientists and medical men wanting to use dead dogs for experimental purposes. One practitioner, a Dr Legg, seems to have been persistent in his attempts to persuade Pavitt to sell him carcasses. To ease the administrative burden on James Pavitt, the Home had just appointed its first superintendent, James Johnson. He was told that he "should hold no communications with Dr Legg" and that Pavitt should be directed "against Mr Legg's applications".

It was a policy that would remain central to the Home's philosophy from that day forward to the present. The Committee made it clear that the Home should never "allow any dogs to be taken from the Home for the purpose of making experiments".

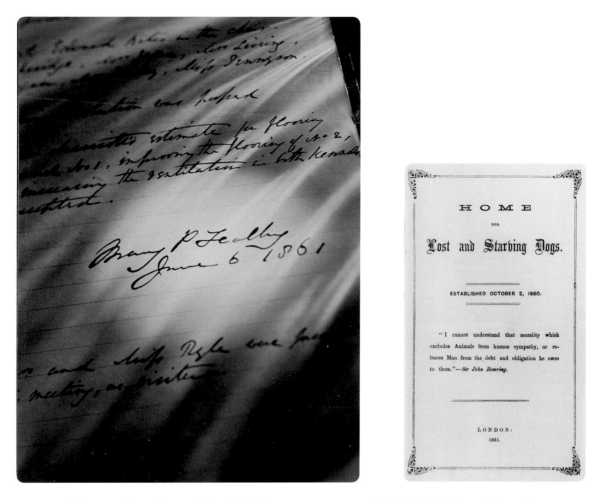

ABOVE LEFT "Unwearied benefactress": Mary Tealby's signature is scribbled in the Home's minutes from 6 June 1861.

ABOVE RIGHT By 1861 Mrs Tealby and her colleagues were able to produce an Annual Report detailing their work.

The Home's high moral stance was admirable, but by the spring of 1862, finances were increasingly tight. To get through the following months belts had to be tightened. In April it was agreed that "in the present the expenses at the Home be confined to things absolutely necessary" and that the Committee would push on with more fundraising activities. They would write to a wealthy aristocrat known to them, Lord Landsdowne, asking him to become a patron, look into holding a bazaar, and fork out on donation boxes – a businessman, Mr Carlton MacCarthy, had visited the Home and shown them a sculpture of a dog that he had turned into a "dog donation box". The Committee ordered six casts at 10s 6d each.

Gifts ranged from a few guineas to a few pennies. They were often accompanied by sentimental notes such as "Poor Touzer sends five shillings" or "In memoriam of Little Trot, six shillings". It all added up. The Home's reputation was growing.

AN EXTRAORDINARY MONUMENT

Wʜᴀᴛ ᴛʜᴇ Hᴏᴍᴇ ʀᴇǫᴜɪʀᴇᴅ most if it was to survive was not money but exposure. There needed to be a change in the general public's attitude towards the Home and its aims. Some ladies on the Committee helped place stories in the newspapers. It was probably Sarah Major who gave one to a writer from the *Friends Review* in 1862. She had written to the magazine encouraging it to visit Holloway and describing a recent arrival:

I happened to be at the Home the other day when a kind man brought in his arms a poor little Scotch terrier whose feet were bleeding terribly. He had worn them to that state in his efforts to find a home, and at last sank exhausted on a gentleman's doorstep. He was placed by the keeper in a pen, with plenty of straw and food.

Next day, he was comparatively well, and jumped upon his benefactor with every demonstration of delight, fondness and gratitude. He had not been in the Home more than three days before he was claimed by a lady in the neighbourhood of Canonbury. This is one among the many instances of the good we may do, and the sufferings we may relieve, of these most intelligent and affectionate of God's creatures – creatures so dependent upon man that they cannot possibly, in large cities, support life without our help.

Such pieces were helpful, of course. But what the Home really needed was a well-known cheerleader capable of persuading people it was a worthwhile venture. In August that year they found one. A rather famous one …

By the 1860s Charles Dickens was the most famous and best-loved author in the English-speaking world. He was also an avid dog lover. Dickens kept a number of different breeds at his homes. In particular, he always had a couple of large, Mastiff-like animals at his country home in Gad's Hill, partly for companionship but also to keep out the local rogues who frequently tried to break in. His favourite dogs were Turk and Linda, the latter a St Bernard. The two dogs had been with him when he had fallen and badly hurt his ankle out walking in the countryside one snowy day. Turk and Linda had crept along at the same pace as Dickens every inch of the three miles home. Among his many other dogs was a small, shaggy white Terrier called Snittle Timbery, given to him by a comedian during one of his lecture tours to America.

Despite his passion for dogs, Dickens was also realistic. When another of his guard dogs at Gad's Hill, a bloodhound-St Bernard cross called Sultan, attacked a small girl, Dickens ordered him shot. Sultan left behind two pups. "One will evidently inherit his ferocity and will probably inherit the gun," Dickens lamented.

In August 1862, he published a piece in his magazine, *All The Year Round*, entirely on dogs. What raised eyebrows among his many admirers, though, was his subject: the controversial, much-ridiculed new Home for Lost and Starving Dogs.

Dickens's writing had always been informed by his social conscience. He had heard that a pedigree "dog show" was due to be held at the Islington Hall that summer. Perhaps through his friend Lord Tennyson, whose sister Emily was a Committee member, he had heard of the Home, a short distance away in Holloway. Dickens sensed a new chance to explore the class divide of Victorian life and penned an article contrasting the two.

He made little attempt to disguise his mild contempt for the people and pets he encountered at "that great canine competition" where, he wrote, there were "many wonderful opportunities for moralizing on humanity":

> Was there not something of the quiet triumph of human success about their [the prize-winning dogs] aspect? Was there not something of human malice and disappointment about the look of the unsuccessful competitors?
>
> Curiously enough, within a mile of that great dog-show at Islington there existed, and exists still, another dog-show of a very different kind, and forming as complete a contrast to the first as can well be imagined. For this second dog-show is nothing more nor less than the show of the Lost Dogs of the Metropolis – the poor vagrant homeless curs that one sees looking out for a dinner in the gutter, or curled up in a doorway taking refuge from their troubles in sleep.

Dickens's description of the Hollingsworth Street mews was as sentimental as it was colourful:

> The Home is a very small establishment, with nothing imposing about it – nothing that suggests expense or luxury. As you enter the enclosure of this other dog-show, which you approach by certain small thoroughfares of the Holloway district, you find yourself in a queer region, which looks, at first, like a combination

of playground and mews. The playground is enclosed on three sides by walls and on the fourth by a screen of iron cage work. As soon as you come within sight of this cage some twenty or thirty dogs of every conceivable and inconceivable breed, rush towards the bars, and flattening their poor snouts against the wires, ask in their own peculiar and most forcible language whether you are their master come at last to claim them?

He found a ragbag collection of breeds there:

A tolerable Newfoundland dog, a deer-hound of some pretensions, a setter, and one or two decent terriers were among the company; but for the most part the architecture of these canine vagrants was decidedly of the composite order.

These vagrants were, in general, typical of the kind of street dogs with whom the reader is so well acquainted … with his notched pendant ears, with his heavy paws, his ignoble countenance, and servile smile of conciliation, snuffling hither and thither, running to and fro, undecided, uncared for, not wanted, timid, supplicatory - there he was, the embodiment of everything that is pitiful, the same poor pattering wretch who follows you along the deserted streets at night, and whose eyes haunt you as you lie in bed after you have locked him out of your house.

To befriend this poor unhappy animal a certain band of humanely disposed persons has established this Holloway asylum, and a system has been got to work which has actually, since October 1860, rescued at least a thousand lost or homeless dogs from starvation …

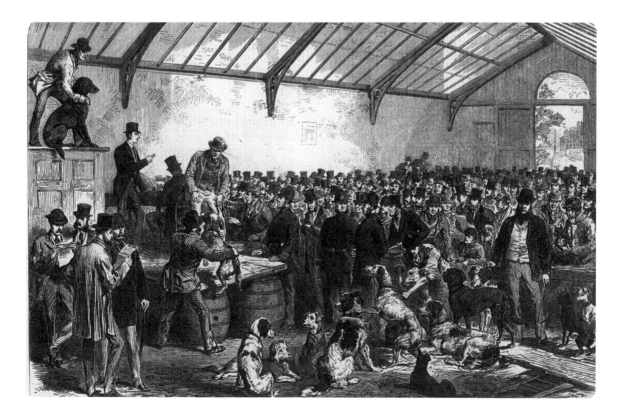

Dickens was fascinated by:

the modus operandi adopted and recommended by the committee of this remarkable institution for preventing the poorer London dogs from going *to* the dogs.

If it should happen in the course of your walks about the metropolis that that miserable cur which has been described above should look into your face and find in it a certain weakness called pity, and so should attach himself to your boot-heels; if this should befall you, and if you should prove to be of too feeble a character to answer the poor cur's appeal with a kick; you must straightway look about for some vagrant man or boy – alas! They are as common in this town as wandering dogs – and propose to him that for a certain guerdon he shall convey the dog to the asylum at Holloway, where he will be certainly taken in, and a printed receipt handed to the person who delivers him at the gates.

Here Dickens added a word of warning:

It is not, upon the whole, considered a good plan to remunerate the vagrant man to whom the vagrant dog has been confided until his part of the contract has been performed, and this same receipt has been obtained. For in the archives of the benevolent society whose system we are examining, there are recorded cases in which credulous persons have handed over the dog and the reward together to some "vagrom man", and somehow the animal has never found its way to Holloway after all.

Dickens then went on to describe how dogs were received at the Home by James Pavitt and his small team of helpers:

The dog has a number tied round his neck similar to those which are suspended to our umbrellas at the National Gallery, and which number corresponds with an entry made by the keeper of the place in his book, stating the date of the dog's arrival, and describing his breed – if he has any – and, at all events, his personal appearance as far as it is describable. The dog's individual case is then considered. If he be ill, and his life is obviously not worth preserving, he is humanely disposed of with a little prussic acid. If, on the other hand, there seems some reasonable prospect of his obtaining a home hereafter, or if he appear to be of some slight value, he is doctored, fed and gradually restored to health.

Dickens clearly spent some time interviewing Pavitt, who provided him with colourful details of the type of medical treatments he and his helpers had dispensed during their first eighteen months in the mews:

Dogs are sometimes brought to the asylum in a most piteous state of exhaustion, and sometimes one of these poor little things will, after receiving a carefully administered meal, curl himself upon the straw and go to sleep for twenty-four hours at a stretch. From the greatest depths of prostration they are recovered by judicious treatment in a wonderfully short space of time.

Intriguingly, Pavitt told Dickens that he and his staff occasionally ventured out into the streets of Islington and beyond:

OPPOSITE Charles Dickens was an avid dog lover and kept a large number of different dogs at his residences.

The society has also employed persons occasionally, to go about the streets and in extreme cases to administer a dose of prussic acid to such diseased and starving dogs as it has seemed merciful to put a quick end to.

At the Islington dog-show all was prosperity. Here, all is adversity. There, the exhibited animals were highly valued, and had all their lives been well fed, well housed, carefully watched. Here, for the most part, the poor things had been half-starved and houseless. At Islington there were dogs estimated by their owners at hundreds of pounds. Here there are animals that are, only from a humane point of view, worth the drop of prussic acid which puts them out of their misery …

Dickens concluded by musing whether he could "discern a great moral difference" between the Islington and Holloway dogs:

I must confess that it did appear to me that there was, in those most prosperous dogs at the "show", a slight occasional tendency to give themselves airs. As to any feeling for, or interest in, each other, the prosperous dogs were utterly devoid of both.

Among the unappreciated and lost dogs of Holloway, on the other hand, there seemed a sort of fellowship of misery, while their urbane and social qualities were perfectly irresistible.

He finished by declaring himself completely in favour of the Home:

It is the kind of institution which a very sensitive person who has suffered acutely from witnessing the misery of a starving animal would wish for, without imagining for a moment that it would ever seriously exist. It *does* seriously exist though. If people really think it is wrong to spend a very, very little money on that poor cur whose face I frankly own often haunts my memory, after I have hardened myself successfully against him – if people really do consider it an injustice to the poor, to give to this particular institution, let them leave it to its fate; but I think it is somewhat hard that they should turn the whole scheme to ridicule, or assail it with open ferocity as a dangerous competitor with other enterprises for public favour …

At all events, and whether the sentiment be wholesome or morbid, it is worthy of record that such a place exists; an extraordinary monument of the remarkable affection with which the English people regard the race of dogs; an evidence of that hidden fund of feeling which survives in some hearts even in the rough ordeal of London life in the nineteenth century.

Dickens's words were heartfelt and hugely influential. He was the most eminent of all Victorian writers, admired by Queen Victoria. Many now began to argue that if Dickens approved of the Home and its objectives, it must have some merit. The article in *All The Year Round* marked a major turning point in the Home's fortunes. Slowly, sometimes grudgingly but steadily, the attitude towards the strange little asylum in Holloway began to change. Looking back at Dickens's intervention years later, John Colam said the debt the Home and its founders owed him was immeasurable: "The truth is that it was not until the late Charles Dickens had come to their rescue that public opinion was moved in their favour." Dickens's words were "at the time worth any sum of money to our cause".

Dickens's piece, helpful though it was in changing attitudes, did little to relieve the financial pressure. Expenses continued to mount, not least the cost of transporting, housing and disposing of dogs. The idea of opening a "receiving house" in central London had been talked about for months. In January that year the Committee had talked about the need for a place "somewhere near the Regent Circus" and agreed to advertise for a suitable site. A plan to open one in the West End was discussed but the annual rent of eighty pounds was deemed "far beyond the present means of the Society".

BELOW "All was prosperity": well-to-do owners and their servants visit the International Dog Show at the Agricultural Hall in Islington, 1865.

Some of the dogs being taken in were too ill or malnourished to be saved and others were too dangerous. The job of disposing of dead dogs had been contracted to a Mr Frazer of Barnet but, in March 1863, he told the Committee he "could not continue to remove the bodies of dead dogs into the community" for less than £28 per annum. Part of this money would be used to buy a "light cart purposely to remove them regularly".

Yet despite the shortage of money, there were signs that the Home was establishing itself as a viable concern. It was a sign of its stability that it held Committee meetings bi-monthly rather than monthly.

By the end of the summer of 1863 the Home had been extended, with the south-east corner of the yard opened up. In July, the Committee had received a note from Mr Marriott requiring them "to decide about the

purchase of the premises". A member, Mrs Hamilton, had recently died, prompting Lord Raynham to adjourn the meeting called to discuss the purchase, "expecting that something in the mean time might be heard from Mrs Hamilton's Executors".

Typically, however, Mary Tealby set to work raising money through other more reliable means. In June 1863, for instance, she staged a bazaar at St James's Hall in Regent Street. Friends were persuaded to bring along "a great many fancy articles" to be sold or raffled. Leading musicians, including Mr H. R. Bird, one of the most popular pianists of the day, agreed to offer their "entirely gratuitous" services.

The event attracted a number of upper-class ladies, including the Dowager Countess of Essex, a supporter of the Home since the beginning. It was such a success that others were arranged for the future. As well as raising money, it cemented the Home's reputation as a worthy cause, certainly among London's female upper classes. As the Home's most loyal supporter in the press, the *Islington Gazette* published a report noting that the charity was now "patronized by many titled, wealthy and eminent individuals".

In October it was agreed that the £550 in the bank "be invested in the purchase of the premises". A sub-committee was set up to "meet Mr Marriott and influence him to take £550 at once and allow the remaining £480 to be left as a mortgage on the estate". Marriott drove a hard bargain. He accepted £600 with £430 left on a mortgage to be paid off in instalments. A resolution was passed that if the Society running the Home was dissolved the proceeds from the sale of its assets would go to the RSPCA.

Finding the right staff remained a challenge. A Miss Hicks, who had been working at the mews as a "nurse", appeared in court that year accused of killing dogs. She had encountered what she had

thought was a rabid dog in central London and – helped by a passer-by – strangled it. Unfortunately, the dog belonged to a gentleman who had left it in the safe-keeping of his hansom-cab driver. The dog hadn't been rabid at all and Miss Hicks had been prosecuted, then convicted at Westminster County Court. A few days later a special Committee meeting on 13 August decided she "be dismissed from any further connection whatever" with the Home. The unfortunate incident served to remind the Committee how lucky they were to have James Pavitt on the Home's staff, overseeing the increasingly demanding inmates of Hollingsworth Street. They tried to show their gratitude whenever they could afford to. On 18 November, for instance, it was agreed to give a sovereign to the keeper so that he "be allowed to purchase soup tickets and a Christmas dinner".

The gesture was a small but significant indication of how relatively secure the Home's finances had now become. A legacy of £500 left by the erstwhile Committee member Mrs Hamilton had helped steady the ship. By 1864 there was only £350 owing on the mortgage for Hollingsworth Street. Apart from that, the Home now had no debt and could put money into improving conditions further.

In 1864 the Home received 2,066 dogs, and that year an appeal was made for receiving houses around London; three were established in Westminster, Chelsea and Bethnal Green. Given the number of dogs arriving at the mews, it was hardly surprising that the Home was becoming a health concern. Pavitt and his helpers did their best to keep the kennels clean but the lack of space and the wretched condition of many of the strays handed in had turned the Home into a potential breeding ground for disease. In January 1864 it was agreed to approach a vet, a Mr Gowing, to ask "for how much he would visit the Home occasionally as required".

In February Mr Gowing agreed to "superintend the sanatory [sic] condition of the Home" for six guineas a year. His first recommendation was that the "cab stables be lime washed".

～

By late 1864 Mary Tealby had become a rare presence at the Home and its Committee meetings. Her father had died in August that year, aged ninety, and she had moved from Victoria Road to nearby Windsor Street. It had been her second loss that year. A relative to whom she was very close, Kate Weale, wife of Robert Weale from Biggleswade, had died in January.

In the months that had followed Mary's own health had deteriorated and she had been diagnosed with cancer. Her strength was already fading and she had written her will in May that year, leaving the little she had to her brother Edward. There was no mention of her estranged husband, which was hardly surprising as Robert Tealby had made no mention of her in his will either. He had died in Hull in March 1862, aged sixty. His few possessions – "a Genova watch" and a "mourning gold ring in which is inscribed the name of my uncle William Tealby" – were left "as a memorial of my esteem and respect" to his "long and faithful housekeeper", Maria Kirton, who was also to be paid an annuity of £30 per annum by Elizabeth Tealby, one of his executors.

In 1865 Mary moved to live with her relative Robert Weale. As the assistant commissioner of the Poor Laws, Weale oversaw the conditions of the country's workhouses but he lived in some style at a spacious property, The Elms, in Biggleswade. Mary would certainly have been comfortable in the house, which boasted a large staff, including a lady's maid, boot-boy, housemaid, and two gardeners to tend the extensive grounds. Edward joined her there.

By May 1865, too weak to travel, Mary had given up attending meetings of the Home's Committee and was sending letters instead, one recommending a cousin, Miss Jarvis, to help with the latest bazaar. In June she wrote suggesting the Committee consider "the French muzzle for dogs". It was her last communication with the Home.

She died on 3 October 1865 and was buried in the graveyard at St Andrew's Church in Biggleswade. Her passing merited only a fleeting mention in local newspapers, none of which noted her connection with the Home. Her gravestone simply read: "Mary Tealby, widow, Born December 30th, 1801. Died October 3rd, 1865." According to probate records, she left "less than £100". Her real legacy, however, lived on back in London.

～

Mary Tealby's death threw the Committee into turmoil. Robbed of its driving force, the Home was briefly rudderless. No reports were produced for most of the year. Eventually, however, Edward Bates, Sarah Major and the other members began to plan for the future.

They were determined Mary would never be forgotten and resolved that every Annual Report published by the Home would begin:

To
the Honoured Memory
of the Late
Mrs Tealby
the Foundress
and Unwearied Benefactress
of this Institution

It appeared in the Home's Annual Report until the 1980s.

~

Three weeks after Mary Tealby's death, Miss Morgan took over as honorary secretary and James Johnson became the first manager, the term "superintendent" no longer seeming to fit. His wage would be "twenty-one shillings per week clear". Pavitt remained in his post and the Home was anxious to keep him happy too. Earlier that year he had been awarded a week's holiday and a "gratuity of a sovereign". Soon his wages were raised to 30s a week. To avoid any friction with Johnson, this included 10s for his wife. Also Pavitt was ordered to keep a book listing everyone who had claimed or purchased dogs and those who called in to make contributions. Unlike some earlier collectors, he seems to have fulfilled the duty honestly and diligently.

Perhaps the most significant other leader to emerge at this time was John Colam, the highly respected new secretary of the RSPCA, and a man who matched his words with deeds. A few years later he became something of a national hero when he ran a one-man protest against attempts to introduce Spanish bull-fighting to England. A team of toreadors and picadors had travelled to London from Spain to perform at the Agricultural Hall in Islington, a short distance from the original Home in Holloway. Midway through the show, as the third bull of the evening was taunted and readied for the kill, Colam had bounded over the barrier separating the audience from the bullring and run across the arena, pursued by a pack of policemen. The sight of the impeccably dressed English gentleman being chased by a collection of constables must have been an entertainment in its

OPPOSITE "They are of every breed and every kind and form of canine beauty": by the 1860s, the Home was taking in dogs of all shapes and sizes.

own right, but it seems the crowd weren't amused. Colam was given such a beating by the police and members of the audience who had jumped into the ring that he spent the next couple of weeks in hospital. His bravery paid off, though: the publicity his protest had generated ensured that the *corrida* never returned. In recognition for his bravery, Colam was awarded forty dollars by a French animal-rights society.

Colam was also a key figure, with Dr Barnardo, in the formation of the children's charity the NSPCC and its American counterpart. He even invented a device to help tram horses release themselves from their harnesses in the event of an accident.

He had, apparently, met Mary Tealby in her kitchen in Holloway and been supportive of the Home from the beginning. Intriguingly, in 1861, soon after the pair had met, Colam sent an RSPCA inspector to be based in Hull, "in consequence of numerous complaints of acts of cruelty perpetrated in Hull". Was this Mary's influence at work? We cannot know. What we do know, however, is that in the wake of her departure his influence – and his family's – was crucial in steering the Home into a new era.

~

In the 1860s, no one could offer a precise estimate of the size of the dog population of the United Kingdom. The only meaningful figure available was the number of dog licences purchased, but that failed to present the whole picture. In the year 1863–4, for instance, the Inland Revenue collected duty on 359,599 dogs, one dog for every sixty-six people in the country. However, it had no idea of the number of dogs that "escape the tax gatherer". Even allowing for the most conservative estimates, there were at least as many dogs roaming the streets and country lanes without licences. Many believed there were in excess of a million in the country, a large proportion of them strays. The numbers were so large partly because the law then stated that anyone found feeding or caring for a dog, even a stray, was liable to pay the annual duty of 12s.

Plenty of people had no sympathy for the dogs. An MP, a Mr Marsh, told the Commons that dogs were a greater public nuisance than foxes. He said that "in Ireland it was universally admitted" that dogs were a complete blight on the human populace. "The curs that abounded in that country bit children, flew at horses, killed sheep and did all kinds of mischief. Indeed, most of the evil deeds laid to the account of the innocent fox were in reality the work of these curs."

By 1867, the problem within London had got sufficiently bad for dogs to be included in legislation introduced to clean up the capital's streets. The new Metropolitan Streets Act brought in a range of traffic measures designed to reduce the number of people being run over in London, a staggering 163 in 1865. As well as banning the removal of ashes or refuse and the driving of cattle or heavy street carts between ten a.m. and seven p.m., the loading of coal at any time other than between one a.m. and seven a.m., it also authorized the Metropolitan Police to seize any dogs found "straying about the streets". If not claimed within three days they could be sold or destroyed. It also allowed magistrates to order the destruction of any dog accused of biting a person.

It was a measure of the position the Home now occupied that it was mentioned during the course of Parliament's debates. In February that year, for instance, during a debate about cutting the cost of a dog licence to 7s per year, a Mr Alderman Lusk, MP, asked about the "Asylum recently established

in the metropolis for Destitute Dogs". Was it intended to levy the tax on the dogs there "which he was told" now numbered three thousand?

It was agreed that charitable institutions should be exempt. But the Government's representative in the debate, a Mr Hunt, "was not aware that the feeling extended to the case of the charitable canine institution". Hansard reported that "he took it that if any persons became owners of dogs within the meaning of the [Metropolitan Streets] Act, even for charitable purposes, they would be required to pay the tax".

The Act placed huge pressure on the police. Fortunately, however, the Home had already begun positioning itself to help with the three "receiving houses" for stray dogs, one in Bowling Street in Westminster, another off the King's Road in Chelsea, and a third in Southampton Street in Bethnal Green. The Act required the police to turn every station in London into a receiving house. The police and the Home quickly realized this wasn't possible. With an adroit piece of political positioning, the Committee opened up a dialogue with the commissioners of the Metropolitan Police, Sir Richard Mayne, and the City of London Police, Lieutenant Colonel Fraser. The meetings weren't conclusive, but they allowed the Home to put down a useful marker.

By July 1868, it was clear that the police were being overwhelmed by their new duties. An announcement that "all dogs which were not very valuable should be destroyed" set alarm bells ringing at the Home. Many seized animals were sold at huge "vagrant dog" auctions across the city. They approached the RSPCA "begging" them to help persuade the police to reject the so-called "Muzzling

OPPOSITE A cartoon portrays "a canine vagabond" confronting a policeman as he tries to seize him under the new Metropolitan Streets Act.

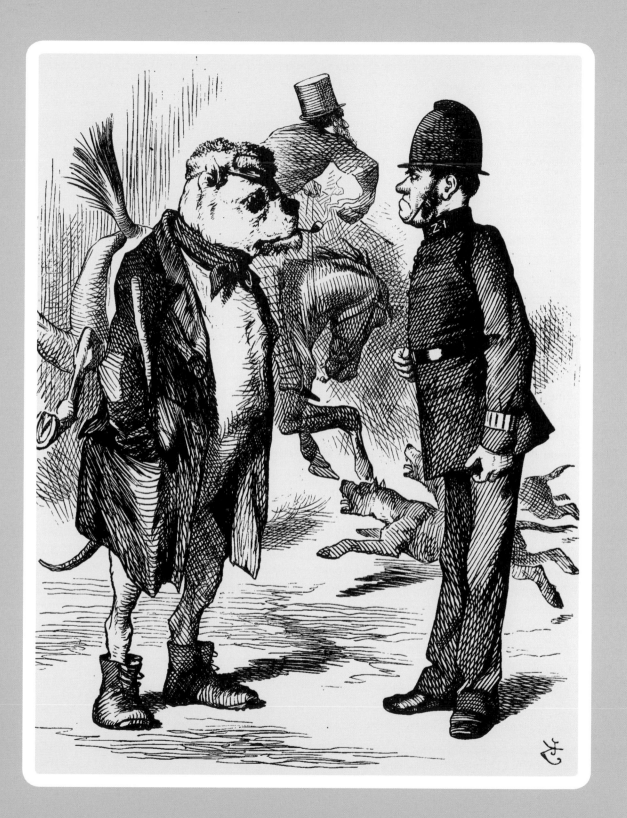

Act". John Colam was soon making representations to the Home Secretary. In December the Home agreed to approach the police with an offer to buy each dog taken into custody for 6*d*. By June 1870 this had been formalized into the beginning of a legal agreement.

In what was to be one of the most significant moves in its history, the Home promised that "every dog brought to the Dogs' Home by any member of the Metropolitan Police Force shall be properly fed and maintained … for the space of three clear days unless it shall be given up to the owner". In addition, the Home agreed to make sure that owners reclaiming their dogs paid for the expenses incurred, and guarantee that, if necessary under the new law, the animal was muzzled. With the threat of rabies always hovering over London, the Home also agreed to keep "separate" any dogs delivered to them suspected of "symptoms of madness". In return the police agreed that, after three days, the dog "shall belong to and be the property of the Association". The receiver of the Metropolitan Police also agreed to pay the Home 3*d* per dog for "food and maintenance", the sum to be repaid when dogs were returned to their owners or sold.

The detailed terms of this agreement would change over the years. The minimum period of stay before a dog became the property of the Home would increase to seven days while the amount payable for each animal would increase slightly, but a fundamental template had been established and the principle remained in place for the next century and more. The Home's arrangement with the Metropolitan Police would safeguard its future.

~

Apart from his obvious gifts as a dog keeper, James Pavitt also seems to have had a knack of charming the press. In the wake of Dickens's visit, a steady stream of reporters and sketch writers made the journey to what one called the "desolate and distant regions" of Hollingsworth Street. They were always made welcome by the keeper, who made sure they had a supply of sentimental anecdotes to take away with them.

In 1867, "Gwynfryn", from the popular *Aunt Judy's Annual Volume for Young People*, visited. Pavitt wasn't soft-hearted by any stretch of the imagination and reckoned that "no dog stealer could possibly escape his penetration", but, watching him deal with people who had come to choose a dog, the reporter was impressed by his ability to match prospective owner and animal: "The keeper, who is very well fitted for his place, and very kind to his charges, knows so well the different qualifications of his *protégés* that he nearly always picks out the right dog for the right person," he wrote, and continued, "The keeper seems to have a stock of appellations which he uses up amongst the dogs and to which they seem to agree to answer at once." Pavitt favoured short, sharp names like Grip and Vixen.

Pavitt, probably with the help of a Committee member, had also come up with an idea to ease a dog's introduction into its new home: he tied a little printed note to its collar that offered sensible and realistic advice about what an owner could expect of their new pet:

The Petition of the Poor Dog to his new Master or Mistress upon his Removal from the Home.
Pray have a little patience with me. There are so many of us shut up together here that the keeper has no opportunity to teach us habits of cleanliness. I am quite willing to learn, and am quite capable of being taught. All that is necessary is that you should take a little pains

with me, and kindly bear with me until I have acquired such habits as you wish. I will then be your best and most faithful friend.

Another note was headed "Advice". It read:

When a dog goes to a new home, care should be taken to prevent his escape until he becomes used to it. A dog must not be expected to act as a guardian until he has learnt to distinguish all the members of the family from strangers, and to feel that his master's home is his own; he will then, no doubts, when occasion requires, be ready to defend both his master and his home.

Gwynfryn told his readers that Pavitt was particularly fond of a couple of dogs. One was a "silky old Pomeranian", who had once been a "drawing room darling". Her mistress had died and she had been turned out into the street. The reporter quickly concluded that the Pomeranian had once "looked down from carriage windows at poor little beggar curs scratching at scraps in the gutter" but "she was a tramp in a Poor-house now". Nevertheless Pavitt "seemed very kind to her" and revealed that a "new lady mistress had taken a fancy to her. So she will die in the Purple after all."

Pavitt's favourite dog, however, was a "little red smooth haired terrier" he called Fan. She had arrived in the Home three or four years previously and had immediately delivered a litter of puppies. "Having had her children born and brought up there no wonder Fan cannot believe it is not her real own home." Fan had been placed in three different homes but each time had returned to Hollingsworth Street. Pavitt admitted that he had already found another home for her but she was "pretty nearly sure to be back again". Gwynfryn concluded that Fan was "an especial pet". Pavitt also talked affectionately about a Lurcher, which – when there was no exercise yard – had acted as "whip to the pack", helping him "hold his pack together, like a shepherd dog with sheep".

BELOW A huge number of strays arrive at the Home. The sign above the donation box reads "Pity the poor starving dogs. Donations thankfully received".

FRESH FIELDS

IN OCTOBER 1869, A MESSENGER delivered a summons to Hollingsworth Street, requiring James Pavitt to appear at Clerkenwell Police Court. It read: "For that there did on the 21st September exist on your private premises a certain nuisance – that is to say, certain dogs kept so as to be a nuisance and injurious to health, and that such nuisance exists through your act, default, permission and sufferance, contrary to the statute etc."

The arrival of a writ was hardly a surprise. The first complaints about noise from the Home had been made in 1862 and directed to the vestry of a local parish church. Nothing had come of them but six years later, in 1868, after being pressed by parishioners again, one of the local ministers, Mr McKenzie, had officially complained to Islington council. A team of inspectors from the health and medical departments had visited the Home but no proceedings had been taken.

By now, however, the complaints had become much more frequent – and serious. This one had been brought by James William Baker, one of the sixty or so residents with homes overlooking the mews. The police had decided his complaint was sufficiently serious to merit a prosecution.

Predictable though it was, Pavitt's summons was worrying. The Committee knew that if he was found guilty it could mean the immediate closure of the Home. In the weeks and days before the hearing a series of contingency plans was put into place. First, Pavitt was instructed to stop taking in dogs in the evenings and a sign saying "No Admissions after 4 o'clock p.m." was placed outside the mews.

PREVIOUS PAGE "The place is a nuisance": by 1870 the Home had outgrown its welcome in Holloway.

On legal advice the Committee also agreed that its solicitor would push for a hearing in a "higher court ... in the event of an adverse decision" in the Magistrates Court. Failing that, they were advised they should ask the magistrate to "stay proceedings ... with the promise that we intend removing to another site".

Most significantly, however, with the latter in mind, it was agreed to form a sub-committee under the Honourable William Byng, charged with finding alternative premises for the Home.

Byng, the second son of the Earl of Strafford, was typical of the sort of useful connection the Home had become so good at nurturing. He was married to a lady from Wellingborough, Northamptonshire, who had probably been introduced to the Home through her friendship with Edward Bates, who had been a priest in the area some years earlier. By a stroke of good fortune, she was also married to the MP for Tufnell Park, the constituency containing Hollingsworth Street, who had proved a useful ally in the past. Doubtless, soundings were taken from him in the run-up to the court case. They proved useful and a list of witnesses who would speak in defence of the Home was soon being compiled.

On the day of the hearing the court was "well attended by the inhabitants of the surrounding houses and also by the friends of the institution". The prosecution produced a stream of witnesses who gave graphic descriptions of the scenes they claimed took place at the Home.

"The howling at night was intolerable and sleep was rendered impossible," the plaintiff, James William Baker, told the court. Not only were people having to put up with the "noise from the 200 or 300 dogs which were often on the premises", the air was also thick with "the stench from the offal on which they were fed, and the open removal of the carcasses of those that were slaughtered". The prosecution said that those with homes backing on to the Home found the "scenes in the yard were of so disgusting a nature that the residents were compelled to desert the back part of their houses entirely".

Another witness for the prosecution, a "City missionary" called Harris, who had "resided at his house more than eleven years", complained that "the whole of his family had suffered in health from the nuisance occasioned, not only by the smell from the manure pit and boiling of the offal, but also from the noise and hubbub".

In all the prosecution produced a dozen witnesses, all of whom claimed to have suffered ill-health because of the goings-on at the Home.

The Home was defended by another Mr Harris. He began by pointing out that "there was no Act of Parliament for keeping dogs from barking". The Home, he reminded the court, was an "institution ... supported by the highest in the land", and described some of the lurid accounts made by the prosecution's witnesses as "gross exaggerations" that amounted to "perjury".

He then produced his own witnesses. A vet, Mr Wilkinson, testified that he had visited the Home at the request of the RSPCA on 30 August that year after a complaint about a dead horse having been seen there. He had found no dead horse and the Home had been "clean" and well kept. "There were about sixty dogs there, and there was no unnecessary smell," he said.

This was backed up by another witness, a police vet, Mr Cherry, who looked over the walls of the mews into the back gardens of some of the adjoining homes and "found them in a very filthy and dirty state ... In one of the yards there were fowls, ducks, fleas and other nuisances," he told the court, to laughter. "The smell arose from those houses."

Two members of the Committee, Byng and Professor William Pritchard, of the Royal Veterinary College, also spoke in the Home's defence. Pritchard had visited the Home on Tuesday of the previous week and "it did not appear it had been got up for his view". He experienced no smell. "The place was paved so that urine and liquid manure could run off and it was covered with clean straw. There was nothing there that could be offensive or injurious to health," he said. He added that he had been "veterinary surgeon to the Dog Show and the arrangements at the Home were better than those at the show".

Byng backed up Cherry's argument and told the court the Home was "more cleanly than those of the persons who complained".

Finally Pavitt took to the witness stand and defended the Home's policies. An uneducated man, he made a convincing argument, although, under cross-examination, he did admit that he had occasionally to resort to whipping dogs to stop them fighting among themselves in the confined spaces of the Home when it was full.

He also offered the court some interesting insights into the life of the Home. He revealed that "the largest number of dogs he had had alive was 110". He said that the straw on which they slept was "turned over daily". He also described how he "boiled the trimmings of bullocks' heads in the evening, but no smell arose".

When all the evidence had been heard it was left to the magistrate, a Mr Mansfield, to sum up. Fortunately he was a dog lover and he gave a long, rambling verdict in which he recalled "stopping with a family where a pack of hounds was kept"

and not hearing "any complaints of their making noises in the night". He also reasoned that Pavitt, whom he described as a "family man", "would not continue to reside on the premises if the nuisance were so great as was complained of". Eventually he dismissed the case, ruling that the evidence didn't "call for his interference with the 'Home'".

The Home breathed a huge sigh of relief, but everyone knew it was a short-term reprieve, not least because there was widespread criticism of the ruling in the press. The *Era* newspaper lampooned Mr Mansfield in an editorial:

> Who but such a profound wit as Mr Mansfield, could have thought of comparing a pack of well-fed and well-cared-for hounds of a gentleman with 200 stray and half-starving curs, brought together from all parts of the Metropolis, especially when the keeper admits that he has sometimes to go among them at night with a whip? Seriously speaking, there can be no question that the place is a nuisance and that it ought to be removed away from the dwellings of man.

The Home had won this particular battle, but knew it had lost the war.

By now it had been established for ten years. It had defied its doubters and established itself as what one newspaper called "a novel and useful charity". It had also learned some valuable lessons, among them the importance of forging alliances with the capital's authorities, most importantly the police. The arrangement struck with the Metropolitan Police in 1868 had been an important turning point. It legitimized the Home in the eyes of not just the police but other authorities. Now the police delivered dogs to the Home on a daily basis.

The Home had also learned to focus on dealing only with London's most deserving dogs. In the original prospectus drawn up by Mary Tealby and her colleagues it had offered dog owners the option of leaving their pets at Holloway as boarders. In theory the idea made sense as it would generate income, but it had not worked very well. Many owners had disappeared without making any payment, leaving their dogs at the Home for months. Many animals had effectively been abandoned. To combat this, the Committee had at one point decided to charge boarders a month's board in advance. But this hadn't worked either so the entire scheme had been dropped. Only strays were accepted.

As the Committee looked forward to the Home's second decade, however, the greatest lesson it had to draw on concerned the Home itself. It was now blatantly apparent that it would have to leave Holloway. On 16 October it was agreed that Byng and Mr Warriner "be requested to see the ground at Battersea". James Johnson accompanied them and they reported back at a meeting on 4 December. The three men had been impressed by what they had seen, a triangular piece of land that was for sale south of the Thames near Battersea Park. It was recommended that every member of the Committee should visit the site.

When they made the journey south of the Thames they discovered that the site was near a railway station and bounded by two main tracks on the London and South Eastern Railway line from Victoria Station. There were a few neighbouring homes, but – given the noise from the railway – the occupants were unlikely to be disturbed by barking dogs. The property was for sale at £1,500, a substantial sum. The Committee was unanimous: it was too good an opportunity to miss. In May 1870 they agreed to make an offer to buy the land for £1,500 and put down a deposit of £100 to secure it.

It was clear that the Home's finances would be stretched to the limit in buying the property. Unfortunately, the Committee lacked a leader with the business acumen necessary to guide them through this minefield. The acquisition and the financial juggling that followed almost ruined the Home.

The London and Westminster Bank agreed to lend £1,500, provided the Home offered not just the old Hollingsworth Street site as collateral but also that five Committee members, Byng, Warriner, Nugent, Hilliard and Morgan, provide promissory notes. They agreed to do so and the deeds were signed in the summer of 1870.

There was no time to spare in getting the new site ready, so builders were immediately asked to tender quotes for erecting kennels and other buildings. A quote of £1,680 from a Thomas Tully of Dalston was accepted and he was told to begin work that summer. From then on, it was a race to leave Holloway and get south of the Thames.

To many Londoners, Battersea was already synonymous with dogs, but for all the wrong reasons. Once little more than an expanse of marshy, frequently flooded land running between Lambeth and Wandsworth, Battersea had been reclaimed from the Thames three centuries earlier. Its rich, highly fertile soil had made it a magnet for market gardeners, who grew fruit and vegetables on the three hundred or so acres of land that became known as Battersea Fields. Battersea provided peas, beans, wheat, melons and other fruit, and produced the best asparagus in London – or anywhere else in England; "Battersea Bundles" fetched high prices in the city's markets.

OPPOSITE One of the most famous Victorian images of the Home, "Table D'Hôte at the Dogs' Home" by John Charles Dollman.

Some of the most successful gardeners were Flemish and it was they who had introduced working dogs to the Fields. In Belgium it was common for dogs to be harnessed to small carts loaded with produce. Visitors to Battersea Fields would routinely see dogs of all shapes and sizes hauling carts laden with fruit and vegetables. Some, inevitably, were driven to breaking point.

It was during weekends that the abuse took on an even darker edge: the poor of south London poured into Battersea's fairgrounds and drinking booths, often to watch spectacles like bull-baiting and cock-fighting. Dogs were heavily involved in bull-baiting, a practice that – unbelievably – was once enshrined in parish law. An incredulous vicar of Battersea, Canon Erskine Clarke, once described how, in his old parish accounts, he had found a string of entries about "butchers being fined for killing bulls without having baited them in the market-place for the amusement of all".

The worst abuse of dogs was reserved for those that pulled carts. At the weekends the carts were transformed into carriages and were routinely filled with two or three people, being taxied to and from the fairgrounds and drinking dens. The dogs were worked so hard that they often died on the street. It was only when it became illegal for them to pull carts, in the 1850s, that the grim spectacle had been consigned to the past.

The irony in the Home moving to an area that had seen such ill-treatment of canines was largely lost on the Committee and the Home's staff as they finalized the move. They had much more pressing matters to worry about.

The Hollingsworth Street property had been put up for sale with the Committee insisting that the agents listen to offers of no less than £1,500, enough to pay off the new bank loan. The manager, James Johnson, was given primary responsibility for finding a buyer, but there were few interested parties.

In the meantime, the cost of building the new premises was already spiralling. The £1,680 agreed with Tully the builder had risen almost immediately. As they had settled into the new Home, Pavitt

and his staff had seen that they needed special accommodation for smaller dogs. In addition to his original contract, Tully was asked to build a special kennel in one of the railway arches.

There were other, invisible, costs. For instance, Londoners had to be told of the Home's move so a series of costly advertisements had to be placed in publications from *The Times* and the *Daily Telegraph* to the *Field,* while cards and flyers were printed to be distributed around the capital. Then the Committee was keen to build a boardroom at Battersea and furniture had to be bought for it. Pavitt and his wife Rosa, who worked in the office, had their wages raised by 5s to 35s a week to reflect the increased workload they were already facing.

Even with a new wave of substantial bequests, the Home was soon feeling the financial squeeze. In December 1871, they had reached the point of desperation. It was agreed to seek a further, even more substantial loan. Another City institution, this time the British Mutual Society, agreed to lend the Home £4,000 with the Holloway premises as security against it. Quite how the Committee succeeded in raising a further £4,000 against a property that was worth significantly less is unclear. In all probability, members had to write promissory notes but the official records are vague. In the short term, the loan allowed the Committee to complete building work and move to Battersea. But with interest being charged at 10 per cent per annum, they were left with a long-term commitment that they would struggle to afford. In 1872, steps had to be taken to "avoid litigation" for unpaid bills, and the Home's manager had been told that he could accept just £1,000 for Hollingsworth Street, "should no better offer be made".

Sarah Major once more tried to rally her society friends by organizing a bazaar in St James's over a weekend in April. She advertised the event widely, asking supporters to help "meet the expense of Painting and Paving the Home and for making certain improvements needful for the convenience of its management and the comfort of its inmates". It did little to ease the financial strain.

It wasn't until December 1874, four years later, that the Committee was able to sell the Holloway property. At first the members seem not to have been informed of the identity of the buyer, who offered a disappointing £900 for the premises. They quickly agreed to accept, though, not least because – combined with a legacy of £1,000 from one of Mary Tealby's original supporters, Mrs Hambleton – it would allow them to pay off half of the massive loan they had taken out with the British Mutual Society.

As the details of the deal became known, however, the members learned that the buyer was none other than James Johnson, now the manager of the Home and soon to be its first superintendent. During the past difficult years, Johnson had already lent the Home £100 from his own money.

> In December 1871, they had reached the point of desperation. It was agreed to seek a further, even more substantial loan. Another City institution ... agreed to lend the Home £4,000 with the Holloway premises as security against it

The Committee seems not to have seen a conflict of interest in that Johnson had, for much of the time, been overseeing the sale of Hollingsworth Street. At a meeting in January 1875, it was unanimously agreed that the Committee "assign the Holloway Property to the said James Johnson for his own use and benefit". In a different age and less desperate circumstances, foul play might have been suspected.

It was only the intervention of Committee member Mary Lloyd that relieved the pressure. In 1876, five years after the mortgage had been agreed, she offered to take over the existing loans, charging half the interest rate, five per cent per annum. When another large legacy arrived that year, this time for £800, the Home's finances finally reached a more stable position.

If the financial side of the Home's operations was precarious, the practical aspect was in better shape. The move to Battersea had been liberating. Its location helped, of course – there were few neighbours to complain of the night-time noise and there was also enough space for dogs to be exercised and run freely. In 1874 the Committee had proudly proclaimed it was experiencing "greatly increased success ... The Home has been visited by many of the nobility and gentry and by great kennel owners and all have expressed themselves very much pleased with the cleanliness and general good order observed."

It was a view echoed by the press. In April 1874 a reporter from the *London Standard* visited "the wilds of Battersea". He, too, was impressed by the standard of hygiene. "All the dogs are well kept, well washed, well exercised and thoroughly well cared for," he wrote. With some pride, he contrasted the Home with a new asylum for dogs that had opened in New York. The latter paid those delivering dogs "according to the value of the animal brought", which made "a perfect nursery for dog-stealing", he reported. Also, after twenty-four hours, dogs of little value were "put into a large vat, which is covered over and water turned in from a hose". He was surprised to find that Battersea was already housing a wide range of dogs:

> They are of every breed and every kind and form of canine beauty, from the little Maltese lion dog that one might kennel in a quart pot, up to a mastiff that would almost require a small house to sleep in comfort ...
>
> The retrievers are the most quarrelsome. The bloodhounds (of which, however, only a few have been taken there) are treacherous and uncertain, snapping suddenly at the man whom they had caressed the day before. The mastiffs alone maintain a sullen dignity, and, unless provoked by an actual attack, will make no quarrel.

He found that "the number of valuable dogs that remains unclaimed is simply astonishing ... Some have very handsome collars on them, which seem to show that they must have belonged to people in good station." As a result, the visitor observed, the Home had become "a perfect mart for buyers ... One retriever was sold for the amount of its keep, which was only twenty-seven shillings, and at a dog show at the Crystal Palace a few months afterwards it took a £30 prize. For anyone that wants to get a cheap and beautiful dog of good breed there are few places in London where they can find themselves more easily suited," he concluded.

CHAPTER FIVE

THE CAUSE OF FEAR

Victorian Britain lived in mortal fear of rabies. Even the slightest hint of an outbreak was enough to induce public jitters and dark humour in the press. In June 1859, "An Ode to Hydrophobia" was published in the *Birmingham Daily Post*:

> A man came down twelve months ago
> And charity was craving
> Muggs' dog he bit him and I know
> He also died a-raving.

Rabies scares also provoked severe reactions on the part of the authorities, often wildly disproportionate to the reality of the situation. In 1830, when the last big outbreak had occurred, there had been what one MP called "general panic" on the streets of London. Dogs displaying anything construed as "madness" had been routinely shot and beaten. Back then there had been no Dogs' Home in the capital to help ease the problem. In 1877, as the first major scare in years erupted, Battersea became the capital's front line in the fight against the dreaded disease.

Early that year the Metropolitan Police were forced to respond to a sudden surge in complaints about dangerous – and potentially rabid – dogs wandering the streets. Constables were ordered to seize any strays they encountered and were free to use as much force as they saw fit. As in the past, the consequences were unpleasant. Aggressive or sickly dogs were routinely beaten and even bludgeoned to death on the streets of the capital, often in front of baying, hysterical crowds. The situation wasn't helped by the ignorance of the general public about the difference between rabies and harmless canine conditions, such as epilepsy.

In an attempt to calm the mood the Home sent out a note to the press, explaining the facts about rabies and detailing an incident that illustrated the panic that had taken hold.

Ignorance of the real symptoms of rabies will inevitably lead to atrocities in our streets. A fit is not a symptom, as is popularly supposed, and no alarm ought to be felt by the public when they see a convulsed dog in the street.

The Hydrophobic Scare.

(Translated from Dog-Latin into Doggerel Verse.)

THE horrid muzzle, in the streets,
  I wear upon my nose,
Makes my tail flag, and quite completes
  The chapter of my woes!

That man in helmet and blue cape
  Has put me in a fog;
He seems to let the thief escape,
  To catch his foe, the dog!

No longer can I rove about
  To keep in health, and thin,
For if I venture to run out
  Sans muzzle, I'm " run in! "

The scare that folks tremble beneath
  Their cowardice reveals,
For, should I grin and show my teeth,
  Why, they show me their heels!

Folks once would stroke me and believe
  Me harmless as a calf;
But *now* no stroke I e'er receive
  Save from a bobby's staff!

I've heard folks sing of " Home, sweet home! "
  Wherever can it be?
I'm sure no dog that dares to roam
  Finds it at Battersea!

Unfortunately people do not stop to reason, but give way to their fears, when they see such an occurrence, and the poor brute is consequently driven up one street and down another at the utmost speed, kicked, stoned and terrorized and maddened into fury, until he bites someone obstructing or pursuing him, whereupon without further evidence he is pronounced mad …

A few days ago, as a policeman was bringing in a half-breed homeless pug to Battersea, the animal had a fit in a street adjacent to the Home. The cry was set up – "Kill him, he is mad"; "Knock his brains out"; "If he bites you, you are a dead man" etc.

Fortunately the dog was taken up by one of our keepers, whose experience enabled him to make a correct diagnosis of the dog's complaint. The dog was brought to the Home where medicine was administered and kindness bestowed upon him. It soon recovered and was subsequently sent to a good home and a kind mistress.

As it happened, the rabies panic soon abated. But the Home learned much about how to manage the outbreaks that would – inevitably – follow. It was one of several important lessons it learned as it settled into its new Battersea premises.

The false accusation that it was a breeding ground for rabies was one of the two most common accusations levelled against the Home during its first fifty years. The other had, if anything, the potential to be even more damaging.

ABOVE By 1881 the Home's Annual Report had become an important publication in which its work could be celebrated and – if necessary – defended.

On, Saturday, 11 March 1882, "an unusually large number of members" crammed themselves into the RSPCA's headquarters at 105 Jermyn Street for the Home's annual general meeting. The throng had come in anticipation of an argument on the most controversial subject of the day, animal experimentation – or vivisection. They were not disappointed. They would witness what was, without doubt, the most dramatic and emotional meeting in the Home's twenty-two-year history.

Feelings about vivisection ran high in Victorian society. Emotions were regularly inflamed by lurid accounts from France and elsewhere on the Continent of what was being done to living animals in the name of science. In the middle of the nineteenth century, for instance, shocked eye-witnesses had described how dogs were cut open an hour or more before experiments took place and then left for students to practise on. One man told of how the leading French scientist François Magendie, regarded as a pioneer in experimental physiology, had tried to expose the roots of the spinal nerves of a dog while it was still awake. Twice the dog escaped and twice it leaped up and put its paws on his face and licked him, as if asking him to stop. On another occasion someone watched him remove "a large round piece" out of a puppy's back "as he would from an apple dumpling".

Campaigners in Britain had been largely successful in outlawing experiments on live – or, indeed, dead – animals and were quick to jump on any institution connected to vivisection. Inevitably, the finger of suspicion had been pointed at the Home, potentially one of the country's richest sources of canine specimens. For obvious reasons, the Home had always been quick to rebut any such suggestion. It had also made its policy plain.

In 1868, a few years after Pavitt had been warned against supplying dogs to the shadowy Dr Legg, a Mr Murphy, a surgeon at the Royal Free Hospital, had written to the Home asking for dogs for his experiments. Horrified, John Colam had sent an RSPCA inspector to explain the Home's position to him. Murphy had been told in no uncertain terms that no dogs would ever be handed over for scientific experiment.

Yet rumours and innuendo were never far away and there were regular unfounded rumblings in the press that Battersea was a source of dogs for the scientific slabs of Bloomsbury and elsewhere. Some, for instance, had their suspicions about the Home's relationship with the police. Rumours of officers selling dogs to vivisectionists weren't uncommon and some put two and two together to make five. In July 1875, in the House of Commons, an MP wondered whether the police were "the principal recruiting officers for this dogs' home". He also wondered "whether the constables, receive any part of the £600 to £800 per annum" that was now being made in dog sales at Battersea.

The secretary of state for the Home Department, Mr Assheton Cross, angrily defended the Home and the police. He said the police were "strictly forbidden to accept any reward or gratuity whatever". He also pointed out that "seizing stray dogs was a very unpleasant and dangerous duty – in which the police very often came out the greatest sufferers of the two".

For a while the Home toyed with the idea of raising the minimum price of dogs to deter the wrong kind of buyers. The logic was that "as dogs could be obtained more cheaply through other sources, the cause for fear would be removed". But the idea was dropped after protests from the public.

At one point, in an attempt to quash the rumours for good, the Committee decided to hire a

retired Metropolitan Police officer to ascertain "whether there can be any foundation for the fears expressed" about Battersea dogs ending up in the possession of vivisectionists. The Home already had a system whereby people buying dogs were required to leave their names and addresses. The policeman spent some time following them home, but discovered nothing "to cause apprehension".

Yet the spectre of vivisection had refused to go away. In that summer of 1882, John Colam again asked an RSPCA inspector to track traffic leaving the Home, in particular dead dogs that were taken by cart to be buried at a Mr Mitchell's farm in Enfield.

A public argument on the subject was bound to result, especially given the individuals now sitting on the Committee. The debate was precipitated by two of its most impressive and formidable members, Frances Power Cobbe and George Fleming.

Cobbe was one of the most outspoken and forceful women of the era. An Irish writer and campaigner for women's suffrage, she was also Victorian England's most visible animal-rights activist and had, in 1875, formed the world's first organization against animal experiments, the Society for the Protection of Animals Liable to Vivisection (SPALV).

In 1867 she had also done her bit to place the Home in the affection of women and children by publishing a sentimental book, *The Confessions of a Lost Dog*. An "autobiographical" tale, written by her Pomeranian Hajjin, it told of how a dog lost on the streets of London could find safety and comfort in the Home for Lost Dogs in Holloway. The book had a happy ending, Hajjin reunited with his mistress. "It is sad to be a dependant on public charity after

> For a while the Home toyed with the idea of raising the minimum price of dogs to deter the wrong kind of buyers ... But the idea was dropped after protests from the public

OPPOSITE "Sketches from the Battersea casual ward": an artist's impression of life at the Home in the late 1880s.

having had so happy a life as mine but I am very, very grateful to you and to all subscribers to the Lost Dogs' Home – very grateful indeed: pray accept all our thanks." Cobbe's influence on the Committee was strengthened even further when it became known that her "domestic companion" was Mary Lloyd, the long-standing supporter of the Home who had helped it out of its early financial difficulties when it had moved to Battersea.

Fleming was one of the country's most eminent veterinary surgeons. After serving with distinction in the Crimea he had become chief vet to the British Army and would go on to found one of his profession's most respected publications, the *Veterinary Journal*. However, it was a piece he had written on vivisection for *Nineteenth Century* magazine that had drawn the crowd to Jermyn Street. In general, Fleming was a strident opponent of the sort of experiments on live animals that had shocked Europe. In his piece, he had argued that the only justification for experiments was for pathological purposes and cited the success of Louis Pasteur. Pasteur had a theory that diseases spread through living creatures via germs. His experiments, in which dogs were injected with viruses including rabies, were intended to prove this and were producing significant results. Fleming ended with a plea that public anger over the emotive subject of vivisection should not lead to scientists like Pasteur being banned from using dogs to conduct pathological experiments.

His piece had gone down well in scientific circles but had aroused suspicion elsewhere, particularly among some members of the Committee, who clearly thought that there might, after all, be no

OPPOSITE The Home's stance against vivisection has remained resolute throughout its history. In this illustration a puppy used in a laboratory experiment is watched by its anxious mother, 1903.

> Cobbe was one of the most outspoken and forceful women of the era ... also England's most visible animal-rights activist

smoke without fire. It was this that had brought Cobbe – and many others – to the RSPCA.

The meeting progressed as normal until the standard motion to accept the minutes was made. At that point Cobbe rose to her feet and demanded that an amendment be made leaving Fleming's name off the list of Committee members. In effect she demanded his removal.

The large audience present didn't know it but the argument had begun in a private meeting beforehand in which Cobbe had called on Fleming to resign his place on the Committee. But, backed by John Colam and a majority of the members, the vet had refused.

Ironically, four years earlier, Cobbe had persuaded Fleming to become superintendent of a veterinary organization, the Brown Institution, precisely because he would stop pro-vivisectionists infiltrating its membership. Yet now she attacked him in what her biographer Sally Mitchell called a "long, vituperative" speech.

She was dismissive of Pasteur's work: "I think this bubble of Pasteur's will burst as soon as most others because it is reared on a false basis." She said that if Fleming remained on the Committee, members were "fully entitled to entertain the suspicion that our Home is likely to become a depot from which vivisectionists may draw their supplies".

Appalled by what he had heard, Fleming, who had come to the meeting with his wife, rose to his feet to defend himself. Addressing Cobbe directly,

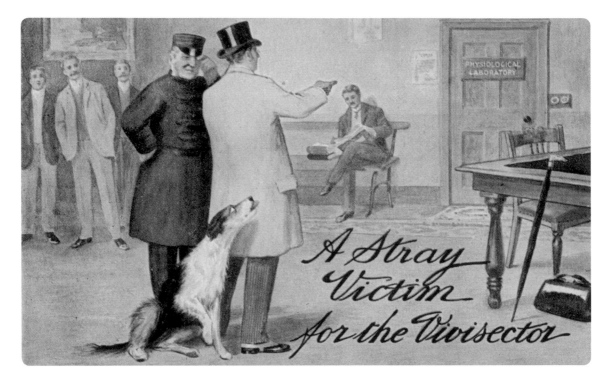

A Stray Victim for the Vivisector

ABOVE The fear of stray or abandoned dogs falling into the hands of vivisectionists was rife throughout the late nineteenth and early twentieth centuries.

he said: "You prefer to perpetuate the dreadful scourge of rabies to the performance of a few completely painless experiments made to prevent it. Ought we not all to be in favour of reducing disease in those creatures which must remain defenceless against contagion if we do not protect them from it?" He made clear again that he didn't approve of "vivisection in its proper sense", only of pathological investigations that did not involve "cutting operations" and were "almost painless". He also repeated his refusal to step down.

A long and heated debate ensued, with a string of members making long and impassioned speeches in favour of both sides.

One of the most heartfelt speeches came from John Colam. No one had done more to rid the Home of the taint of vivisection than he. Before he had become more heavily involved in its running, Colam had had his reservations about the way the Home disposed of dogs and told the Committee so. "The affairs of the Home were in a state of great confusion; they were in a very loose condition, indeed, as regards the disposal of the dogs; for nobody could possibly say what became of them, as no record was kept," he said later.

Indeed, Colam had made it a condition of his joining the Committee that "certain improvements indicated by me, to save the dogs from the agonies of the torture-tables should be made before I would consent to join". So he found Cobbe's suggestion that Fleming might use his influence to "bribe or coerce the manager into a conspiracy to perform experiments at the Home, or connive at the disposal of the dogs for that purpose elsewhere" as "a downright attack on the honour of Mr Fleming and of everyone else on the Committee".

Tempers flared at several points. During his speech John Colam accused Cobbe of distorting what Fleming had said. She snapped that she had been coming to meetings more often than him. But as the meeting continued it became clear that no one thought Fleming was arguing that the Home should hand dogs over to vivisectionists. He had been writing as a scientist, not as a member of the Home's Committee.

Ultimately Cobbe's motion was not accepted. Her reaction was as dramatic as it was predictable. In a fit of pique that, according to Sally Mitchell, "showed Cobbe's stubborn unwillingness to compromise", she resigned from the Committee. In what was almost as big a blow to the Home, Mary Lloyd also resigned.

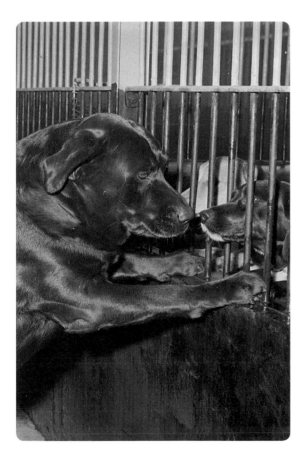

The meeting was a watershed in the Home's history. It confirmed what it had always sensed: that any links between Battersea and vivisectionists would be ruinous to its reputation. In succeeding years, it frequently conducted investigations into the destination of dogs leaving the Home.

In the year after the meeting, inspectors from the RSPCA were hired under the "control and direction" of Mr Colam to carry out a more extensive investigation. Colam set them to follow sixty people as they left the Home to make sure they were going where they claimed. "I can now state with precision that in sixty consecutive cases recently investigated every dog was found in the place where it ought to be," he told the Committee.

On another occasion the Committee decided to engage a detective, a Mr Limeburn, to secretly follow dogs leaving the Home, particularly if they had been bought in large numbers. Limeburn tracked people all over London and beyond for several weeks but found nothing untoward.

To make its policy absolutely clear a new series of "Bye Laws" was introduced in January 1884. They included a requirement that every member of the public buying a dog or a cat at Battersea sign a legal agreement promising that "animals shall not be sold for the purpose of physiological, pathological, toxicological or other experiments being made on them" and that they should never be sold to "any person giving his address at a hospital". In that area, at least, it probably owed a debt to the combustible Miss Cobbe.

LEFT During the late nineteenth century the Home fought fiercely to protect its reputation as a safe haven for all dogs.

NEW ARRIVALS

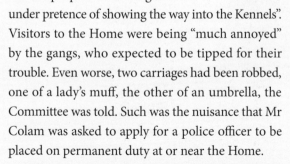

IN THE AUTUMN OF 1882 THE Home was attracting a new breed of visitor, some more welcome than others. Young men and boys had begun hanging around the entrance "for the purpose of holding horses or under pretence of showing the way into the Kennels". Visitors to the Home were being "much annoyed" by the gangs, who expected to be tipped for their trouble. Even worse, two carriages had been robbed, one of a lady's muff, the other of an umbrella, the Committee was told. Such was the nuisance that Mr Colam was asked to apply for a police officer to be placed on permanent duty at or near the Home.

However, it was the arrival of another unruly collection of street dwellers that transformed the Home in a more positive way. That autumn, London's stray cats were finally welcomed through the Battersea gates. Cats – like dogs – had been a part of London's social landscape for centuries. They were, for a long time, considered symbols of good luck, and were woven into the City's legends, most notably the fourteenth-century tale of Dick Whittington. Yet they were also associated with strange superstitions. It was believed that mummified cats brought luck to new buildings and sacrificial cats were often placed inside walls during construction. When one of the City's finest churches, St Michael Paternoster Royal, destroyed in the Great Fire, was rebuilt in 1694 by Sir Christopher Wren, a cat was sacrificed and buried in the foundations.

For hundreds of years, huge numbers of cats had roamed the city's streets, with some areas becoming particularly popular. In the thirteenth century, there were so many strays living in Gresham Street, in the City of London, that it was known variously as

Cattestrate and Cattestrete. Other areas were known as "cat streets", including Clerkenwell Green, the Obelisk in St George's Fields and the alleys off Drury Lane in the West End.

London's cats were, of necessity, creatures of the night, scavenging for food and up to mischief. Dickens compared them to the lowlife of the city: "They leave their young families to stagger about the gutters, unassisted, while they frouzily quarrel and swear and scratch, and spit, at street corners," he wrote of the "city cats".

As a result, cats received a mixed reception from Londoners. "The day was when no cat could appear in the streets of Bethnal Green without being hunted or maltreated," an East End resident once told the social historian Charles Booth.

But as the nineteenth century drew to a close there had been, again, a sea change in people's attitudes. Booth described how in Whitechapel he had seen a prostitute wandering the streets handing out meat from a basket to every stray she came across. She was, in her own way, doing what Mary Tealby had done. It was inevitable that the Home should consider taking in cats as well as dogs.

It was not quite as straightforward a matter as it might have been. By the late nineteenth century an estimated three-quarters of a million cats roamed the streets, a large proportion of them in a parlous physical state.

As secretary of the RSPCA, John Colam understood all too well the resistance people had to treating cats as anything other than public pests. He

BELOW The Home faced legal hurdles when it considered taking in cats, since they were not technically "goods and chattels" in the same way as dogs.

Temporary Home for Lost and Starving Dogs.

❖ BAZAAR ❖

It is proposed to hold a BAZAAR of FANCY-WORK, etc., on TUESDAY, WEDNESDAY, and THURSDAY, July 10th, 11th, and 12th next, at 105, Jermyn Street, (by kind permission of the R.S.P.C.A.), in aid of the funds of the above HOME.

Friends who may be disposed to aid in promoting this object, by preparing articles for sale, will much oblige by communicating with the Manager and Secretary, Mr. Thomas Scoborio, at the Dogs' Home, Battersea Park Road, London, S.W.

ABOVE Fancy work: early fundraising efforts consisted mainly of bazaars run by female supporters of the Home.

recalled once how, in the mid-1860s, when the Dogs' Home was still struggling for acceptance, he had sent an RSPCA officer to Marlborough Street magistrates seeking a "summons in the case of cruelty to a cat": "The magistrate, whose name for obvious reasons I will not mention, refused to grant the summons and sent word by the officer that he desired to see me," he recounted. "Accordingly I went up to the Court and saw him in his private room, when he asked me what I meant by these proceedings, and whether I did not know that cats were vermin."

Colam had persuaded the magistrate to prosecute, drawing on the law to point out that cats were as protected from cruelty as any other animal. But the incident had illustrated the levels of prejudice many felt. There were legal hurdles to overcome too, primarily that cats weren't considered to be "goods and chattels" as dogs were. "The law lays down certain provisions of

relief through the police with respect to dogs, but in the case of cats there is no law enabling us to deal with them," Colam told the Committee in 1881. "Thousands of poor strays are found in our streets and squares. The police cannot take up cats, neither can private individuals, so that there is no legal way of getting a cat into the Home."

A wealthy patron, Richard Barlow Kennett, seems to have been the driving force to change Colam's mind. In September 1882, honouring the wish of his wife, a supporter of the Home who had recently died, he offered to donate £500 if the Home welcomed cats as boarders.

At a Special Meeting held on 10 November, it was resolved that both dogs and cats be accepted as boarders, "provided always that neither … be

received into the Home to be treated as patients". A space of about 150 feet by 50 was found within the grounds and new kennels and an exercise yard were built – Barlow Kennett laid the foundation stone. The outer eastern wall, adjoining the street outside, was raised by four feet. Most significantly, the Home began renting two of the railway arches under the London, Chatham and Dover Railway line, adjoining the yards, and converted one into a temporary home for cats.

The Home knew that cats would be less financially viable than dogs, so an appeal was made to cat lovers for funds to build a more permanent home. A small number of donations trickled in, but the response was nowhere near as strong as it was when a dog appeal was made. As the first strays were put on sale, a similar picture emerged. Dogs had always helped to pay their way with the fees that owners paid to reclaim or rehome them. Cats proved almost impossible to sell or rehome. "No hope could be held out to reduce the expense of the cats by any such payments," the Committee quickly concluded.

of the Home, specimen of a be wished for. he wanted it to secretary looke dog indeed ; The owner kr would purchas nately, the dog bit snappish, and just paid a c money as ator done. It was to The master le

ABOVE The first accommodation for cats was built thanks to a £500 donation from a Mr Barlow Kennett.

The new arrivals gave fresh impetus to a change the Home had been contemplating for some time: a more humane and effective method of euthanizing animals. Several members had become uncomfortable with the long-standing practice of putting dogs to sleep by administering prussic acid. "All who have seen an animal die by this means (and I have seen many scores) must be struck by one fact, namely that however quick the acid may operate, the animal always suffers one terrific spasm before life is extinct," one

OPPOSITE Donations for the Home were even collected by some of its previous residents, such as this stray named Bruno, "one of 4274 dogs rescued in 1889".

Committee member, Professor Pritchard, said. "The pain experienced during that moment is indescribably bad." The arrival of large numbers of cats at the Home would require even more animals to be euthanized in cases where they were too ill, dangerous or decrepit to be kept alive. The issue suddenly became a priority.

The Home enlisted the help of a scientist and inventor, Sir Benjamin Ward Richardson, who had been proposing the use of a "narcotic vapour [carbon oxide gas]" to euthanize animals

ABOVE Many owners brought their sick and infirm dogs and cats to Battersea to end their lives as humanely as possible.

for more than a decade. He had been experimenting with a small anaesthetizing chamber: in this the dogs would be overcome almost immediately and it produced a death that was "absolutely free of pain". Ward Richardson claimed that, compared with other known means of the day, this method stood "far ahead on every ground of practical readiness, certainty and humanity" and presented the Committee with a long list of objections to the existing form of euthanasia used in the Home. Apart from the "moral and physical" issues it raised, he was worried that administering the lethal dose of prussic acid was a demoralizing and dangerous business for the keepers.

The Home agreed with Ward Richardson that the arrival of cats made the work of the keepers even riskier and reported: "It would be almost impossible to administer Prussic acid to cats without incurring great risks to the hands and faces of the servants of the Home." Committee

members subsequently tested the idea on the newspapers and were "greatly pleased" by the reaction of the *Pall Mall Gazette* and the *Daily Telegraph.* Building started in late 1883 and Ward Richardson personally supervised the construction of the chamber to ensure that the process would be as quick and painless as possible for all parties. It was given its first trial in May 1884 and was quickly adopted as the official method of euthanasia; a sad but necessary and accepted practice that remained in place at Battersea throughout the Victorian era and beyond.

"Go home? He'll be cremated first!"

ABOVE The idea of keeping cats and dogs on the same premises seemed comical to some in the press.

OPPOSITE Cats at first proved more difficult to rehome than dogs. By the turn of the nineteenth century the cattery was full to capacity.

~

As the Home entered a new era, it bade farewell to the man who had, perhaps more than anyone else, been at the sharp end of steering it through the difficult early days. James Pavitt's health had been deteriorating for months. Concerns had been raised at his ability to carry on working – both physically and mentally – and the man whom Colam called "the best dog doctor in the United Kingdom" had been called in to talk to a sub-committee headed by Colam in May 1882 to discuss a retirement pension.

But Pavitt said he did not wish to retire. He said his judgement was unimpaired and his only physical handicap was a "stiff joint in his right elbow", which had its root in "a twist that a powerful dog gave the joint as he was removing it out of the pen about 4 or 5 years ago". Pavitt was also questioned about changes he had made to the diets of the dogs and was asked to ensure that neither he nor any member of his staff take "gratuities" from members of the public.

To have his authority challenged in such a public way clearly upset him. The Committee offered to start negotiations about a pension for him but before they could begin he had fallen ill and, in October 1883, James Pavitt died. The Committee recorded his passing: "needless to say that the Home had lost an old servant, whose unprecedented knowledge of the treatment of dogs rendered his services of great value to the Home."

His wife resigned a few weeks later, "having obtained another appointment", but his son-in-law, George Tagg, who had been Pavitt's assistant for ten years, was promoted to the role of keeper.

The winds of change were blowing through the administrative offices too. When James Johnson had died in 1877 his replacement as manager had been Thomas Scorborio, an ex-RSPCA superintendent. After six years at the

> "Needless to say that the Home had lost an old servant, whose unprecedented knowledge of the treatment of dogs rendered his services of great value to the Home"

Home, however, the ageing Scorborio tendered his resignation in 1883 under something of a cloud. That year the Committee introduced a new set of bye-laws that required an "intelligent, practical and, above all, humane superior officer". Why Scorborio fell foul of these requirements is unclear. He was replaced as manager, the post now known as secretary, by Charles Colam. He and his younger brother Matthias were sons of John Colam, both of whom became associated with the Home. Colam was introduced to the Committee as offering, "besides an intelligent mind, an acquaintance with the habits of dogs, and practical knowledge of their wants". He had to steer the Home through a potentially rocky period, which proved rather rockier than anyone could have anticipated.

OPPOSITE **The Home has proved endlessly fascinating to artists. These drawings show scenes of daily life.**

WHERE LOST DOGS AND THEIR OWNERS ARE REUNITED: THE DOGS' HOME, BATTERSEA.

THE REMOVAL OF LOST DOGS FROM A POLICE STATION: EVERY DAY VANS FROM THE DOGS' HOME, BATTERSEA, COLLECT OVER A HUNDRED STRAY DOGS.

THE ARRIVAL AT BATTERSEA: DOGS BEING UNLOADED FROM THE COLLECTING-VANS BEFORE BEING EXAMINED AND CLASSIFIED ACCORDING TO BREED AND CONDITION.

THE RECEIVING-SHED AT THE DOGS' HOME, BATTERSEA: HERE EVERY DOG IS GIVEN A COLLAR WITH A NUMBER ON IT BEFORE BEING TAKEN TO AN APPROPRIATE SECTION OF THE KENNELS.

ALTHOUGH the Dogs' Home, Battersea, has come to be regarded as a London institution, there are many people who have but little idea of its real functions. Our Special Artist, Captain Bryan de Grineau, has recently visited the Home, and on this page and the following pages we reproduce the drawings which he made there. In 1860 the Dogs' Home was founded by a Mrs. Tealby. It was then in Holloway, but later moved to its present home at 4, Battersea Park Road, London, S.W.8, where it is situated within three minutes' walk of Battersea Park Station. Every day a list of stray dogs from widespread police stations is sent to the police station at Nine Elms, where it is collected by a representative of the Dogs' Home, and later in the day the collecting-vans proceed to the allotted districts to fetch the lost animals. When they reach the Home they are examined and divided into categories according to sex, breed, condition, etc. There are usually about 400 dogs in the Home at a time, and they occupy a series of kennels built beneath the arches of the railway station, which can be seen in the drawing on pages 522-523.

DINNER-TIME—A NOISY AND WELCOME PART OF THE DAILY ROUTINE: THE COST OF MAINTENANCE AND COLLECTION OF EACH DOG AMOUNTS TO OVER TEN SHILLINGS A WEEK.

DRAWN BY OUR SPECIAL ARTIST, CAPTAIN BRYAN DE GRINEAU, AT THE DOGS' HOME, BATTERSEA.

A LOST DOG FINDS A NEW OWNER—DOGS MAY NOT BE SOLD UNTIL SEVEN CLEAR DAYS HAVE ELAPSED.

MAN'S TRUEST FRIEND

THE HOME FELT PROUD THAT it had taken in very few dogs with rabies during its twenty-five-year history. Yet, despite the breakthroughs being made by Pasteur, in the late nineteenth century the scourge of "hydrophobia" was still present in the dog population. Typically, the Home admitted around a dozen or so rabid dogs per year. In 1885, however, the number rose suddenly and sharply. In the first quarter of that year, twelve rabid dogs were diagnosed at the Home. The Committee decided to act on this immediately, introducing a series of new measures.

First, it was decided that dogs to be offered for sale should be kept for a minimum of five rather than three days. It was also decided to build two new temporary kennels to isolate infected dogs. The measures failed to have much impact. In the next four months, twenty-three rabid dogs were admitted and another twenty-five during the last four, ten in December alone. The consequences were predictable.

The sudden jump in numbers was perhaps unsurprising given the increase in dogs arriving at the Home. Stray dogs were once more being hauled off the streets in vast numbers, many having been brutalized and even killed. Panic was building, and again Battersea was bearing the brunt.

New legislation meant that the Metropolitan Police were bringing dogs not just from the inner London area but from the outlying districts too, a total area of more than seven hundred square miles. By the end of the year the Home had taken in an unprecedented 25,578, a rise of 10,806 on the previous year.

PREVIOUS PAGE Special "isolation kennels" were built to accommodate dogs feared to be infected with rabies.

The increase in rabies cases caused all sorts of problems. Extra staff had to be taken on to deal with the heavy workload, especially in terms of euthanasia as a large number of dogs were now being destroyed daily.

A rabies outbreak always left the Home vulnerable to other threats too. One woman from Bedford wrote in to complain when the dog she bought at Battersea developed what she thought was rabies. The dog had been shot before he bit someone. Fearing a potentially devastating legal action, the Home's honorary vet, Mr Sewell, was asked to look into the case. To everyone's relief the dog turned out to have distemper.

Then, in November, a Mr T. S. Price wrote a powerful letter to *The Times* describing scenes he had witnessed during a visit to Battersea. He wrote that the crowded conditions meant "the disease of rabies would be more likely disseminated than prevented". Charles Colam sent a stern denial, laying out the steps the Home was taking to prevent the illness while also pointing out the extra workload they were suddenly struggling with. But a quarter of a century after its fight to establish itself, there was again a sense within the Home that the public mood might be turning against it.

Fortunately, one person felt quite the opposite.

~

The Royal Family had taken an interest in the Home since 1879. That year the Prince of Wales, later to become King Edward VII, had visited it with the Queen of the Belgians. They left impressed by the conditions and working practices they had seen.

TEMPORARY HOME FOR LOST AND STARVING DOGS.

FOOD and Shelter are required every day for thousands of Lost Dogs and Cats rescued from the streets and starvation. All Animals are kept seven days, to enable

owners to regain their property; new homes are found for unclaimed animals, or they are mercifully put to death.

HELP IS URGENTLY NEEDED.

ABOVE The Home's Annual Reports featured appeals for funds that tugged at the heart-strings, as this example from the late nineteenth century illustrates.

In 1884 Queen Victoria's youngest son, the Duke of Albany, had inspected the Home. By now there had been a whole range of improvements to the site, including a meeting room for the Committee and a house for the secretary. The Duke was so impressed by the work being done there that he bought a Fox Terrier, which he took home with him in his carriage. In April that year both princes agreed to become patrons.

OPPOSITE Queen Victoria photographed at her desk in the company of one of her Dachshunds, possibly Waldie, around 1865.

‘ In the grounds at Windsor there was a particularly impressive monument to Deckel, a Dachshund she [Queen Victoria] had acquired soon after her marriage to Prince Albert ’

LEFT "No one loves Dogs more than the Queen or would wish to do more to promote their comfort and happiness. They are Man's truest friend": Queen Victoria pictured with her family, including her dogs.

Queen Victoria had been a dog lover since her youth and her estates were dotted with memorials to favourite pets. In the grounds at Windsor there was a particularly impressive monument to Deckel, a Dachshund she had acquired soon after her marriage to Prince Albert. An inscription on the tomb read: "Here is buried Deckel, the faithful German Dachshund of Queen Victoria, who brought him from Coburg in 1845. Died August 10th, 1859. Aged 15 years." Another Dachshund, named Boy, had died three years later, in 1862.

It seems that the Queen had closely followed the news of the problems Battersea was having in dealing with the huge new influx of dogs. She felt sympathetic and was inclined to offer a helping hand. But before doing so she wanted a report on conditions there from a most trusted member of her household staff.

ABOVE Tales to tell: a drawing of one of the Home's Committee meetings during the 1880s, under the leadership of the loquacious Sir George Measom.

Towards the end of 1885 she sent her private secretary, Sir Henry Ponsonby, to visit the Home. He travelled to Battersea twice altogether and was pleased to see that the dogs were "comfortably housed and well treated and that the kennels and grounds were so cleanly kept". His positive comments produced an immediate result.

On 16 December, Charles Colam received a letter from the Privy Purse Office at Buckingham Palace containing a donation of £10. It was the first the Queen had made to the Home and provided a much-needed boost. But there was even better to come.

Queen Victoria spent Christmas at Osborne House on the Isle of Wight with her family. Three days afterwards Ponsonby wrote to Lord Onslow, the president of the Home, confirming that the Queen would from now on "subscribe £10 yearly to the funds of the Institution".

No one was happier at the news than the sitting chairman of the Committee. George Measom was a resourceful character who had made his fortune writing a series of books listing the nation's railway timetables. Since then he'd lived off the ongoing royalties and devoted himself to writing boys' adventure books and chairing various organizations, including the RSPCA, the Cancer Hospital and the Home.

Measom's popularity with charities was understandable. A century or so later, he would have been known as a master networker. He told once how, while out walking in Scotland, he had passed a lady with her Collie. After engaging her in conversation, he had given her a copy of the Home's last Annual Report. "I never leave home without two or three reports in my pocket," he admitted. His policy paid off. "Two years later we received from the executor of the lady £200," he reported.

OPPOSITE Master networker: Sir George Measom, photographed shortly before his death in 1901.

A loquacious and colourful speaker, his addresses to the Committee tended to be as epic as they were entertaining, often featuring poems he had plucked out of a newspaper or even penned himself. One read:

> I'm nothing but an ugly dog,
> whose home is on the street,
> I trot along the pavements
> with my weary muddy feet,
> Or crouch aside to envy gallant dogs
> who flourish by
> With dainty jingling collars,
> and self-complacent eye.

Measom also had a tendency to get carried away emotionally, a weakness that showed itself when he announced Queen Victoria's decision: "Her Most Gracious Majesty the Queen has not only sent a donation but has kindly added her name to the list of subscribers for £10 per annum," he said, to what were described as "loud cheers". This was the signal for him to wax lyrical about his monarch:

> As the arm of justice we are told is long enough to reach the wrongdoer, so the tender heart of our beloved Queen goes out towards suffering whether felt by man or beast.
>
> It is almost impossible to speak without a feeling of emotion concerning the Queen of these realms. Every day some fresh instance occurs of her goodness, not only to her people but when within her power to all created things in the United Kingdom.

Whether or not Measom's loyal outpouring was intended to ingratiate the Home – and himself – with the Queen is unclear. The chances are that it wasn't. But when the Home followed up her donation with a letter to Sir Henry Ponsonby asking whether the Queen would be willing to become the Home's official patron, Measom's widely reported speech can't have harmed their cause. Soon the Home received one of the most important notes in its history. "Most certainly. No one loves Dogs more than the Queen or would wish to do more to promote their comfort and happiness. They are Man's truest friend," came the reply, with some of the key words underlined by the royal pen.

The importance of Victoria's patronage couldn't be overstated. It gave the Home the seal of Establishment approval it had long sought. It also dealt its detractors a mortal blow.

Queen Victoria proved to be a far from passive patron. As other organizations she supported knew only too well, once she got involved she seldom took a back seat. Quoting an ex-Cabinet minister, "who knows the Queen very well", the *New York Times* reporter in London once revealed that Victoria was "especially vehement in antagonism to vivisection. Of his own knowledge, he said, whenever an anti-vivisection society seemed to be lagging in its public propaganda, its noble Chairman got a letter from the Queen stirring it up to fresh exertions." So, she was soon taking "a great interest in this Battersea Dogs' Home".

Frequent notes and letters were soon being despatched to George Measom and the Committee. In March 1886, Measom acknowledged her interest by saying that: "The Committee feels the deepest gratitude to Her Majesty for her sympathy with their work during a period of anxiety, caused by the recent prevalence of rabies. This has been abundantly evinced by her inquiries respecting your means and resources."

Fortunately there were issues outside the Home to distract her as well. In May 1886 she was particularly angered by an incident in London's

Baker Street, which became a *cause célèbre*. A Miss Revell had opened the door of her house to discover a police constable and an inspector beating a dog with their truncheons. Miss Revell recognized the dog, a Spaniel, immediately. She had seen it inside a neighbour's home earlier that day and told the policemen as much. The officers, however, were adamant that the dog was "mad" and needed to be dealt with and ignored Miss Revell's pleas to take the dog into her house. She went inside and produced a pitcher of water, which she proceeded to throw over the policemen. She was cautioned and charged.

As the police continued to beat the dog, a large crowd gathered to watch the gruesome spectacle. One boy passed out from the sight. The beating went on for three-quarters of an hour before the bloodied and battered dog was strapped to a water car and taken off "to be finished at the station". Its carcass was eventually delivered to Battersea.

Miss Revell was fined for her actions but when a letter was published in the *Spectator* public feelings ran high. In May 1886 Queen Victoria wrote to Sir Henry Ponsonby: "Read last night … about dogs and lost order. I protest vehemently against such tyranny and cruelty …" Then she sent a note, via Ponsonby, in response to a letter from Miss Revell, expressing her horror and outrage.

Her Majesty cannot sufficiently express her horror at the statements so frequently made in the newspaper of cruelty inflicted on dumb creatures, especially on dogs, "man's best friends". The Queen has desired me to forward your letter to the Secretary of State for the Home Department with a request that he will enquire into the circumstances of the case you have communicated to Her Majesty.

The Queen was so horrified by the account of the attack in the *Spectator* that she demanded a full inquiry. Commissioner Warren of the Metropolitan Police defended his men's actions strongly when the Home Secretary asked him to explain the case. He said that Ms Revell's letter was "bristling with false statements and exaggerations". He also tried to lay some of the blame at the door of the Home. "The Secretary neglected to have it examined and hence this prevents the police constable proving that the dog was mad." He also criticized the way in which the public had been stoked up into a frenzy:

A dog may be healthy at one time of day and in a dangerous condition at another. During the last 20 days we have had two cases in which dogs led by their owners have suddenly become mad and their owners have requested the Police to kill the dogs. 56 dogs have been killed in the streets in the last 25 days – of these 16 were rabid and the remainder mostly suffering from epilepsy and dangerous to the public.

Warren said there had been "much malice shown in the manner in which certain persons have endeavoured to break down and injure the police constables who killed the dog".

The Queen didn't pursue the matter further. But the press continued to heap pressure on Warren to the point at which he resigned shortly afterwards.

∽

More and more cats were now arriving at the Home. During 1888, 343 cats came into Battersea, a rise of 66 on the previous year. Of these, 112 were boarders, 198 strays and 23 to be destroyed in the lethal chamber. But the new arrivals brought with them an all too familiar problem.

That year the Home had been shocked by a case of cruelty against cats heard at Guildford Magistrates Court in Surrey. A man called McConnell had been found guilty of extreme violence to three of his dozen or so cats. During the course of the case it emerged that McConnell had acquired his cats from Battersea. An inquiry was held and Matthias Colam took the blame. He had been at a meeting of the Committee in Jermyn Street when McConnell had come into the Home and persuaded the staff to sell him a dozen cats. Now he introduced a new rule that cats couldn't be sold when he was absent from the Home if there were "the slightest grounds for suspecting they are required for an improper purpose".

The fact that many cat owners were bringing their old and infirm pets to be put to sleep at the Home demonstrated social acceptance of the humane method of euthanasia it had adopted. The general verdict was that it was one of the great humane inventions of the age. Its acceptance was, in part, down to the Home's openness. Members of the public were allowed in to witness it in use, provided they weren't there to "gratify curiosity" or for "a love of sensational spectacle".

The chamber had made Ward Richardson something of a celebrity. He had gone on to invent a version for use by the police. When he turned up at the 1889 annual general meeting he was given a warm welcome. "I am indeed very proud of its success," he said. "You and the public have thanked me over and over again for the introduction of this method of destruction." He called it "a death so merciful that no man or woman can ever expect to meet with as peaceful an end".

Significantly, during that year, five rabid dogs had turned up at the home, been quickly diagnosed and put to sleep. Given the terror that rabies continued to instil in the public, it was this that Richardson regarded as the chamber's greatest value to the Home: "The enormous benefit which arises from the removal of such dogs out of the streets to the Home is incalculable. Those five animals if left to stray about might and very likely would have communicated the disease to at least fifty of their own species and thus the poison of rabies would have spread in a few towns to an alarming extent involving most likely in its ravages the loss of many human lives."

News of the chamber spread far and wide and solicited enquiries from as far afield as France, Germany, Italy, India and South America. Although it was viewed as a revolutionary and overwhelmingly positive advancement, the publicity it attracted threatened to overshadow much of the more important work the Home was doing at the time. Many dogs were being reunited with their owners or sold to good homes. In 1887, for instance, just under 25 per cent of all dogs were "permitted to live and fulfil a career of usefulness", John Colam told the AGM. He was acutely aware that the dark side of this statistic was that 75 per cent of dogs had not left the Home. But he justified the deaths with a simple illustration. That year, 13,000 dogs had been removed from the streets:

What would have happened if they had been left in the streets? Why in the first place there would have been 13,000 cases of individual suffering … untold misery and privations, whilst they are subject to the kicks and blows of cruel or thoughtless persons.

But in order properly to estimate the magnitude of the evil, it must be remembered that these thousands of ownerless dogs would soon increase in compound ratio. Thus before long … we should have had, instead of 13,000, 130,000 starving creatures, whose presence in the thoroughfares of this metropolis, besides being a misery to themselves would be a danger to the public.

This was greeted with loud cheers. Next he told his audience that there had only been two cases of rabies in 1887 and went on:

Let us pause for a moment to consider what would have happened as regards that epidemic if the 13,000 dogs brought to the Home had been allowed to remain in the streets. The record concerning the recent epidemic of rabies would have been vastly different to that we present before you today.

If this work had been left to the Police, there would have been no lethal chamber and crematorium to perform a last act of mercy. The animals would have been drowned in vats, the water gradually rising to the required height, or perhaps their brains battered out, or possibly, the work of destruction might have been carried out by poison, all of which methods have been followed by Police in other cities.

Colam was a hard-headed pragmatist. He knew what the options were.

The heavy burden being imposed on the Home was unrelenting for, as well as undertaking this level of euthanasia, it also had to deal with the disposal of animal carcasses. For many years, the remains of dead dogs had been taken to a farm in Enfield where they were buried. In 1886, however, that contract came to an abrupt end.

At first the Home tried to resist, but John Colam could see the writing on the wall: "It is not easy to provide a place for the reception of a large number of dead bodies like those we have to dispose of.

> **Many dogs were being reunited with their owners or sold to good homes**

You cannot dig pits and bury them. There are no cemeteries for dogs," he told the Committee, adding that the only alternative was cremation.

So it was that, in June 1886, it was agreed that "arrangements be made" for the building of a small crematorium. A builder, a Mr Neil, was given the contract at a cost of £624. The Home was soon making an appeal for funds to help with the construction. It raised only £245. Fortunately, Mr Barlow Kennett once more came to the Home's aid, advancing the Home £1,000 that had been left to him in trust by his late wife. Work on the crematorium was complete by the end of the year.

Given the interest she had taken in the Home's affairs to date, the Committee, rather naïvely, decided to tell Queen Victoria about its decision to build a crematorium. She was not best pleased. In an abrupt reply, Sir Henry Ponsonby said she was opposed to the idea. In a second letter on the same day she suggested that the bodies be disposed of by having quicklime thrown over them.

Charles Colam wrote a long letter back explaining the difficulty the Home had in finding a burial ground that would be large enough, let alone the expense. The Queen's reply was again brief. She let it be known that her opinion was unchanged but that, while she couldn't stop them going ahead with their plans, she would not contribute any money towards the building of the new crematorium.

From then on the Home was much more circumspect in its dealings with the Queen.

GOODS AND CHATTELS

QUEEN VICTORIA'S PATRONAGE had an immediate impact on the Home's fortunes. Her support was a signal for the rest of London's high society to follow suit. In 1888 the Duke of Westminster allowed a group of fundraisers free run of his home, Grosvenor House on Park Lane, for a grand concert.

Aristocrats and politicians rubbed shoulders with famous actresses, like Ellen Terry and Fay Lankester, and the event raised £420. Soon afterwards the well-known animal painter Yates Carrington contributed drawings to accompany a moving article in the *Pall Mall Gazette*. An appeal accompanying the piece raised a healthy £360. Combined with the funds from other recent bequests, the proceeds from the two events allowed the Home to pay off a loan of £1,000 extended by the RSPCA five years earlier.

The Home's fashionability proved more than a passing fad. In the following year, 1889, Ellen Terry performed in a play called *Monte Carlo* at the Lyceum in the presence of the Prince of Wales. Again all the stars performed "gratuitously", with proceeds going to the Home. Other events followed in years to come, raising yet more much-needed funds.

The popular singer Hayden Coffin was receiving so many requests for autographs that he'd had a card printed. It read that he would only sign his name on receipt of a postal order made payable to one of three charities, one of which was the Home for Lost Dogs. His autographs raised "large sums" apparently.

In the immediate aftermath of Queen Victoria's patronage however, legacies and donations from the wider public fell. In 1886, for the first time ever, the

Home reported that while in the past it had been "under deep obligation to benevolent deceased friends … during the past year such benefactions have unhappily been absent". There were two possible explanations. The first was that Queen Victoria's blessing was assumed to be enough to guarantee the Home's future. The Home, however, blamed a mischievous newspaper piece that had suggested it had received its biggest ever legacy, an incredible £10,000. The story was widely circulated in the press, prompting the Home to issue an official denial: "The statement was unwarrantable, as there is not the slightest foundation for it, and the repetition of the fabrication throughout the land has caused money to be diverted from the Home," it complained.

The sudden dip in donations and legacies couldn't have come at a worse time. As a result, the Home had to take out two separate loans to finance the crematorium. For the first time since the move to Battersea, it was in debt, to the tune of £2,000. "I am sorry that it has been necessary to go to so great an expense but what could we do?" a contrite president, the Earl of Onslow, said.

High society might have taken the Home to its heart, but there were still those who refused to accept its rightful place in the legal landscape. Challenges to its practices in the London courts were far from unusual. In April 1887, a man named Richard Yeoward visited the Home in search of a dog for his family in nearby Clapham. He immediately fell for a lively black and tan Collie, which had been found wandering on the Holloway Road in north London ten days earlier.

Yeoward paid fifteen shillings for the dog and took him home that day. Knowing the dog had run

ABOVE The Home had to go to court to establish its ownership of stray dogs that remained within its walls for more than three days.

away in the past, he and his family immediately put their address – 5 Abbeville Road, Elms Park, Clapham – on a metal tag attached to its collar. It proved an astute move. During its first four months with the Yeoward family the Collie ran away three times, but each time was returned safely, thanks to the address on its collar. When, on the afternoon of 18 July, the dog ran off for a fourth time, the family's luck ran out. Three days later, they were visited by a man called William Manners.

Manners informed Yeoward that the dog was in fact his and that he had been looking for it since April. He had come to the house to tell him that he intended to keep it. A furious Yeoward visited Manners at his home in Borough near London Bridge but was unsuccessful in retrieving the Collie. Determined not to let the matter go unchallenged, he applied for a summons against Manners for "detaining his dog". The case was heard at Southwark Magistrates Court but was rejected. The magistrate ruled that dogs were not "goods or chattels" so Yeoward had no right to claim the dog as his own property.

The ruling horrified the Home and highlighted an issue that had been a nagging thorn in its side for years: its legal right to sell dogs. Despite the powers given to it under its agreement with the Metropolitan Police, there were still those who questioned its right to claim ownership to the strays that remained in its care for longer than three days. The Home's case wasn't helped by the fact that the law was applied erratically.

The first legal challenge to its legitimacy had come in 1879 when another man had brought a case against the Home at the local Lambeth Stipendiary Magistrates Court. He had lost his dog but had failed to turn up to collect it from the Home within three days. He argued that the Home had no legal title to the strays in its care and therefore should not have sold his dog. The magistrate rejected his case, ruling that:

> According to the Metropolitan Streets' Traffic Act, the Police had power to seize dogs found running loose in the street and to take them to some place where they must be kept for three days. If at the end of that time the dogs are not owned they may be kept, sold or destroyed. The Police by arrangement send all dogs to the Home, the managers of which therefore have power to sell them. The sale in the present case was clearly a proper one, and the defendant had, without doubt, forfeited all right to the dog through his own neglect in not going to the Home or to the Police with regard to his loss within three days.

The case was widely reported by the newspapers and was greeted as a major boost by the Committee for giving "confidence to purchasers and authority to your manager".

As Richard Yeoward took his case against William Manners to court, the Home assumed that the same principle would apply. However, according to the Southwark magistrate, it didn't. The case set alarm bells ringing at the Home, where they knew that if buyers were unsure of the legality of buying a dog from them their chances of rehoming would be seriously damaged. The Committee decided it had to intervene on Richard Yeoward's behalf.

The Home applied to the High Court for a ruling that would compel the magistrate to issue a summons against Manners. John Colam appeared on behalf of the Home and was successful in persuading the justices that the word "goods" did in fact refer to dogs. The High Court effectively ordered the lower court to issue the summons and hear the case. A few days later Yeoward was able to reclaim his dog from Manners, although the latter's final words to his new owner was that he would soon "run home". But that was the least of the Home's worries. They had taken an important step towards establishing a precedent.

It was a problem that would arise again, regularly, and seven years had passed before the precedent was finally set in stone.

The landmark case involved a Lambeth horse dealer, Carl Meyer, who had bought a dog from another man called, confusingly, Beyer. Beyer had bought the dog, "a valuable mastiff", from the Home in May after it had been unclaimed for a week. He had paid a pound and sold it on to Meyer for £3 10s, pocketing a handsome profit.

The day after Meyer had collected the dog, he had been walking down the Strand in central London when he was accosted by a theatrical agent called Carlton. Carlton had been adamant that the dog was his and had begun shouting and making a scene. When he'd tried to take the dog's lead from Meyer there had been a struggle and a policeman had intervened. When the situation was explained, the policeman had asked both men to accompany him to nearby Bow Street police station to sort the matter out. Eventually, and reluctantly, after several hours, Meyer agreed to leave the dog at the station. In the wake of the incident, however, he brought an action for assault and false imprisonment.

The case was heard in the High Court by Mr Justice Lawrance. The judge made it clear that Meyer had bought the dog in good faith and legally. "It seems that when a dog which wanders from its owner is found by the police, the owner can claim it within three days, but if it is unclaimed within that time it may be sold or destroyed. It might be sold by law to anybody and the person to whom it is sold has a good title," he said. Importantly, he underlined that it didn't matter whether a dog was bought from the police or not. He also established the Home's legal status: "The Dogs' Home is a valuable institution which takes care of dogs found wandering about. It makes no difference to you or me, if we lost a dog, whether it was in the hands of the police or at the Dogs' Home; the law is the same; if it is kept for three days at the Dogs' Home and is not claimed, they are entitled to sell it."

The judge ruled in Meyer's favour and awarded him £5 in damages. More importantly for the Home, it set a precedent that could be used if any similar actions arose. It was invoked many times in the century that followed.

≈

In 1889, the Home lost its last founding member, Sarah Major. Its elder statesman, John Colam, paid a heartfelt tribute to her at the annual general meeting, explaining to the newer and younger members how great the odds against them had been when she and Mary Tealby had opened the Home thirty years earlier.

The Home was originally started in a back kitchen in Islington. I remember very well how impossible it was to find accommodation for even a small number of dogs without arousing the indignation of neighbours. At that time there was no moral force at the back of our cause – indeed there was nothing but odium.

Hence the pioneers of our cause, who fought for it at a time when it was unfashionable, when we had no Royal patrons, noble presidents and wealthy supporters to shield its founders from ridicule, deserve more than a mere passing reference in our Report.

As the original founders of the Home faded from the scene, the Colam family's contribution had become more and more significant. John Colam remained the Home's éminence grise, the wise old bird of the Committee. His son, Charles, remained a force on the Committee but had been replaced as secretary by his younger brother Matthias at the end of the 1880s.

Matthias Colam had suffered a difficult beginning at the Home. In 1890 he had dismissed a member of staff, a clerk called Edward Walton, who had been suspended for being drunk and abusive as well as selling a dog at a reduced price and pocketing the difference, probably to fuel his drinking. His dismissal wouldn't normally have merited any great debate by the Committee, but Walton proved to be a troublemaker.

OPPOSITE "Lost and Found": the moment when owners and their dogs are reunited has always been emotional, as this image, from around 1900, shows.

ABOVE Since its earliest days, Battersea has regularly received deliveries of entire litters of puppies, found abandoned on London's streets.

Upset at being dismissed, he accused Matthias and Charles Colam of embezzling subscriptions and donations to the Home. The allegation was so serious a sub-committee had to be formed to look into it. The Colam family had been among the Home's staunchest and most loyal allies for more than twenty-five years, so the inquiry left a nasty taste in the mouth. To no one's surprise, however, the brothers were completely exonerated of any suggestion of wrong-doing and Walton's accusations were dismissed as "utterly worthless".

Walton was forced to write a grovelling – not to mention rambling – letter of apology to the secretary:

I am sorry to say that I have made most offensive accusations against Mr Matthias Colam which I am unable to establish and the Chairman having assured me that all the items which I thought had been omitted from the cash book have been duly entered in it and that all my accusations are therefore groundless, I feel that I ought to withdraw the charges that I have made against the Secretary and admit that I was mistaken and not justified in making them.

To compensate him for "the great anxiety caused to him by Walton's conduct", Matthias Colam was paid £10.

By the 1890s, the Home was coming to be regarded as one of London's most heroic, entertaining and even romantic institutions. Its annual general meetings were, by now, widely reported in the newspapers and the Committee members loved nothing more than giving verbose speeches on matters relevant – and sometimes irrelevant – at them. The chairman, George Measom, was, without doubt, the greatest supplier of opinions, anecdotes and assorted ramblings. He regularly read out epic poems, and on one occasion from "Dog and Man" by Henry Downes:

> His master's voice was harsh and gruff,
> Coarse and hard his hand, but Ruff
> Could not worship him enough.
>
> Many a rent the curious eye
> In his raiment might descry,
> But Ruff could no defect espy.
>
> Of food and drink but little store
> Had he: he was old and poor,
> But the dog did him adore.
>
> His limbs were weak, his pace was slow,
> His friends were gone, his lot was woe,
> Humbly behind him Ruff doth go.
>
> Only this one faithful thing
> Did unto his fortune cling,
> Unto Ruff he was a king.

Other members of the Committee revelled in the opportunity to recount funny or touching stories from the Home. One, the Reverend Montague Fowler, told a particularly affecting tale about how the Home had reunited him with his small Aberdeen Terrier. The little dog, with his "long body and short legs", had "lost himself in the streets":

I advertised for him and went to all sorts of expense and trouble to find him. The moment our advertisement appeared I received letters from different people assuring me that our little pet was in their possession and saying, "Will you come and look at it?" I remember starting out in a cab on one of these excursions and when I arrived at the house I was shown a very large poodle which of course was not mine.

No sooner did I get home than a similar letter awaited me and I tore off again in a hansom, only to be introduced to a giant Pomeranian dog and this sort of tour went on for a week. Well, I was getting very tired of this and it seems my little terrier was too, for when he had had enough of gipsy life he appears to have walked up to a Police Constable and asked to be taken to the Dogs' Home where I ultimately found him.

The little chap was unutterably miserable with nervousness and showed unmistakably the mental trials and sufferings he had undergone. Of course this recovery was a great joy to us and I am afraid people do not realize to what extent the Home helps them in matters of this sort.

Newspaper editors had latched on to the Home as a source of stories too and regularly despatched their reporters there on the lookout for entertaining items. One of the earliest stories to capture Fleet Street's imagination had been that of Peter, the faithful sidekick of Charles Peace, a daring house burglar and one of the most infamous criminals of the era. Peace became a household name, thanks to his habit of regularly eluding the police, often by adopting disguises. When, in 1879, he was finally arrested, tried and hanged for a murder he claimed not to have committed, his dog Peter was entrusted to the care of Battersea.

Peter had been Peace's accomplice during many of his crimes, including his final, fateful, break-in at a house in Blackheath. His great talent was in warning the master criminal if anyone approached a house he was burgling by growling quietly under the door. His life among the London underworld proved very useful at Battersea. On arriving at the Home, he was assigned to one of the night-watchmen and during his eight years in service proved his best ever watchdog. If a row broke out in the kennels Peter would warn the watchman and lead him straight to the right kennel and point out the villain of the piece, a former staff member recalled years later.

Other, less colourful, dogs attracted the newspapers' interest too. In the 1890s, several papers reported how a Bloodhound sold to a Member of Parliament, Mark Beaufoy, produced a litter of puppies, one of which grew into one of the most famous dogs on the show circuit, Cromwell "champion bloodhound of the world".

The papers also lapped up the story of a dog called Bluebeard, which kept returning to Battersea. Four times Bluebeard had been placed in respectable homes but four times he'd reappeared like the proverbial bad penny. On one occasion the keeper had heard a "tap tap tap at the entrance" and opened the Home's distinctive red gates to find Bluebeard knocking on the wood with his paw. Whenever he returned he headed straight for his favourite kennel.

Even the Home's staff had developed a gift for self-publicity. In 1899 the secretary, Matthias Colam,

> On one occasion the keeper had heard a "tap tap tap at the entrance" and opened the Home's distinctive red gates to find Bluebeard knocking on the wood with his paw. Whenever he returned he headed straight for his favourite kennel

told the story of a Pug that had been brought in one day by a policeman. It looked in good health and was wearing a collar and chain with a "blue ribbon of feminine tenderness and a mistress's care attached to it", he told a newspaper reporter.

Dog thieves routinely loitered outside the Home, watching new arrivals. The Pug had barely settled into his new kennel when a suspicious-looking character appeared at the entrance, announcing that he had "come to claim my dawg".

"Oh, indeed," said Colam. "And what is it like?"

"Oh, he's a pug," the man said, "and 'eve gawt a collar and chain an' a bit o' blue ribbon on the collar!"

"And when did you lose him?" Colam asked.

"Yusterday."

Colam quietly told one of his staff to take the blue ribbon off the newly arrived Pug and put it on another.

When the dog was brought out Colam asked the rogue if he recognized it.

"Rayther," he said. "Nussed 'im from a pup, didn't I, Rover?"

"Rover" showed no sign of recognition.

When Colam opened the register he asked the man again when he had lost his Pug. "Yusterday."

"Then it can't be your dog, for it was brought in a fortnight ago."

The newspapers lapped up that story too.

The Home's fame had spread far beyond London and Battersea had become the prototype for numerous other animal sanctuaries and refuges around Britain and the world. Overseas visitors regularly came to the Home to study how things were done. In 1894 Dr Carl Schneider, from Cologne, spent a day there and, back in Germany, wrote an article that shone a revealing light on its day-to-day routine. He was impressed by its efficiency and openness and that "any respectable person is allowed to inspect free of charge. A clerk will enter your name and address and soon you find yourself in a labyrinth of sheds, the inmates of which are asserting themselves to the best of their ability." Conditions inside the kennels were equally admirable, with dogs well fed and exercised.

As soon as the dog has got reconciled to his new surroundings and kennel mates, his condition is by no means the worst. He is fed on scientific principles: he receives hounds' meal (a mixture of meat and meal) and duly soaked in water the well known Spratts Meat Biscuits, which are prepared as a tempting morsel for the canine palate.

He obtains exercise in the playground, a railed-in enclosure behind the kennel where he may run and romp to his heart's content; a shed-roof protects him from the rain and he can take his rest on a couch lined in the winter with straw.

Like most visitors, Schneider was moved by the faces of the dogs:

It is sheer despair that is depicted on most of the canine faces; despair at the discomforts of confinement, the unaccustomed surroundings, the impending doom.

I shall not forget for a long time to come the look on the face of an aristocratic Collie; he looked at me with human eyes, whimpering and whining and unfolding his troubles to me in an exquisite dog language, moving body and tail in every possible posture of entreaty and abject submission, and when I moved away, he pressed his nose and paws against the railings and emitted a cry such as might burst from the shipwrecked on a barren island, who sees the sail on which he built his hopes of deliverance disappear on the horizon.

He saw the other side of the Battersea story too:

When a dog is claimed the meeting between master and dog is a most touching scene. As soon as the animal hears the sound of his master's voice, he jumps about as if demented, then circles around him with mad leaps, his eyes sparkle with joy, and, when he has been redeemed, he rushes out without even casting a farewell look upon his less fortunate fellow prisoners.

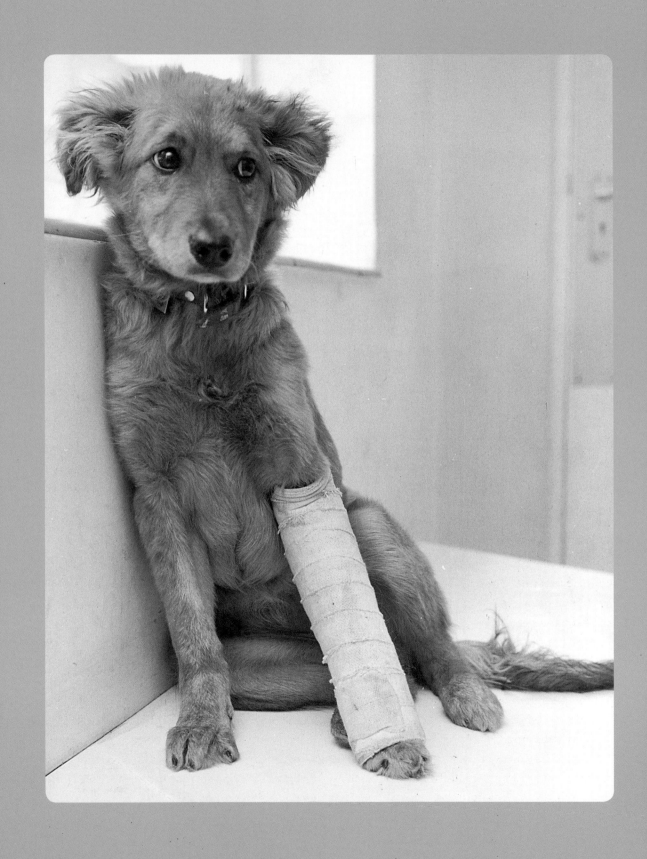

CHAPTER NINE

200 DOGS
PER DAY

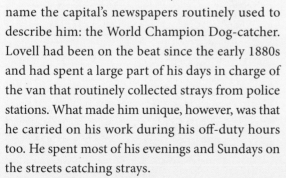

IN THE FIFTEEN OR SO YEARS since he had joined the police force, Constable Robert Lovell's exploits had made him a household name, at least on the streets of London. Most knew him by the name the capital's newspapers routinely used to describe him: the World Champion Dog-catcher. Lovell had been on the beat since the early 1880s and had spent a large part of his days in charge of the van that routinely collected strays from police stations. What made him unique, however, was that he carried on his work during his off-duty hours too. He spent most of his evenings and Sundays on the streets catching strays.

Lovell was proud of his celebrity and his record. "In the course of my career, I have personally captured many hundreds and handled many thousands of all kinds of dogs, from St Bernards

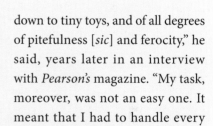

down to tiny toys, and of all degrees of pitefulness [*sic*] and ferocity," he said, years later in an interview with *Pearson's* magazine. "My task, moreover, was not an easy one. It meant that I had to handle every dog caught in the Metropolis several times to take it from the station-yard and secure it in the van, and thence, at the end of the journey, to take it before the authorities at Battersea."

It was hardly surprising that Lovell picked up his fair share of nips and bites: "I have been badly bitten several times, on three or four occasions so severely that I was compelled to go on the sick list." He seems to have been lucky to have got off so lightly. He reckoned he had caught as many as six dogs mad with rabies, safely getting them to Battersea alive so that the authorities could investigate their condition.

PREVIOUS PAGE A cartoon celebrates PC Robert Lovell, the "Champion Dog-catcher" who delivered as many as 127 dogs a day to Battersea.

Lovell seems to have been fast and fearless. According to him, he was far from the only bobby who walked around ready to pounce on strays:

Almost every constable carries a piece of strong whipcord, with a running noose, ready in his pocket.

As soon as the dog comes within arm's reach, the noose is slipped over his head and round his neck. If of a ferocious nature, another noose is fastened tightly around his muzzle. With the whipcord cutting into his neck, if need be, the most spiteful Retriever or Collie recognizes that the inevitable has happened and gives little trouble in being conveyed to the station. That is the method by which I have captured hundreds of Bulldogs, Mastiffs, Newfoundlands, Collies, St Bernards and other big dogs.

The *Pearson's* interview was accompanied by a cartoon of the PC lassoing a stray like a cowboy landing a steer.

Asked on his retirement to nominate the busiest time of his career, Lovell had no hesitation: "1896," he said, with a mournful shake of his head.

In February 1896, the Home received a letter from the London County Council. It laid

BELOW "What in the world have you got on your heads?" Muzzles became the subject of dark humour in the press.

out the rules for a new muzzling order that was to be introduced. Once again, fear of rabies was circulating. The police had introduced a strict rule that all dogs must be muzzled and were empowered to seize any that were not. The letter told the Home that the police would convey "all dogs to the Dogs Home where they must be kept for a period of five days". After that Battersea was free to do as they wanted with them. The council said it was "prepared to pay the sum of fourpence in respect of each dog taken to the Home in pursuance of these Regulations".

The order caused the biggest influx of dogs in Battersea's history. It came into force on 17 February 1896. During the next fifty days, until 9 April, the Home took in a staggering 11,399 dogs at a rate of 232 a day. A large proportion was brought in by Robert Lovell who, at the peak of the muzzling order, was delivering three or more vanloads, each holding from thirty to thirty-five animals, to Battersea every day. By Lovell's reckoning he took as many as 127 dogs on a busy day. During the course of "my busiest year's work … I conveyed 3,331 to Battersea," he said.

The rabies scare wasn't without foundation. In March, a man in East Ham had been bitten by a black Retriever that had been diagnosed with rabies. Immediately a new rule was introduced at the Home, requiring that "keepers and yardmen wear gloves during the time of receiving dogs into the Home". Yet the muzzling order was hugely unpopular with the public and the letters columns were full of complaints. Newspapers ran cartoons and odes in protest. One began:

> The horrid muzzle, in the streets,
> I wear upon my nose,
> Makes my tail flag, and quite completes
> The chapter of my woes!

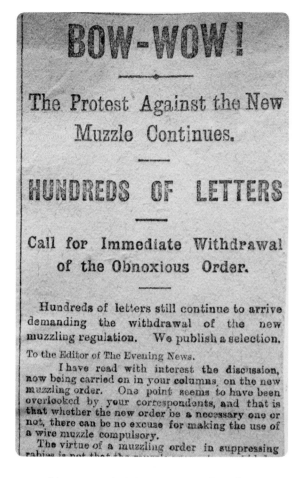

ABOVE Newspapers led the protests against the "obnoxious" muzzling orders and received hundred of letters, making it a topical issue.

> That man in helmet and blue cape
> Has put me in a fog;
> He seems to let the thief escape,
> To catch his foe, the dog!

By February 1897, the weight of complaints – and the fall in the number of rabies cases – prompted the London County Council to lift the order. Dogs were once more allowed to wear only a collar with a name and address "legibly engraved thereon". But it lasted for just sixty-one days: when suspected

ABOVE At the height of the rabies emergencies, Battersea's exercise areas became overrun with dogs.

new rabies cases cropped up in April, a new order was introduced by the Board of Agriculture. This time it was even stricter, requiring that dogs must wear a particular wire muzzle rather than a leather one.

This prompted even more complaints, particularly about the more expensive and scarce wire muzzle. In April 1897, the *London Evening News* printed hundreds of letters from angry people. One writer complained about what he called the "crackbrained muzzling edict":

In times of panic it is perhaps excusable and natural for boards to lose their heads under the pressure of red tape, but as the collective efforts of the principal veterinary surgeons of London appear to have been unable to produce a rabid dog, the only object that can be seen for enforcing the present order seems to be a desire upon the part of someone – I don't know who – to do for a friendly wire worker.

Another wrote:

It is a great shame that dogs have ever had to wear muzzles and the cranks who proposed them ought to be made to wear one themselves as they are a great deal madder than the dogs are or are ever likely to be.

This wasn't a unanimous opinion. One woman described to the *Evening News* the scene in Clapham:

We suburban residents are suffering from a "plague" of dogs and it has been positively unsafe to send our children alone on to the neighbouring commons, from the number of vicious half-bred collies, fox-terriers and mongrels that infect them and the neighbouring roads. Seventy dogs on Clapham Common counted in ten minutes … and three children bitten on one Saturday afternoon, and it is a "shame to muzzle the poor things"!

While the city argued the pros and cons of the order, the Home had to deal with its impact. The reintroduction of the order caught many by surprise, sparking widespread panic among owners whose dogs were suddenly hauled off the streets. A reporter from the *Sun* was at the Home during the first days after the new order had come into force:

The suddenness with which the reversal of the order was decreed took most people off their guard and the result has been that the police have been acting like amateur acrobatic cowboys in every quarter of London during the past five days. The inquiry department was besieged by people of all classes whose dogs had fallen victim to Robert's vigilance. It was truly a motley gathering. The West-end lady, armed with a docket authorizing inspection was jostled by the wife of the tradesman or the can-and-muttered coster, who drove up in his barrow and moke to enquire for his missing tyke.

During the first week that the order was enforced 1,192 dogs arrived at the gates. Only a very few – thirty-eight – were reclaimed. Protests against muzzling continued throughout the year, but as the numbers of dogs arriving at the Home continued to surge, there were reminders of the very real threat that rabies posed.

In November 1897 a rabid dog was admitted to the Home. As it was being processed, one of the receivers, Mr Crumpter, was bitten on the arm. He wasn't wearing the regulation gloves and required emergency medical attention. The wound was cauterized, then a specialist doctor was called in to treat him using the French Buisson system, using drugs developed by Pasteur.

There was widespread admiration – and sympathy – for the job the Home was doing during the extended crisis. News of the strain it was under

Under Arrest.

ABOVE As the nineteenth century muzzling acts took effect, the sight of dogs being seized by police officers became commonplace.

ABOVE "Dogs by the cartload": an illustration evokes the scenes inside Battersea's over-crowded kennels during the rabies crisis of 1896.

even reached the Royal Household. In January 1897 the Home received a letter from Osborne House. It revealed that "the Queen has expressed the intention of increasing her subscription to the Temporary Home for Lost and Starving Dogs from £10 to £15 per annum". Her only worry was that dogs were being destroyed too quickly. "I hope I am right in informing the Queen," her private secretary continued, "that valuable animals are kept for a considerable time before being disposed of, as I know this is the hope of Her Majesty."

The Home assured her it was doing its best, but the truth was that, with the muzzling order back in place and no prospect of it being lifted in the near future, it was being overwhelmed. Hemmed in by the railway line and the adjoining yards, the Battersea site was simply too small. It had to expand. But how?

The idea of opening a second Home had been percolating quietly for years. Staff and members were keen on a quieter, more sedate establishment, where the emphasis would be on rest and recuperation, ideally in a countryside location. There were attractions from the business point of view too. As well as creating much-needed new kennel space, a new Home would open up the prospect of once more earning money from paying boarders and from charging owners for holding their dogs in compulsory quarantine.

By 1896, the number of dogs at Battersea had swollen exponentially with the new muzzling order, and a new Home had become a priority. As it approved plans for a second Home, the Committee argued that the new premises would also be a fitting gesture to coincide with the Diamond Jubilee of its patron, Queen Victoria.

It was agreed to begin searching for a site where, in the Committee's words, "the better class of dog could be sent so that an effectual effort may be made to improve their condition, restore them to health, and save a large number of them from the Lethal Chamber …"

The first option considered was to buy some open space not far from the Home owned by the Southwark and Vauxhall Water Company. When the agents revealed the land would cost £7,500 an acre, however, it was quickly agreed that the price was "quite prohibitive". Members cast a wider net and soon found for sale an area of open fields in Hackbridge, Surrey. The site was eight miles from Battersea, on the London, Brighton and South Coast Railway, opposite Hackbridge station. When

ABOVE Battersea's staff always used innovative methods to persuade dogs to exercise properly!

the chairman and Matthias Colam travelled there at the beginning of April 1897 they immediately declared it "desirable in every way": "They found it to be a rich pasture, very picturesque, well shaded with trees, with abundant water supply."

The price was equally appealing at £400 an acre. When the Home started negotiating this was reduced to £380. The Committee quickly struck a deal to buy an eight-and-a-half-acre plot for just over £3,000. A bargain it might have been, but it was still a huge sum at the time. To finance the building work, an appeal was launched that quickly raised an anonymous £1,000 donation.

Work began immediately on a reception building that was "spacious, light and sanitary and possessing every facility for receiving and examining the dogs as they enter the Home". The bills were soon mounting: fencing, draining and laying concrete foundations at the new Home cost more than £500. Tenders for the building work ranged between £1,200 and £1,500. The Committee also ordered the building for £80 of a special van capable of transporting dogs between Battersea and Hackbridge.

By August 1898, the Committee was ready to hire the new Home's first resident keeper. Of the three candidates to make the final interview, it was agreed that the most suitable was a George Tobutt. He had provided excellent testimonials

ABOVE "The Dog's Paradise": an artist's impression of the idyllic "country home" at Hackbridge in Surrey.

George Measom, as usual, made a hyperbolic speech in which he called the Home "one of the most beneficent schemes ever inaugurated for the benefit of dogs". He also revealed that, on hearing of the extension to the Home, Queen Victoria had sent a message saying "she would be glad to know" of it.

The Duke of Portland caught the mood best. "Instead of calling it a Home for Lost and Starving Dogs it ought to be called the Dogs' Paradise, because I am sure dogs cannot fail to be happy when so many provisions for their happiness have been made for them," he said, to applause and laughter. "If I have a fault to find at all it is that the dogs here may be made too happy, for as you are all aware, dogs are very intelligent creatures indeed, and if it comes to be known they are made so happy here, I am afraid that sometimes their masters will have very considerable trouble in preventing their being lost."

He reminded everyone of the role Mary Tealby and Sarah Major – "two kind and humane ladies" – had played in establishing the Home "in spite of much opposition and ridicule". He also paid tribute

and was interviewed by a three-man board. They unanimously agreed to give him the job at a wage of 30s a week. He and his wife would also have use of the cottage that had been specially built at the Home, as well as "gas, coal, water, rates, taxes and uniform free of charge".

On Saturday, 29 October 1898, Lord and Lady Portland opened the Hackbridge Home. Despite the "damp weather" a large contingent of press was on hand to record the event. In many ways, it was the first official opening that the Home for Lost and Starving Dogs had ever enjoyed and the Committee made the most of it.

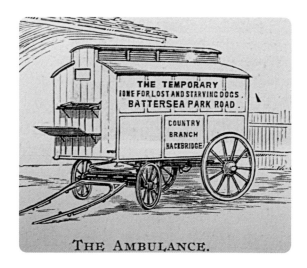

ABOVE Keepers were given the most up-to-date vehicles to ferry dogs to and from Battersea.

ABOVE "So many provisions for their happiness": Hackbridge prided itself on the quality of its kitchens.

ABOVE "Most beneficient": the Hackbridge kennels were more spacious than those at Battersea.

to two donors, an anonymous lady who had given £1,000 and a Mrs Grove Grady who donated £1,200 for the new Home. He concluded on a serious note, reminding the crowd of the muzzling order and the rabies threat that had forced Battersea to extend its operations into the Surrey countryside.

"During the first year of the present muzzling order no fewer than 42,614 dogs were admitted – the largest number ever received in one year," he said. The cause represented by Battersea and now Hackbridge was "not only one of mercy for lost and starving dogs but also one of necessity in such a vast metropolis as London, where an enormous amount of homeless dogs must be a source of danger in the streets and also a source of spreading that most horrible disease, hydrophobia".

The opening ceremony generated a large amount of publicity, but there was no time to dwell on it. The next Monday morning, George Tobutt and his staff began the hard work of dealing with the overspill of dogs still pouring into Battersea because of the muzzling order.

The Committee members were aware they had taken a risk by locating their second Home in such a relatively isolated spot and had to work hard to

sell it from the very beginning. Members were encouraged to "endeavour to visit the place and do all they can to induce their friends to journey down and interest themselves in the undertaking". It even suggested members take a day trip to the Surrey countryside. "For cyclists the run from town is a most agreeable one of about nine miles over excellent roads the whole distance," it said. "Arrangements will be made for taking care of cycles and afternoon tea." Unsurprisingly, perhaps, there were few takers.

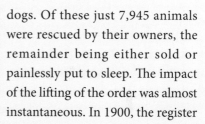

FOR THE CREDIT
OF THE HOME

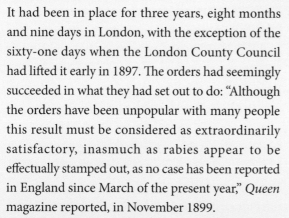

Tʜᴇ ʙᴇɢɪɴɴɪɴɢ ᴏꜰ ᴛʜᴇ ɴᴇᴡ century brought mixed blessings. The most welcome news was that the muzzling order had finally been abolished. The legislation was withdrawn on 27 October 1899. It had been in place for three years, eight months and nine days in London, with the exception of the sixty-one days when the London County Council had lifted it early in 1897. The orders had seemingly succeeded in what they had set out to do: "Although the orders have been unpopular with many people this result must be considered as extraordinarily satisfactory, inasmuch as rabies appear to be effectually stamped out, as no case has been reported in England since March of the present year," *Queen* magazine reported, in November 1899.

But a terrible price had been paid. During that time the Home had taken in an incredible 106,353 dogs. Of these just 7,945 animals were rescued by their owners, the remainder being either sold or painlessly put to sleep. The impact of the lifting of the order was almost instantaneous. In 1900, the register recorded the arrival of 16,731 dogs – a drop of 2,924, or around 15 per cent, on the previous year. Further falls would follow.

There was also positive news from Hackbridge, where a new infirmary had been built for sick dogs. The more genteel surroundings of the Home were already having an impact on the condition – and saleability – of the dogs kennelled there. Of the 376 sent to Hackbridge in the first year of the new century, 215 – almost 60 per cent – had gone to good homes. "The animals taken there find not only a refuge from suffering but a veritable haven of rest," the Committee reported.

PREVIOUS PAGE The lifting of the muzzling orders eased the pressure on the Home as it began a new century.

The success of the second home had also come at a price, though. The 1900 accounts showed that, for some reason, Hackbridge had made "a considerable loss". The secretary, Henry Ward, had promised to see whether he could make the home more profitable, but had warned that Hackbridge was "not a commercial undertaking and cannot be financially remunerative". This was especially worrying given that the Second Boer War, which had begun in 1899, had taken its toll on donations and there had been "a marked falling off of receipts".

The most painful loss the Home suffered, however, was personal. Queen Victoria died on 22 January 1901 aged eighty-one, prompting the following encomium in the Home's Annual Report:

> The memory of Her Majesty's sympathy will remain, even beyond the lives of your Committee; while deploring the loss your cause and the nation have sustained, the recollection that the foremost lady in the world, out of the fullness of her compassionate heart gave to lost and forsaken dogs her benevolent sympathy and support, and her gracious countenance and commendation of your Committee, will remain as a sacred memento of her reign.

The words might have tripped off the silver tongue of George Measom, but the Home had lost him too. He had retired through ill-health halfway through the year, and had died shortly before his eighty-third birthday.

≈

The Home could take great pride from the fact that while it was no longer Europe's only home for dogs or cats it remained by far its best known and respected. On the Continent, successful dogs' homes had been established in Berlin, Antwerp and Amsterdam. Closer at hand, refuges had been opened in Liverpool, Manchester, Birmingham, Bristol, Leeds and Glasgow. Even smaller towns now had their sanctuaries. A lady called Mary Wemyss, who had been on friendly terms with Thomas Scorborio before his resignation in 1883, had founded a Home, based on Battersea's principles, in Gloucester. Sadly, many had fallen foul of the kind of troubles that had afflicted the Home since Mary Tealby had first opened its doors.

A cats' home in Haverstock Hill, north London, founded by a Miss Morgan, had succeeded in attracting patronage from a number of well-heeled ladies, including the Princess of Wales. But there were serious questions about Miss Morgan's finances and the *Truth* newspaper had published a long exposé of how she was channelling the thousands of pounds she was raising each year into her own pocket. The paper's call for the Home to be "suppressed" soon led to its demise.

The key to Battersea's success lay in its relationship with the police and London's other authorities. If Committee members ever wondered how the Home might have fared had it not forged its links with the Metropolitan Police and the London councils, they only had to look across the English Channel to Paris.

The French capital had had a comparable dog population to London and its upper classes liked to think themselves as humane as, if not more so than, their English counterparts. Yet it had only been in the early 1880s that a lone campaigner, the Baroness d'Herpent, had opened a dogs' home in the Levallois-Perret area. Like London's Miss Morgan and, indeed, Mary Tealby, she had begun

ABOVE **By 1900, five hundred cats each year were being housed at the Home.**

the venture after separating from her husband, the Baron d'Herpent. During her twenty years' running the home, she had fought against dire financial problems, local complaints about the noise and smell, and even a fire-bombing that killed sixteen dogs. She refused to put down any animals that arrived at her home and considered her greatest duty was to keep dogs from the city's official dog pound – the notorious Fourrière.

The pound was a magnet for dog stealers who, according to one campaigner in the city, "make a living by enticing and stealing dogs of no matter what size or species and claiming a bonus of from 1 franc 50 cents to 2 francs from the Fourrière authorities". A reporter from the Paris-based *New York Herald* managed to infiltrate the pound and found that dogs were being disposed of in barbaric circumstances.

The pound's most vocal critic, a Mademoiselle Neyrat, had travelled to Battersea to see Ward Richardson's euthanizing chamber and had been sufficiently impressed to raise two thousand francs for a version to be built at the Fourrière. But she was told that it was "impossible" for the institution's governors to accept it. "As I have said and will continue to say, the Fourrière is a disgrace to Paris," she protested.

It would take four more years to get the message through but, eventually, Benjamin Ward Richardson was personally invited to Paris by the *New York Herald* with a view to persuading the Fourrière to take a new version of his chamber. Reluctantly, the authorities agreed.

For all the progress it had made, Battersea could not afford to be complacent, as it soon discovered. In October 1902, the Committee heard of "serious irregularities" at Hackbridge. The second Home had continued to be a loss-

115

making operation, but worrying rumours were circulating. Two Committee members, Colonel Parr and Professor Pritchard, were despatched to the Home to investigate.

The most concerning reports that had reached Battersea had come from a keeper called William Wolven, who had made allegations against head keeper George Tobutt and his son, Frank. Wolven claimed that he had seen Frank, who ran his own kennels nearby, loading sacks of dog biscuits on to a horse and trap. He also revealed that he and other members of the Hackbridge staff had been ordered by George Tobutt to work at Frank's kennels in nearby Carshalton during the Home's hours of business. There, they had recognized a large number of items from Hackbridge, including mops, brooms and watering cans.

Summoned to explain himself at a meeting with Parr and Pritchard, George Tobutt admitted lending his son a small amount of biscuits at one point but said they had been repaid. He blamed Wolven's attack on the fact that Wolven had wanted to rent the kennels Frank occupied but had been refused.

Parr and Pritchard weren't terribly convinced by his story. They asked Tobutt why there had been a "great increase" in the amount of food being ordered at Hackbridge. The quantity of biscuits used during the first nine months of the year had gone up by two tons and much more meat was being ordered too.

Tobutt blamed the rise in biscuit consumption on Wolven overfeeding the dogs. The increase in meat was the butcher's fault, and he said he had visited him to "remonstrate".

The Committee considered the evidence and unanimously agreed that Wolven's evidence was "maliciously designed to incriminate Tobutt and his son". Wolven was dismissed with one week's pay. They weren't so naïve as to believe Tobutt,

though, because they knew of the financial troubles he'd been having. In 1900 and 1901 Matthias Colam and the secretary Mr Ward had learned that Mr and Mrs Tobutt had run up huge debts in Hackbridge and in Brighton where they had lived before moving to Hackbridge. Colam had feared the damage this might do, so "for the credit of the Home" he had personally agreed to pay off the monies owed on condition that the couple incurred no more liabilities and repaid him privately.

Disappointed by the keeper's behaviour, the Committee censured George Tobutt for letting his staff work at his son's kennels during normal hours. He was ordered to appear at a full Committee meeting so that he be "sternly reproved for his delinquencies and admonished to pay strict attention to his duties in future".

If the Committee had hoped that was the end of the matter, they were sorely disappointed. A few weeks later, in December 1902, a "burglary" was reported at Hackbridge. The contents of the Home's cash box –

ABOVE Illegal dog-dealing was rife in London. This article entitled "Where To Procure A Dog For Nothing" imagines a cunning dog thief at work.

£4 10s – had been stolen. However, an investigation revealed some alarming facts. On the night of the burglary, the fierce guard dog that was normally kept in the house had been shut out for the night, while the back door of the house had been left open. The cash box had, unusually, been left downstairs in an unlocked cupboard. It also transpired that there had been another theft a few weeks earlier.

Colam must have felt personally responsible because he read out a statement at the next Committee meeting, detailing the Tobutts' financial difficulties. He also explained that, despite previous help given to them, they were now in a worse state than ever. They "had made no effort to discharge any of their debts but had on the contrary incurred fresh debts in violation of a promise made by them in writing to pay their way in future". Mr Ward had complained "several times" that money received by the Tobutts had "not been promptly paid over".

The Committee wanted to dismiss the family immediately but Colam argued they should be given a final chance. Reluctantly, the Committee agreed.

It wasn't long before they were regretting it. In May 1903, George Tobutt was regularly found drunk while on duty. Again Colam tried to help him and spent time talking to him at the Home. Tobutt had confessed that he had been arguing with his wife and had turned to drink. Now "the desire for drink possessed him to such an extent that he felt he could no longer resist it". He had "begged that he might be put away in some asylum or home for inebriates at the expense of the Committee". He had suggested that his son Frank take over the role of head keeper in his absence.

The Committee rejected almost all of Tobutt's requests. Tobutt agreed that his wife would pay the fees for his treatment from her wages. He was dismissed immediately.

> The key to Battersea's success lay in its relationship with the police and London's other authorities

As he walked out, his son Frank walked in. Frank had worked with his father at the Brighton Dogs Home and now agreed to wind down his operation at Carshalton to take over George's role.

In November Mrs Tobutt sent a letter saying Frank had contracted a "serious illness". Two Committee members, Wragg and Pritchard, travelled to Hackbridge. They were horrified by what they saw. The infirmary was filled with thirty-three sick dogs. Of the thirty-eight more in the kennels, thirty-five were "so diseased as to be unfit to be placed with other dogs". Only three were in good health.

"We think that this branch of the Home is unquestionably saturated with disease and that very stringent measures must be adopted, and at once, to render it otherwise," they reported. The situation was dire. There weren't enough staff. There was no system distinguishing corridors from kennels or for identifying dogs. The large open spaces and exercise yards seemed unused. The two men felt "compelled to strongly recommend that this Branch be closed *pro tem* and that the whole of the dogs there be put to sleep". "Under no other circumstances can the kennels be thoroughly fumigated and disinfected and rendered a fit habitat for healthy dogs in the future."

As if this was not bad enough, there was a clear feeling that the Tobutts had defrauded the Home. When Henry Ward took a careful look at

"In October 1912, the Home began to witness a new ritual ... lines of dog and cat owners would form outside the Home, their sick pets curled up in their arms"

RIGHT The Home opened a twice-weekly outpatients clinic which immediately drew queues of dog and cat owners eager to obtain "advice free of cost" for their pets.

the register of dogs for Hackbridge he found there were at least sixteen fewer on the site than in the books. The accounts were in a "very unsatisfactory state": "He was unable to get any money out of Mrs Tobutt in settlement for dogs sold in September and October."

George Tobutt had written to the Home asking to be allowed to leave his confinement to help his son but his request was refused. The Home had had enough of the Tobutts and a motion that "the entire Tobutt family be dismissed immediately from the service of the Home" was passed. It was also agreed that all dogs be brought back to Battersea and destroyed, that the Home be closed and the entire staff given two weeks' notice.

It was nothing short of a disaster for Battersea.

Publicly, the truth was glossed over. At the annual general meeting, Henry Ward reported merely that "drastic changes" had been needed at Hackbridge. After what he called a period of

LEFT Henry J. Ward, the hugely popular secretary credited with putting the Home on "an organized footing" as it began the twentieth century.

"renovation and purification", however, the Home was reopened "under much more favourable circumstances than formerly". Hard lessons had been learned. The mistakes of Hackbridge would not be made again.

~

On 27 February 1903, *The Times* carried a notice "respecting stolen dogs". It explained that "persons who have lost dogs" should go to Battersea "where upwards of thirty dogs supposed to have been stolen are being held in separate compartments and may be inspected pending proceedings at Marlborough Street Police Court for dog-stealing and dog-starving".

Dog theft had always been a problem in London, but had become increasingly sophisticated. Often the thieves would work as a double act, usually a seemingly innocent couple out for a stroll. When they spotted a desirable dog, the woman would make a fuss of it while the man put powdered baked liver into his trouser turn-ups. Enticed by the smell, the dog would trot obediently along behind the couple.

One owner told the *Daily Mail* of how her daughter spotted their black toy Pomeranian walking off through Kensington Gardens with a "correctly dressed" man and a "fashionably clothed" woman. The little girl challenged the couple as they put the dog into a cab, shouting, "That's my dog."

Sometimes the thieves demanded ransoms. Montagu Williams, a well-known writer, admitted he had paid twenty pounds to be reunited with his dog. More usually, however, the dogs were sold to buyers around the country. Large depots had been set up in the East End of London for redistributing dogs from the capital to the rest of the country.

The case at Marlborough Street related to one such operation and involved two of the most serious offenders yet caught, William Lee, known as the Chinaman, and a German bootmaker called Conrad Jaeger. Embarrassingly for Battersea, the Home had been inadvertently caught up in Jaeger's massive operation. That year two keepers, Hale and Andrews, had been caught taking money from him. The pair had been supplying Jaeger with a large number of dogs and had also been altering the official Battersea receipts so that he could claim to his clients that he had paid more than he actually had. They were dismissed.

On a more positive note, however, the notice in *The Times* signalled a new development in Battersea's relationship with the police. Until now, it had been standard practice for the police to retain stolen dogs in their possession while proceedings were brought against dog thieves. At the end of the case the dogs that remained unclaimed were sold by public auction. Now, however, Commissioner Edward Henry had agreed that stolen dogs should be housed at Battersea. The arrangement meant they were "kept under more favourable conditions". Those that remained unclaimed would be sold "for the benefit" of Battersea. The Home had been lobbying for this for some time and had even invited Edward Henry to take the chair at the AGM that year. The new arrangement had its downside, of course. Once more, the numbers of dogs coming into the Home was likely to rise.

~

Numbers were on the increase in the cattery, too, something of a relief after the troubles it had endured. Since taking its first animals in during the

early 1880s, the Home had found it a challenge to get used to the very different demands of stray felines.

It wasn't for want of trying. As the 1899 Annual Report put it, "every care was bestowed upon these unfortunate, forsaken animals". At one point, the Queen's "dog and cat doctor", Mr A. J. Sewell, had been "in constant attendance upon them". Yet caring for them could, at times, be a frustrating and thankless job. Outbreaks of illness among cats were common but the main problem was that they were so difficult to rehome. Even those who were boarding proved problematic. "I would sooner have a hundred dogs than one cat," the superintendent complained in 1896. "The cats pine for their owners and go 'off their feed' so persistently that we have often to write to people gone away into the country to come back and fetch them."

Compounding the problems, some owners seemed to treat the Home as a hotel for their cats. Many were brought in at Christmas time, as their owners headed off to the country for the holidays. In 1897, it was revealed that one cat had lived there for fifteen years, since the very first cat intake. Another lady kept fourteen there, only taking them out when she needed to show them at a cat competition.

In general, the staff preferred caring for the strays, which were much easier to deal with. "They have had a taste of adversity and they are only too grateful for a chance of appreciating the shelter and food given to them," a member of staff told the *Saturday Journal* in 1896.

By the turn of the century around five hundred cats a year were being housed at the Home, around two hundred of them boarders. The strays' time at the Home would consist of "6 to 14 days during which they were properly fed and cared for, in the hope that some of them might be purchased".

In its Annual Reports the cats' department was generally damned with faint praise. In 1899 it was working "in a satisfactory manner"; a year later it had "maintained its usefulness". Hardly ringing endorsements.

Since the turn of the century, however, there had been a sudden rise in arrivals. By 1903 cats were coming into the Home at a rate of roughly one a day. Matthias Colam and his staff didn't need to look far for the reason behind the new influx. Almost half of the animals were being brought in by the same person, a mysterious, well-heeled lady, who turned up several times a week with stray cats she had found on the streets of central London. She had brought in 161 of the 385 cats that came in during 1902 and 132 of the 358 that had arrived in 1903.

All sorts of rumours had begun to fly about her identity. In his speech to the annual general meeting that year, Matthias Colam found it necessary to defend her, denying that she was "affected with a mania for stealing cats": "She is a person of means, and she uses her means for carrying out a work of humanity that she has set her heart on," he added, refusing to identify her. In many ways the mysterious lady was an echo of Mary Tealby. "She practically says, 'I cannot do much in this world to make it better but I pity stray cats and whenever I see them starving I stretch out a hand to rescue them'," Colam said.

There was no question that life for London's stray cats had improved enormously in the twenty years since the Home had taken in its first feline inmates. As Colam explained, back in the 1880s "boys in the street used to think it fair game to pick a stone up and throw it at any passing cat". Now serious consideration was being given to introducing the same licensing system for cats that was being used in New York. "The acknowledged feeling nowadays is that cats are not only domestic favourites and pets, but are protected by the law equally with dogs, and this asset has promoted our cause greatly," Colam said. But now they – like the dogs – were arriving in such numbers that they would soon need more space.

With this in mind, the Committee had made attempts to buy railway arches from the London, Chatham and Dover Railway Company but had fallen frustratingly short. In October 1905, however, they got wind of the fact that five railway arches and a large parcel of land were about to be vacated by the railway company. The Committee seized the moment and snapped it up, although it took until July 1906 to conclude negotiations with the railway, whose representatives, at one stage, wanted to put the Home on a short lease with just a week's notice to quit.

Appeals were made for the £2,000 the extra building work would cost. Raising the money proved hard, especially when the treasurer, Guy Guillum Scott, fell foul of a conman. He took a phone call from someone asking whether he would meet with the nephew of America's best known philanthropist, J. Pierpont Morgan. An excited Scott had looked up the tycoon in *Who's Who* and discovered listed among his many recreations "dog fancier".

"I have come from my uncle, who is anxious to know something of the Home and its work," the nephew said, on arriving at Battersea.

Scott explained the plans to expand the site and the man asked about its cost. Scott told him they'd raised half of the money they'd need. "You may put my uncle's name down for £1,000," the young man said, to Scott's delight. He added that Scott could put J. P. Morgan down for an annual donation of £50 as well.

The man confirmed his offer on the back of his business card, which read G. W. Morgan. He promised the cheque that Friday.

Scott's excitement was short-lived. The following day the man turned up at the Scotts' front door in some distress. He had lost his watch and £12 on the nearby streets and asked for a short-term loan. A few days later, when Scott went to the address on the business card he was introduced to the real G. W. Morgan. Needless to say, the impostor was never seen again. "You may well imagine how galling it was to be imposed on in this way when we appeared … on the eve of realizing so much for the benefit of the Home," a red-faced Scott said, recounting the episode to the Committee.

The first phase of the new work was converting the five arches into kennels and turning the open land into an exercise ground for the dogs. After that, work would begin to improve some of the old buildings, many dating back to 1871. Given that the development was the most significant the Home had undertaken since its move to Battersea, it was decided to hire a top architect.

The job was given to Clough Williams-Ellis, a rising star in the London architectural world. Williams-Ellis, a clergyman's son from North Wales, was a colourful character who had become an architect after failing to complete a natural-sciences degree at Cambridge. He was very much a man of the new century and found the Committee and the chairman, in particular, Sir Guillum Scott (the father of Guy), amusing throwbacks to the Victorian era. He described Scott as "a charming old barrister who still rode to his chambers in the Temple on a smart little cob, his trousers strapped beneath his boots, a low-crowned top hat on his venerable head. His speech and elaborate manners matched his old-fashioned dress and he was a great stickler for the precise observance of etiquette and protocol."

Despite this, he accepted the job, which he later described as a "rather odd commission": "For the most part it was a matter of reorganizing the layout of the existing huddle of odds and ends of buildings into a coherent and readily workable entity, and exploiting the newly acquired arches under the railway that crossed the site, all with such seemliness as I could contrive, which was somewhat minimal," he wrote. He clearly found the work a little dull so tried to entertain himself by adding interesting details. "I was permitted to do a little face-lifting of the office block's street front and slightly to embellish the entrance and boardroom," he wrote.

His greatest piece of mischief, however, was a plan to build an elaborate pavilion in the middle of the yard. It seems he was amazed when he was given permission to go ahead.

LEFT Guy Guillum Scott, the innovative secretary who steered the Home into a new era in the 1900s.

On some pretext or other I did get away with a little two-storeyed pavilion with a cupola and a weather vane atop its steep pantiled roof, and an elegant outside timber stairway round it. Though leading up to only one small room for which I had invented some more or less plausible function, it was condemned to be torn down as a fire risk until I found someone who claimed that he could render it fireproof.

On 8 August 1907, two and a half years of planning and construction work came to an end with the opening of the new, radically redesigned Home. It was the biggest outlay on building that the Home had made since moving to Battersea. The 1907 accounts showed that the work had cost £3,277.

It seemed money well spent. Even Clough Williams-Ellis's folly proved more than just an eye-pleaser: the pavilion was designated the new cattery and proved as practical as it was pretty. It even boasted stoves to warm the place during winter, and seemed to attract even more inmates. During its first year, the Home took in 787 stray cats, an increase of 103 on 1906.

On 1 January 1906, yet another new piece of legislation came into force, one of the most significant – and lasting – statutes affecting Battersea and its work. The Dogs Act recognized that dogs were legal "chattels" and that, as a result, the police had a responsibility to deal with any lost, stray or stolen items of such "property".

The Act allowed a police officer to seize and detain any dog found in a public place that he had "reason to believe" was a stray, regardless of whether it was wearing a collar or not. The owners of dogs with identification around their necks would be notified of a dog's seizure, but "dogs will be liable to be sold or destroyed if not claimed within seven clear days after the service of the notice".

It was the final provision that had the most serious implications for the Home. Since the 1880s, it had kept lost and stray dogs for a minimum of five days before it could rehome them. The new law would require it to keep every animal for an extra two. In the run-up to the legislation being passed by Parliament, the Committee had fought hard against it, sending a deputation to Whitehall to argue their case – unsuccessfully as it turned out.

The Act also shifted responsibility for collecting and disposing of stray dogs from local authorities to the police. In Battersea's case this meant the onus shifted from the London County Council to the Metropolitan Police, which meant that the Home had to negotiate a new agreement with the police.

There was much that bothered the Home in the new legislation. One Committee member, Leonard Noble, admitted that, days before the legislation came into law, he had broken one of its conditions, that anyone finding a stray dog should contact the police. Noble had seen "a wretched dog on a doorstep" when he was leaving the St James's Theatre. "I took it along with me to supper at Princes' and afterwards conveyed it to my home in the country."

It was only three days later that he got his servant to polish the dirty collar. When he did so, it revealed that the dog came from a house on the same road as the St James's Theatre – King Street. "Which proved to me that I had actually stolen the creature from its own doorstep," he explained.

"Now it is obvious that if this Act had been in force I might have had to appear before the magistrate as a dog stealer."

But there was little that the Home could do to stop it being introduced. Instead it had once more to start planning for the massive influx of dogs it could expect when the new legislation came into force. "It is quite obvious that the number of dogs in residence at the Home must be largely increased and that the new arrangements must entail a considerable increase of expenditure for extended accommodation, more food and a larger staff of attendants," the Committee concluded, in its annual general meeting that year.

The economic burden of dealing with this would test the Home to its limits. "This additional responsibility causes your Committee much anxiety as to their financial position in the future," the Committee worried.

~

On the morning of 1 October 1909, the streets of London were treated to a new and eye-catching sight. The pair of gleaming scarlet Dennis motor vans was being piloted by smartly uniformed "chauffeurs" and bore the same gold-lettered livery: 'Temporary Home For Lost & Starving Dogs, Battersea & Hackbridge, Patron: H. M. The King. President: The Duke of Portland K.G.'

The striking vans – complete with yellow wheels – had been rented from a car-hire company, Thomas Tilling Ltd, in Peckham, as part of a three-year contract. The Home had also hired seven non-motorized vans, six horses and another half-dozen drivers. For 25s a week the drivers would "drive and look after each horse and van". To help them do this the Home had also taken delivery of quantities of "harness, forage and shoeing".

The agreement included a clause under which the Home could hire extra horses at 7s 6d a day, "should the work required to be performed by any of the horses be beyond its capacity". It was a sensible provision, given the amount of mileage the new fleet of collection vehicles would have to rack up.

Since the introduction of the Dogs Act, the area the Home was expected to cover had expanded beyond all recognition. According to the secretary, Henry Ward, the catchment area now represented a huge sweep of the metropolis "as far as Staines in the west, Epsom, Banstead and Kenley in the south and Belvedere, Erith and Bexley in the east". The new area went "beyond the twenty-mile radius" the Home was previously required to cover, Ward added.

While the horse-drawn vans made collections from the seventy-eight police stations in the "county of London", the motor vans had been recruited to cover the forty-nine stations outside the metropolis. To give itself a chance of covering the entire southern area, one of the vans would take its dogs to Hackbridge, rather than Battersea.

Ward admitted it was an ambitious plan. "We thought we would have a shot," he said. "It is a big task and will cost us about £2,000 a year. The police will, of course, bear part of the expense, but there is no doubt that a considerable sum will have to be raised by our supporters if the work is efficiently to be maintained."

On their first morning in service, the two motor vans brought in forty dogs, half the number they'd have been expected to collect. The numbers would soon rise, but in one respect, Ward had already succeeded. He and the Committee had hoped that the unveiling of the vans would generate much-needed publicity and funds for the Home. Sure enough, photographs of the distinctive vehicles appeared not just in the mainstream newspapers but in the automotive press too. In the first days of October, the Home received so many requests to see the vans that Ward organized a special parade of the vehicles in Battersea Park. Hundreds turned up to watch, donating handy amounts of money at the same time. Battersea's distinctive red vans were soon greeted with cheers and smiles by schoolchildren all over the city.

For Ward it was a rewarding and quietly symbolic moment. Weeks later he announced his retirement after sixteen years as secretary. He was to be replaced by a younger man, Guy Guillum Scott. Ward was a modest man, but he accepted the universal praise that came his way as the press devoted pages to his departure in December. "When he took up the position … the dogs were

housed in shelters made of corrugated iron and wood. Now all the houses are made of brick and are fitted with the most modern appliances," the *Evening News* reported. "I think I may fairly claim to have put it on an organized footing," he said.

Like everyone else connected to the Home, Ward's greatest terror had been to find that a Battersea dog had been sold to a vivisectionist – or worse. He retired happy in the knowledge that he had never sold a dog to an undeserving owner. He recounted the case of a "foreigner" who had come to Battersea wanting to buy eight or nine Fox Terriers for a French vineyard "to protect the vines from stoats". Ward had been suspicious and turned him away.

His darker memories were mixed with happier ones. To *Reynolds* magazine, he told of a dog that had arrived at the Home from Bristol. It was apparently fond of jumping on board moving vehicles and somehow climbed on to a train bound for London's Paddington Station. It had spent several months wandering the streets of the capital, by which time the Home was used to receiving regular weekly visits from its owner, who travelled up to London from Bristol every week. "The owner sent us a description of his lost pet. We entered that description up in our routine book, and in a few days we were fortunate enough to have placed in our hands an animal which appeared to resemble the one wanted." Ward described the reunion between the man and his dog as "most affecting".

On another occasion, a man had been reunited with his dog – "an undistinguished pedigree" – after a week. "You would have been surprised to see the amount of gratitude in that animal's face. Just as he

1. Front of the Dog Licence Card.

Dog Licence, 1909.

Name...................................... No................

Address..............................

Official Completion Stamp.

Inland Revenue.

3d.	3d.	3d.	3d.	3d.
3d.	3d.	3d.	3d.	3d.
3d.	3d.	3d.	3d.	3d.
3d.	3d.	3d.	3d.	3d.
3d.	3d.	3d.	3d.	3d.
3d.	3d.	3d.	3d.	3d.

LEFT In 1909, the dog licence cost seven shillings and sixpence and could be paid for in threepenny instalments.

was leaving us the dog gave three joyous barks, and, as an afterthought, ran up to the head keeper, gave him an almost human look, and licked his hand before departing."

His favourite stories were of two very different dogs. One was a Scotch Terrier, which he had sold to a police inspector. The little dog was "fond of taking long walks. This happened so many times that he came to be picked up in almost every part of London," Ward said, relishing the retelling of the story to the newspapers in December, days before his departure. The dog was always returned safely, however. "When its little legs were tired it would pick out a policeman and sit up and beg to him in the street," he explained. "Nothing would induce him to leave the constable who was ultimately compelled to find the name on his collar and send him home again. This happened time after time."

His other favourite was Nellie, the adopted dog of London's cab drivers. An Irish Terrier, Nellie had been "the sport of the bad boys of the locality" where she was found, Shoreditch. "The cabbies took pity on her, fed her and clubbed together to pay for her licence." Ward went on to describe how Nellie was often to be found enjoying a free ride in one of their cabs.

The bravest dog Ward had ever encountered during his time at the Home was a black Retriever that had been sent from Battersea to Burma, where he became the pet of a serving officer in the British Army. One day the officer was in a part of the country occupied by the local dacoits. "Being unarmed they thought their last hour had come, but the Retriever sprang at the dacoits with such ferocity they were for the moment dismayed and the officers were enabled to run away."

The dog was "speared" but the owner returned later to "avenge his death", Ward said.

Ward was clearly one of the most popular members of staff the Home had known and was given an unusually grand send-off. As well as receiving a Sheffield tea service, he was also the guest of honour

at a special dinner held at the Hackbridge Home. The evening was clearly a raucous affair as, "with no ladies present to inhibit the proceedings", it ended in the small hours with all the men linking arms and singing "Auld Lang Syne".

Guy Guillum Scott was a very different character from Ward. He was, by nature, an administrator, and had cut his teeth on the committees of various charities. He was soon making his mark on the Home. In October 1912, the Home began to witness a new ritual. Every Tuesday and Thursday afternoons, at around two thirty, lines of dog and cat owners would form outside the Home, their sick pets curled up in their arms, or in cages or even in prams. At the suggestion of Scott, John Stow Young, the much-respected vet at the Hackbridge Home, had begun travelling up to Battersea to hold an outpatients clinic for "those who were really unable to pay the usual charges for professional services to obtain for their dogs and cats advice free of cost".

Twice a week, for three or so hours, he would check the assembled animals for illness, diagnosing everything from fleas and flaky skin to diarrhoea and distemper. The sessions were an instant success. Guy Guillum Scott was soon reporting that Stow Young's clinic was "alleviating a good deal of suffering". Within a few months a sponsorship scheme was introduced to help more people benefit from the outpatients service. For every five shillings subscribers put into the Home, they would qualify for a letter "entitling one poor person to free Veterinary advice for their dog or cat". Members were soon taking advantage of the offer in large numbers.

The success of the outpatients clinic contrasted starkly with the disappointments that were being

OPPOSITE From October 1909, the sight of Battersea's liveried vans became a familiar one on the streets of London.

experienced in the cattery. Despite the increase in numbers since the opening of the new quarters, the Home's feline population had continued to cause problems. Illness remained rife – so much so that by 1913 the Home had virtually given up trying to prevent it. As the Committee reported that year,

Serious outbreaks of disease of a highly contagious nature almost invariably make their appearance every year in Cats' Homes in London, however well managed they may be.

Very little appears really to be known, even by the most experienced members of the profession, about feline disease. No amount of care, disinfection, or the most scrupulous cleanliness, seem of any avail to prevent sudden outbreaks of illness ... while it is well known that a cat, when once ill, offers little constitutional resistance to sickness, and speedily succumbs without apparent cause.

It was therefore decided to stop taking in boarders in the cattery at Battersea. From now on, only strays would be accepted.

By 1914, the Home was increasingly using the revitalized kennels at Hackbridge as a commercial operation, in particular charging for boarding. In the late autumn of that year, the country home welcomed a very unusual party of guests: ninety-nine Canadian Husky-type dogs.

They had been ordered by Sir Ernest Shackleton, the adventurer, who was in the final stages of organizing his latest expedition to the Antarctic. The grandly named Imperial Trans-Antarctic Expedition aimed to complete the first land crossing of the continent. The dogs, a mixture of breeds, mostly

The SHACKLETON Trans-Antarctic EXPEDITION.

The Expedition, which this Week Takes its First Definite Step on its Adventurous Journey, is Here Fully Described in "Sphere" Diagrams and Pictures.

SOME OF THE 120 DOGS WHICH THE SHACKLETON EXPEDITION WILL EMPLOY

ABOVE Canine celebrities: the canine members of Ernest Shackleton's Antarctic expedition drew huge crowds when they were kennelled at Hackbridge in 1914.

Huskies but also Husky-Collies, Husky-wolves or Husky-St Bernards, were to be Shackleton's primary land transport during the epic crossing.

Many of the dogs were semi-wild and extremely hard to handle. Fortunately, the Home had just the man to cope with the challenge. Since its earliest days, Battersea had attracted an eccentric mixture of workers, many of whom found it as much of a refuge from the outside world as the dogs did. None, however, was quite as colourful as George Wyndoe.

Wyndoe had arrived at the country Home after many years' working on fairgrounds. His main occupation there seems to have been selling "patent medicines" – dubious-looking linctuses and pills that promised to cure all ailments. There had been times when the job had been bad for his own health.

Everyone who met Wyndoe agreed that he was blessed with the "gift of the gab". An inveterate story-teller, he once told how, after a successful day hawking his medicines, he had run out of supplies. Fortunately he had some empty bottles and had filled them with tap water. When someone discovered this he had had to run for his life.

OPPOSITE In safe hands: a new arrival fresh from one of Battersea's vans gets a first glimpse of its new home.

Wyndoe quickly established an understanding of Shackleton's wild pack and took responsibility. The Committee had agreed to let the dogs stay at Hackbridge for two months free of charge. It was a calculated gamble, but a successful one. The publicity value was worth much more than the boarding fee. The Home reckoned the dogs helped raise an extra £12 in donations on the previous year in the money boxes.

Shackleton was a hugely popular public figure and the presence of the dogs at Hackbridge immediately drew large crowds. Wyndoe's lively commentary added to the appeal. His relationship with the sleigh dogs became so strong that when the time came for the expedition to sail for South America, Shackleton asked him to accompany them.

He sailed to Buenos Aires with the dogs from Plymouth in August 1914, apparently working wonders with them on the long and often treacherous sea crossing. He had remained there until they set off into the lower reaches of the south Atlantic. He wasn't asked to go on Shackleton's ill-fated adventure, which would see the adventurer and his men stranded on the ice for almost two years before returning safely to Britain in the summer of 1916. By then Wyndoe, and many of his colleagues at Battersea, had been recruited for a very different expedition: a few days before Wyndoe and the Shackleton dogs sailed, Britain had gone to war.

> Shackleton was a hugely popular public figure and the presence of the dogs at Hackbridge immediately drew large crowds

FOR KING AND COUNTRY

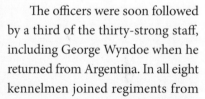

B Y THE SUMMER OF 1914, DARK clouds were gathering over London, England and the Empire. Following the assassination of the Archduke Ferdinand in Sarajevo, the great powers of Europe were lining up for a confrontation that was already being talked of as "the War to end all Wars".

In August 1914, Britain joined the war being fought on the Western Front. The mass mobilization of troops that followed had an immediate impact on Battersea. Three members of the Committee, the secretary Guy Guillum Scott and executive members Colonel William Elliott and Lieutenant Colonel Thomas Cochrane, joined up instantly. So too did the Home's vet, John Stow Young, who was offered and accepted a commission in the Army Veterinary Corps.

The officers were soon followed by a third of the thirty-strong staff, including George Wyndoe when he returned from Argentina. In all eight kennelmen joined regiments from the 15th Hussars and the Royal Engineers to the Berkshire Regiment and the 18th Hussars. All were promised their jobs would be there for them when they returned "so long as they were not disabled from performing their usual duties".

It was not only the men of the Home who were asked to make their contribution for King and Country. Early in 1914, the Home received a letter from Lieutenant Colonel E. H. Richardson, an expert police and military dog trainer. He had been pressing the army authorities since before the war to form a specialist canine brigade, at first to work with the ambulance service across the Channel.

PREVIOUS PAGE Dogs of war: members of the Army's canine division on parade.

A couple of years earlier, Richardson had encountered a distinguished-looking German on a Scottish moor, buying top-quality sheepdogs. He wanted them for a new military school in Berlin. By 1914, Richardson had learned that the Turkish and Russian armies had similar establishments in Constantinople and Petrograd. He was playing catch-up and wanted to train as many dogs as possible. His first batch of recruits was mostly from Battersea.

Richardson was very particular about the breeds he took with him. Lurchers, known as the poacher's dog, were considered the best all-round war dogs while Airedales, Collies, sheepdogs, Whippets, Retrievers and Deerhounds were

regarded as good messengers and sentries. Great Danes, Boarhounds and Mastiffs were regarded as the best watchdogs. Richardson had little time for Poodles and other dogs with "gaily curled tails", which pointed to a "certain levity of character quite at variance with the serious duties required!"

By the start of 1915, a large contingent of dogs had been kennelled at a makeshift camp near Shoeburyness, not far from the Channel in Kent. The location had been chosen because of its closeness to the giant guns that were positioned nearby and were firing across the Channel. They stayed there for five or six weeks and were then sent to France. During their five-week training, dogs were taught to squeeze, wade, jump and swim

BELOW With admissions rising and sales falling, staff who remained at Battersea during the war had their hands full.

Dogs were put through their paces at the Shoeburyness training camp for the "canine brigade".

their way through obstacle courses filled with water barrages and to surmount barbed-wire fences.

Initially they were used as ambulance dogs, sent out to search for injured men, but they also began to show themselves as useful messengers. As the Flanders fields were transformed into a hellish landscape of shell holes, mud, smoke, gas and water, the dogs' superior sense of direction and speed proved of vital importance.

Richardson's dogs covered themselves in glory, winning many "mentions in dispatches". During a major German assault, the British lines were cut off by a massive artillery barrage. A Highland sheepdog was given a message calling for reinforcements and ran two miles in ten minutes through mortar and artillery fire to reach a French colonial division. The French were able to send up reinforcements avoiding what would have been "a terrible disaster" for the stranded British troops.

Dogs weren't just useful during rearguard actions. During one British assault, as the troops pushed on, a dog was sent back to Brigade Headquarters carrying crucial information in a map. The journey, across cratered and muddy terrain, would have taken a man an hour and a half but the dog did it in twenty minutes. Collies, sheepdogs, Lurchers, Welsh and Irish Terriers all performed heroically, but the most famous dog to emerge from the campaign was an Airedale from Battersea. His name was Jack.

According to his proud commander, Jack was already a veteran of the Russo–Japanese War a decade earlier. Jack and another recruit – a Scottish sheepdog – had, he claimed, been an invaluable help to stretcher-bearers in the Russian Army as they searched for fallen comrades in millet fields. The high plants had made spotting injured soldiers well nigh impossible but Jack and his sheepdog companion had been able to sniff them out with ease. How Jack had managed to serve a foreign army in a far-off campaign a full fourteen years before he arrived in France is something of a mystery. It might have been that he was the original Jack's offspring. Whatever the truth, he found immortality when he served with the Sherwood Foresters in France.

ABOVE A Sergeant of the Royal Engineers (Signals) slips a note into the cylinder attached to the collar of a messenger dog in Étaples, August 1918.

Jack had been despatched to deliver a request for reinforcements when his battalion got trapped under enemy fire. He had been forced to pick his way through a ferocious bombardment. He was hit twice during his two-mile journey but got the message through just before he died of his terrible wounds. His story became one of the most oft-told of the war and was being retold twenty years later.

He was one of the heroic animals that *The Times* had in mind when, in December 1918, a leader said: "it is only right that the national service of the brave dogs of Britain should receive mention."

For those that had remained at the Home, life was difficult too. Tillings of Peckham were still supplying the vans and drivers for the Home's collections, but with men constantly being called up, the quality of the service had suffered badly and the Home had been given a series of young, inexperienced and careless drivers.

In April 1915, Battersea wrote to Tillings complaining about the "state of the motor vans" and of one vehicle in particular that was "not a credit either to your firm or to us".

Tillings simply replied that there was a "very great difficulty in getting men": "We are very lucky, I think, to get the vehicles driven at all just now. If you say anything to a man he leaves – that is

ABOVE Battersea cared for many canine victims of the war. This messenger dog arrived with leg injuries sustained in a mustard gas attack near Nieppe Wood in May 1918.

the position of the labour market just at present. We will, however, do the best we can for you."

Soon afterwards Tillings had written complaining that prices had risen so steeply that they were making a "considerable loss": "The case is so serious and so unprecedented that we are bound to come begging," the company said, before asking for an extra 3s a week for the two "chauffeurs" they were supplying. In the end the Home agreed to pay up on condition that Tillings "see that thoroughly suitable steady chauffeurs are provided who will take care of the vans, stay with them and not drive them about recklessly … Latterly there has been too much tendency to make the motors a school for boys, who knock them about and drive recklessly all over the place," Guillum Scott wrote.

With rationing in place, the commodities the Home relied on were hard to find. Food supplies, in particular, were hit hard. The scraps and offal it needed were dwindling, as was another staple, dog biscuits. One member of staff, a Captain Bathurst, told the *Field* that suppliers like Spratts simply couldn't get their hands on the "miller's offals and damaged grain" that were being substituted for the normal wheat or rye flour. As a result the dogs' rations were down to the absolute minimum. "It is impossible to ration dogs any more than they are being rationed at present and keep them in good condition," he said. "A good-sized dog needs half a pound of dog biscuits a day besides scraps. Now he will not be able to get the biscuits."

As the city's menfolk marched off to war, the Home was receiving more dogs than normal. Bathurst and his staff had begun to take in hundreds of pets that had been simply abandoned in the parks and streets of London. Many people brought dogs into the Home and some desperate owners were taking off their dogs' collars, tying a piece of string around their necks and dropping them off at Battersea, claiming they had been found as strays. "A woman who did this the other day broke down and wept when she left the dog who tried hard to go with her," Bathurst explained.

The Home was now holding on average four hundred dogs. Before the war, many men had come for guard dogs to watch over their households while they were away at the front. With the campaign now under way, sales were dwindling. The result was that Bathurst and his staff could no longer keep dogs for the full seven days before putting them to sleep. Inevitably, the Home's finances suffered too. The 1917 Annual Report revealed that legacies and donations were down, as were earnings at Hackbridge. The drop in quarantine receipts was predictable, given that many dogs weren't being admitted into the country because of shipping problems caused by the war. The loss was exacerbated by the death of the Home's best fundraiser, a black Retriever called Sam: according to the Committee, he was "very clever at poking his nose into everybody's hand". His passing "no doubt explained the diminution of receipts under that heading".

To make matters worse, the large number of dogs that were returning from France as companions to soldiers had caused health problems. During the summer of 1915 the kennels were closed because of an outbreak of distemper. The keepers blamed it on the "stray dogs picked up by the troops in the trenches, villages and deserted farmhouses of France … Several of these dogs were allotted to Hackbridge and their subsequent history made it quite clear that they brought the disease with them."

There was also mixed news from the front. In 1916 George Gridley, who had joined the Home as a cycle boy in 1911, died in France while serving with the Royal Berkshire Regiment. Then, in 1917, Mr Shiell, who in his thirteen years at the Home had risen to head clerk, drowned on New Year's Eve when his ship was sunk by an enemy submarine. A kennelman called Wilkins, who had joined the Royal West Kent Regiment, had been "somewhat severely wounded while serving in the trenches in France".

There was better news of other members of staff, however, in particular the Home's vet, John Stow Young. He had joined the Royal Veterinary

ABOVE With the war finally over, Battersea was the scene of many a tearful reunion, as this line drawing illustrates.

Corps and had been in charge of a party of young vets when they had come across a large group of distressed and wounded horses near the village of Guy in northern France. The animals had apparently stampeded after being bombarded by heavy artillery fire. Young took charge of the situation and, with his men, rounded up the petrified horses. A large number of wounded

men were also in the area. Young and his group placed them on the backs of the uninjured horses and led the party to safety in the face of a new bombardment. Then they used the horses to carry away a cache of arms and equipment that would otherwise have fallen into the hands of the advancing enemy forces. He was awarded the Military Cross for "conspicuous bravery and devotion to duty".

In 1918 Stow Young returned to the Home, as did three kennelmen, Ball and Brenchley from Battersea and Ball of Hackbridge. They discovered the Home had a new secretary. Back safely from France, Guy Guillum Scott had decided to step down from the role while remaining on the Committee. Responsibility for the day-to-day running of the Home passed to Guy Rowley. He faced a baptism of fire.

ABOVE The end of the war brought a new influx of dogs, this time soldiers' pets which returned from France with diseases, including rabies.

ABOVE When the keeper's away! Kittens at play in the cattery.

The return of the troops brought with it a range of problems. The war years had been "the most difficult and trying period the Home has ever had to face", the Committee's Annual Report for 1918 admitted, with the lack of dog food the biggest problem. As hundreds of thousands of men and women returned to London and the south-east, the situation worsened. Already, during the summer of 1918 the Home Office had suggested to the Home that they should destroy all unclaimed dogs after just three days. The idea was met with horror. Apart from anything else, the keepers would have no opportunity to get a dog ready for sale. The Home didn't want to appear unpatriotic or disloyal to King and Country, but in a stiffly worded letter they registered how much they "deplored the proposal". The Home Office acknowledged receipt of the letter and never mentioned the idea again.

By the end of 1918, there were more pressing problems to occupy everyone's minds. Spanish flu was spreading around the towns and cities of Britain with alarming speed. Also, in Devon and then Cornwall, rabies returned to the UK for the first time in years. The Ministry of Agriculture put into place a set of draconian rules banning the movement of dogs without permits, but it had little effect.

With so many people returning from the war – many with dogs they had befriended in France – the flow of dogs around the country was uncontrollable. At London's railway stations scores were found hidden in suitcases and kitbags. Many more arrived in the capital undetected.

Battersea was asked to help. The RSPCA struck a deal with the Committee to send five hundred dogs to Hackbridge, to be supervised by Captain Stow Young. In return for a fee of 10s per week for every dog, the Home agreed to construct new kennels and other buildings to accommodate the influx. It had little impact on the spread of rabies.

By April 1919 there were outbreaks not far from Hackbridge, and a rabid dog attacked a family in Acton, leaving the mother, father and daughter in need of emergency vaccination. Soon there were 800 reported cases nationwide. In May, London became subject – once more – to a muzzling order. Stocks of wire muzzles were nowhere near adequate

> The Ministry of Agriculture put into place a set of draconian rules banning the movement of dogs without permits, but it had little effect

ABOVE A contented soul: one of the feline residents of the era.

and the streets of London were soon overrun with abandoned dogs.

Battersea's vans were swamped. "Extra vans were put on, some of them doing double journeys and even furniture pantechnicons were utilized," the Home reported. Yet more dogs were delivered each day from the main railway stations, where owners were being told they could not travel with their pets and were abandoning them in large numbers, particularly at weekends and during holidays.

Miraculously Battersea escaped the disease, even though, during 1919, the Home took in 16,856 dogs. But the impact on the Home was huge, not

OPPOSITE It's playtime at Battersea as its canine residents enjoy a run around in the exercise yard.

least financially: between May and September that year, when the muzzling order had been lifted, it was not allowed to sell dogs to the public.

The other major problem the Home faced lay with its staff. Many of the men working at Battersea and Hackbridge were veterans of the trenches. Some had returned with physical injuries. Others bore psychological scars. As a result standards were not what they had been prior to the war. At Hackbridge in particular there was a general "lack of organization", which was "no doubt due to the difficulties of the War and to the subsequent demobilization". The regimes at both Homes had always had a military streak, with keepers expected to parade first thing in the morning for inspection and superintendents acting like drill sergeants. At Hackbridge, where a man called Stuart was superintendent, there was dissension in the ranks. The men's work had been considered "not what it should be" and Stuart had been told to "lick them into shape".

This didn't go down well with many of the keepers and a man called Tomlinson hit back, accusing the superintendent of a range of crimes, ranging from the trivial, such as "lack of tact" and using "obscene and filthy language", to more serious offences such as "stealing meat" and keeping well-bred dogs out of visitors' sight so that he could personally sell them to "well-known fanciers and dealers".

Tomlinson was sacked for his insubordination but Stuart was told to change his ways. Many of the men who worked in the Home had fought heroically for King and Country. "While he was expected to maintain order and discipline in the Yard it was not possible to exercise the same methods in civilian life as were applicable to the army," he was told.

Nevertheless, the end of the war marked a new dawn for the country. Battersea, like the rest of the nation, entered that era with a quiet optimism.

THE
LOST LEGIONS

THE 1920S BEGAN WITH SOME of the most positive news the Home had received in years. In January 1920 Guy Rowley reported that the number of homeless dogs found wandering the streets was at its lowest level in recorded memory. "The stray dog has practically disappeared," he said. The root of this sea-change wasn't hard to diagnose. "The rationing restrictions during the war, the high cost of foodstuffs and the rabies regulations have greatly decreased the number of dogs in London," he explained to the *Morning Post*.

Even better, from the Home's perspective, demand for dogs now outstripped supply. With the country returning to some semblance of normality, those who had lost or sold their dogs during the war were now finding themselves new companions. Queues outside the Home were commonplace and

many left Battersea disappointed: "Every dog that is sound and healthy we keep until we can sell it. There has been a great demand for dogs during the last fortnight and if we had had another three or four hundred we could have sold them," Rowley explained.

The Home's finances were in rude health too. Its operations were more business-like – and profitable – than at any time in its sixty-year history. During 1922 the Home managed to pay off an overdraft of almost £2,500 and invested almost £1,400, the result of a series of sound business decisions. In 1921, it had ended its contracts with Tillings, the van-hire company, and bought its own fleet of three vans, saving £1,300 a year.

Also in 1922, the Home took the bold step of allowing advertising, not just on the side of its new vans but in its Annual Report. The first ads, printed in that year's summary, were for Garstin's Tonic Dog Soap and Osoko, "The paramount dog food", manufactured by Spillers. They were clearly seen as a success: the following year the Report carried five pages of ads, ranging from dog foods by Spillers and their big rival Spratts, a shampoo and a range

ABOVE In 1922 the Home's Annual Report began carrying advertising, such as this advert for Osoko dog food.

of "leather dog requisites" produced by a rather unlikely-sounding company, H. L. Barkway.

The Home began to take a more modern approach to publicizing itself too. It knew the public had a huge affection for dogs and cats, especially those with sentimental stories attached to them. For the first time, it focused on this as a means of spreading the word about its good works. It may have discovered the power of the well-placed story by accident. In March 1918, the *Daily Mirror* ran a photograph of a black Pekinese that had arrived at Battersea. The caption said that Princess was the smallest dog at the Home and was destined to be destroyed if a good home couldn't be found soon.

According to Henry Selby, the story had been written without the Home's knowledge or explicit permission. A man had visited a few days earlier and "received permission in the ordinary way to inspect the Home". As he wandered the kennels he had been allowed to take some photographs. The Home couldn't have anticipated the response in the days that followed the story's publication. In all, Selby said, it had received "1,500 letters, eighty-eight prepaid telegrams and forty unpaid telegrams … We placed a man on a chair to answer telephone calls all day. At one time a considerable crowd gathered outside the home. Offers varied from ten shillings to eight guineas." In the end – rather suspiciously – the dog's owner contacted the Home, claiming the dog "had been stolen from her in January".

Selby told the Committee, almost apologetically, that the incident had been a "great inconvenience". However, it had opened the Home's eyes to something it had long suspected but never been prepared to test: it was sitting on an endless supply of happy – and sometimes not so happy – stories. In the wake of the Princess story, it began to let them seep into the public domain.

ABOVE Photos of Battersea including its staff and residents, such as this, became popular with the newspapers during the 1920s.

It also tapped into the power of celebrity. Members of the Royal Family aside, the most prominent person to be associated with the Home at this time was the Prime Minister, David Lloyd George. He had fallen for and adopted a massive St Bernard called Riffel while on holiday in Switzerland and had put the dog into quarantine at Hackbridge. The Home sensed an opportunity to publicize its less-known work as a quarantine centre and put out a story. Riffel briefly became a celebrity, particularly when the time came for him to leave Hackbridge and make his home at 10 Downing Street.

Soon the *Star* was reporting that "staff at Downing Street is still busy mending the carpets and putting the furniture back where it came from". Later it was revealed that Riffel had had to be moved to larger premises in case he "brought the Government and the Foreign Office down" with him.

Such light-hearted publicity couldn't fail to help the Home's cause. Neither could tales of

heroism, of which there was also no shortage. The most striking came during the rabies scare in 1919, when two ladies discovered a dog trapped under the electrified railway tracks at Gloucester Road tube station. When they alerted the staff they were told the dog had been there for some time. Many attempts had been made to rescue it but all had come to naught. The dog was too terrified to get itself into a position where it could be lifted free.

Three days later the ladies returned. When they heard the dog's plaintive cries still echoing down the tube tunnel they decided to take matters into their own hands. The following night, just after one a.m. when the power supplies were switched off, the two ladies squeezed down a manhole from the street above into the tube station dressed in overalls and equipped with a strong rope, some titbits of meat, an electric torch and a dog collar. They picked their way along the darkened platform, eventually finding the dog. Even then the rescue wasn't complete. Just as they were about to reach the street, the dog wriggled free and they had to chase back down into the tube station to retrieve him again. He was taken to Battersea where he made a rapid recovery and soon went to a good home.

Stories about Battersea dogs became a staple in the nation's newspapers. The most amusing was about a champion Greyhound, Oak Top, which was sensationally stolen from its kennels at the Catford Stadium in south-east London. The newspapers were full of speculation about what had happened to it. To everyone's surprise, however, Oak Top turned up at Battersea. The keepers had grown suspicious one morning when a streaky ginger Greyhound arrived in the back of one of the collection vans. When they gave the dog a thorough wash they discovered it was Oak Top. His captors had dyed him ginger but had abandoned him when the colour had begun to run.

FILM STAR FROM THE BATTERSEA DOGS' HOME

Scruffy Climbs the Ladder to Fame

A MONGREL

Tinned Salmon Was the Way to His Heart

new film star who will soon have all the world at his feet has been found in the Battersea Dogs' Home.

He has no resounding high-born name and no ponderous pedigree stands to his credit. His name is Scruffy, rescued from obscurity for a paltry seven and sixpence, and last of

Mr. Bernard Brown.

He ignored them. They offered him quite expensive chocolates. Scruffy intimated that they made him sick.

As a last resort they tried him on tinned

Dogs owned by celebrities predictably took up the most column inches. One of the biggest stars of the 1920s, the actor, acrobat and singer Lupino Lane, told one of the funnier – if less credible – stories about the time he visited the Home and took away a Bull Terrier. Walking home, he had become worried about the dog, which was panting heavily and seemed distressed. On passing a veterinary surgeon's he called in to have the dog checked out. He emerged an hour later with not one dog but five. The female Bull Terrier had given birth to four puppies. Quite how the Home's vets had missed the pregnancy was never satisfactorily explained.

When the great British film director Alexander Korda asked his cameraman Bernard Brown to find a star for a new movie he was planning called *Wharves and Strays*, Brown ended up at Battersea. Korda wanted a cute mongrel but after Brown had auditioned more than four thousand dogs around Britain, he hadn't found one that had the character Korda was looking for. His luck changed at Battersea. The moment he walked into the holding kennels he was greeted by a Scottish

ABOVE The press went to town with the tale of Scruffy, the Battersea dog who became a movie star.

Terrier-sheepdog cross called Scruffy, standing on his hind legs yapping.

Brown immediately knew he had his dog and took Scruffy home. Training him wasn't easy. When Brown took Scruffy to Hampstead Heath for his first sessions, he discovered that the dog only responded to treats of tinned salmon, unlike most normal dogs. Scruffy was made of the right stuff, however: Korda offered him a six-film deal including *The Private Life of Scruffy*.

He cost Brown 7s 6d but Scruffy was soon so famous he had to be insured for £400.

Scruffy was the first but far from the last performing dog to emerge from Battersea. In 1932 the singer Gracie Fields, then one of the country's most popular rising stars, borrowed a group of dogs from the Home to appear in a film called *Looking on the Bright Side*. Newspapers latched on to the story, many of them wondering whether some of the animals would have to be put down before the film came out if they didn't find new homes. Inevitably the Home was overwhelmed by offers to take them in. One, an Airedale, remained with Gracie Fields, becoming a lifelong companion.

Battersea dogs became well known for their ability to perform unexpected roles. A few years after Scruffy rose to fame, another dog, Crab, was cast in a Shakespearean role. He was chosen by one of the day's leading comic actors, Jay Laurier, to star with him in *Two Gentlemen of Verona* at the Memorial Theatre. The role required the little ginger mongrel to play along with some of Laurier's comic antics. He won glowing reviews, with one leading critic writing: "This dog is an unconscious comedian."

The other staple diet for newspapers was the sadder and more sentimental stories that the Home turned up on a regular basis. In 1923, another dog hit the headlines. The little Fox Terrier had been living under the Law Courts in London for years, where members of staff had been secretly feeding her. She was eventually caught by the RSPCA and was due to be destroyed when Battersea intervened and found her a home in Hendon. It was some time later that workmen at the Law Courts discovered the Fox Terrier's hideaway – and two hundredweight of bones.

The story of a dog called Florrie was particularly touching. Florrie had lived with an ex-serviceman called George Clark. Since returning from the war, he had struggled to find work. As the economic conditions worsened during the 1920s and 1930s he despaired. Eventually he put his last few pennies into the gas meter at his dingy London bedsit, lit his oven and stuck his head inside. He was found by the police when Florrie's plaintive howling alerted neighbours.

Florrie was sent to Battersea and quickly found a home with a well-to-do family in Chelsea, but

refused to settle there. On at least two occasions, the faithful dog ran back to the bedsit where she stood waiting for her old master to return.

Of all the stories told about Battersea dogs during this period, however, the one that caught the public's imagination the most was about Pip, the lion pup. Pip's rather adventurous tale had begun when the popular animal photographer, explorer and big-game hunter Cherry Kearton had visited the Home. He wanted a small dog to take with him as a companion on an African expedition.

ABOVE Sentimental stories and images featuring children and their dogs helped to publicize the Home's work.

He chose Pip because "She had a silly little stump of tail, which began to wag as soon as she saw me. I stood in front of her kennel and laughed: the tail wagged faster than ever."

Kearton's expedition was to east Africa and the Masai region of Kenya and northern Tanzania, where he planned to take extensive photographs of lions in their natural habitat. He was a fearless soul and one day set off to photograph a pair of large lions that had been seen in the bush near his camp. He was accompanied by eleven Masai warriors with spears and four Somali horsemen. As they marched off into the bush Pip ran alongside them, barking playfully, seemingly excited about the adventure.

The party soon came across the two lions, which reacted violently to their presence. Eventually one ran away, but the other disappeared into a dried riverbed. Kearton sent Pip towards it, hoping she would simply point to the lion's position. But, to the amazement of the adventurer and the Masai, the little dog ran directly to where the lion was hiding.

Moments later there was a huge roar and Kearton assumed the worst. When he approached the riverbed, however, he saw the lion lying dead with Pip holding its tail. She had somehow worked out that one of the Masai had managed to get behind the lion, when it had attacked, and was poised to strike with his spear. The dog had gone for the lion's tail in an effort to distract it, which had given the hunter enough time to land a killing blow.

The custom among the Masai was that the person who claimed the tail of a lion was also entitled to its mane, so the little dog from Battersea was duly awarded the honour, with the nickname Simba, meaning "lion" in Swahili.

OPPOSITE Dog ownership was never more fashionable. A lady dog lover is here photographed in May 1927.

Kearton wrote about Pip's exploits when he returned to London and the story was picked up by newspapers and magazines all over the country. Pip – or Simba, the lion pup, as most people knew her – was for a brief time easily the most famous and admired pet in Britain.

Stories like Pip's and Scruffy's were always positive to the Home. Invariably there was a trickle of donations or – even better – legacies after a particularly heartrending tale appeared in print. But there was a deeper purpose to publicizing the positive side of the Home's work. Battersea's success in transforming the lives of ordinary dogs helped counter the arguments of those who still argued that such "lower-class animals" didn't merit a place in British society. However, sixty years on from the days when Parliament routinely heard dogs condemned as worthless curs, there were still plenty of heirs to the Earl of Hardwicke. In 1922 the editor of *Dog World*, Phyllis Robson, wrote an astonishing piece in which she effectively called for the extermination of all mongrels. It was a response to an article by Hannen Swaffer in the *People* in which he had, light-heartedly, argued that mongrels were actually superior to pedigree breeds because they were "the dog that adopts you". Robson argued: "It would be better if the mongrel could be swept away, the public educated to keep only pedigree dogs which cost exactly as much to maintain and are worthier of the tradition of a

> Pip – or Simba, the lion pup, as most people knew her – was for a brief time easily the most famous and admired pet in Britain

nation of dog lovers." She was clearly influenced by the then fashionable eugenics movement, which argued human evolution would benefit if those with perceived "genetic defects" were discouraged – or prevented – from reproducing. Popular in the 1920s, it had faded by the 1940s but only after it had been taken to its gruesome extreme in Nazi Germany. Robson wrote:

It is not to be denied that the pariah dog of the streets, living by its wits to gain food and shelter, acquires a fox-like cunning which may be mistaken for sagacity. When given houseroom it may even be worthy of Mr Swaffer's sentimental affection. But no amount of special pleading will persuade me that the promiscuously begotten cur of mixed breed can in any circumstances whatever be essentially wiser, more tractable, more faithful or more lovable than the descendant of ancestors that have been purely bred on eugenic lines to a perfection of type and the highest standard of mental efficiency.

The *People* gave Robson's view an airing but printed alongside it another story provided to the paper by Battersea. Widgeon, a Labrador Retriever, had been picked up and brought to the Home earlier that year. A Mr Thursby had come to the Home soon afterwards and bought Widgeon for 12s 6d. Within months Mr Thursby was exhibiting Widgeon at dog shows where he had become an instant star. "He won two championships and four first prizes. Widgeon's cash value jumped up as a result and he was worth almost his weight in gold," the *People* reported. Mr Thursby was so pleased with his new dog that he had a portrait of Widgeon commissioned and presented it to Battersea. The *People*'s message was unmistakable: if all mongrels had been exterminated *en masse* we would never have discovered the Scruffys and Simbas of the world. As the paper put it: "The lost legions of stray dogs have reason to wag their tails proudly."

DOG LICENCE DAYS

THE OPTIMISM OF THE EARLY 1920s was short-lived. In 1929, the Wall Street Crash set in train a worldwide economic decline. America's Great Depression spread across the Atlantic, and by the early 1930s unemployment in Britain had risen from around a million to 2.5 million. It would reach three million within a year. The Home's financial position suddenly became perilous again.

Fortunately its heartland, London and the south-east of England, was less hard hit than Scotland, Wales and the north of England. In 1930 alone the Home received just over £20,000 in legacies, an unusually high amount. It had also learned the useful habit of earning money in unusual ways. That year it sold a young fox that had been found in St John's Wood and kept at Battersea for a week. It had also received a generous donation from the owner of a

grey parrot that had been handed in to Gerald Road police station. But there was no escaping the dire financial circumstances at home and abroad. As a result, significant changes were soon afoot.

In 1931 it had been suggested to the Home that it should take advantage of new provisions under the Companies Act, which allowed it to become a registered charity. After much debate it was agreed to incorporate the Home that year, although the certificate of incorporation was not finally granted until August 1933. The move made sound legal and business sense and followed the example of other charities, like the RSPCA. Despite this, however, some Committee members were horrified, convinced the Home had been turned into a money-making business. Others had to reassure them that "The objects of the Association

PREVIOUS PAGE Dogs and cats, large and small, have always received the best possible care at Battersea.

are in no way altered, nor are the methods by which it has been carried out for over seventy years in any way changed."

Other institutions were battening down the hatches to survive the financial storms ahead, among them the Metropolitan Police. In July 1933 the Commissioner gave notice that he was going to terminate its contract with Battersea to receive and deal with stray dogs under the 1906 Dogs Act. Another canine charity, Our Dumb Friends' League, which ran a home in Willesden, north London, and a Mr Sellar, who had taken in dogs in the East End, received similar notices.

New tenders were invited for each of the different regions. Battersea bid for – and won – the contract for south and north-east London, partly because of the death of Mr Sellar. The contract for north-west London was retained by Our Dumb Friends' League, although the police were keen for Battersea to open a north London home and lobbied hard for them to do so for many years.

For now, though, the Home's new catchment area was enough. To deal with the huge new influx of dogs this would entail, the Home knew it had to acquire new premises, somewhere north of the river Thames within easy reach of east London. There would be a price to pay for this: it soon became apparent that the Committee would have to close its country home in Hackbridge.

Hackbridge had continued to be an expensive part of the Home's operations. For the past decade or more, its upkeep had stretched the Home's finances to the limits. Its problems were many, not least that people frequently failed to pay for the boarding and quarantine accommodation it provided. Its location and lack of publicity also meant that the kennels were often underused or empty. In 1921 a sub-committee had met to decide whether "we recommend the committee to retain Hackbridge". If the answer was yes, "to what other uses do we recommend it should be put?" At that time, it had been agreed to stick with it and make the Home a more attractive environment for potentially lucrative boarders.

In 1931 money had been spent to modernize the so-called army kennels there, and a disused kennel had been transformed into what even the Committee admitted "might be described as the most luxurious cat-house in the world". Every

LEFT New Year's Day would bring a queue of apprehensive owners, often children, ready to hand over their dogs on "Dog Licence Day".

ABOVE Dog ownership remained popular, despite the harsh economic climate.

cat had a room and an outside run of its own. Yet its remote location meant that the Home still didn't attract people in the numbers that came to Battersea. The hope was that the improvements would be "an attraction to so large a part of the dog and cat owning community that enough animals will be sent to Hackbridge in future to negative [sic] the high overhead charges".

Numbers had continued to slide, and in 1933 the decision was finally taken to sell the Hackbridge Home, lock, stock and barrel. To the Committee's relief, a deal was struck with Spratts, the dog-food company, which ran a boarding kennels and quarantine station nearby. They made an offer to buy Hackbridge and its land for £10,000. They also agreed to take on all of the staff – with one notable

exception: Captain Stow Young, the Home's vet. Spratts had their own team of vets.

John Stow Young was by now approaching retirement and, in recognition of all he had done for the Home, the Committee at Battersea agreed to award him compensation. He was able to leave the Home for a quiet life after three decades of service.

A new Home was found in Bow, east London. It was smaller and less well appointed than Hackbridge, but had the advantage of being within easy reach of the easterly parts of the city. It was soon busy.

As the Depression deepened and unemployment spread, at Battersea the office staff had more work than they could cope with, answering the hundreds

NEW YEAR DEATH KNELL
FOR HOMELESS
DOGS.
—
FAITHFUL PETS
WHICH CANNOT
BE PAID FOR.
—
HEARTBROKEN
OWNERS.
—
IF you have a hard heart you can
stand on Chelsea Bridge
these days and watch heart-broken
dog-owners leading their pets to
the Battersea Dogs' Home.

NOT A DOG'S CHANCE remains for
these little chaps unless they are

ABOVE With the nation in the depths of a Depression, the seven shillings and sixpence that the dog licence cost was beyond many Londoners.

of begging letters they were now receiving from distraught dog owners. In the past, the nearer it had got to Christmas and New Year, the more desperate their tone had become, as 1 January was Dog Licence Day, when owners were required by law to pay their annual "dog tax". At least that particular pressure was now beginning to ease.

The licence had been introduced in 1796 by William Pitt and an MP called Dent, who had argued that it would reduce the number of stray rabid dogs wandering the country. The duty, originally set at half a crown, had earned Dent the nickname Dog Dent. It was introduced partly to raise revenue from the more than one million dogs that were then at large in the country but partly to tackle other social and economic problems.

It had always been controversial. Ever since the original tax had come into force, politicians had argued over whether it should be abolished, cut or increased. Amendments calling for certain breeds and classes of dogs, such as working dogs, to be exempted were common. The debates often shone a revealing light on the British people's special

affection for their dogs – the well-bred ones, at least. In 1878, for instance, it had been proposed in the Budget that the annual dog licence fee rise from 5s to 7s 6d. By now, there were thought to be 1.5 million dogs liable to pay the duty. The extra half-crown would raise hundreds of thousands of pounds, even after exemptions, which now included guide dogs for the blind and Collies, used by shepherds and farmers. There were those who thought it should have been doubled to 10s. One MP thought that would "have the effect of ridding the country of something like three fourths of the dogs", which he regarded as "a wretched nuisance to the public".

The proposed rise produced a predictable outcry among the grander members of Parliament, however, many of whom ran large packs of hounds as well as farms. Lord Randolph Churchill was among those who pleaded for a special case, in his case for masters of hounds to be allowed a discount. He made his appeal to the Chancellor because he "represented one of the best sporting counties in the Kingdom – Devonshire – the home of wild sports and of the red deer".

Eventually it was agreed that the tax would rise to 7s 6d and apply to all dogs over six months rather than the two months originally proposed.

The impact on Battersea was almost immediate. Each year around Christmas, the number of strays would suddenly spike upwards and people would turn up at the gates announcing they could no longer afford to keep their dogs. The most significant numbers always turned up on the day the licence had to be renewed, 1 January. Licence Day had always been a black day in the Battersea calendar.

OPPOSITE In 1920 the Home began buying dog licences for the poor who would "otherwise have been compelled to part with their dogs".

ABOVE The youngest canine residents of the Home make a splash at bathtime.

In 1905 the Home's secretary, Henry J. Ward, wrote to *The Times* complaining that because of the "large number of dogs that are turned adrift when licences become due, the Home is very crowded, the admissions averaging 171 per day (upwards of 200 were received on two days this month)". But by the 1920s it was getting darker still.

The Home had always tried its best to help the most deserving cases. Since 1920 or so, it had regularly bought a small number of dog licences to be given to "poor people residing in the Metropolitan area who would otherwise have been compelled to part with their dogs". With hundreds of thousands of people losing their jobs, however, there simply weren't enough licences to go round. As a result, New Year's Days had become reruns of

the same familiar and depressing scene. Regardless of the weather, the staff would open the gates to find long queues of apprehensive owners and their dogs snaking down towards Battersea Park. Many of the men, women and children clinging to their dogs were in tears. Aware of the pathetic scenes that were now unfolding on a regular basis, the newspapers were always ready to record them. Photographs of children kissing their dogs goodbye and then staring under the gates for one final glimpse of their best friend became staples.

To the Home's annoyance, the papers usually – and conveniently – overlooked the fact that the vast majority of the dogs were found homes. The only exceptions were the sentimental happy-ending stories that cropped up most years, like that of Peggy, a Terrier who had been dropped off by a little girl called Gladys Higgs – she hadn't been able to raise money for a new licence at the end of

1929. According to the *South London Press*, "long after the door had closed upon her", Gladys had "stood outside and cried and cried" and "could not be persuaded to leave the doors of the home".

Apparently Peggy was about to be put to sleep when the stage manager of the Globe Theatre, Bernard Howard, arrived looking for a dog to appear in his new play *The Street Scene*. He soon spotted Peggy and whisked her away to the West End where, "after being fed with bones, sweets and biscuits, she was told to act". Peggy apparently was a natural performer and was hired for the role of "Queenie, a New York tenement mongrel". News of the dog's remarkable rise to fame was soon all over the papers with a photo of the new West End star.

When Gladys saw the picture she headed straight to the Globe where, according to one report, Peggy "danced excitedly round her former

BELOW Each December, hundreds of dogs like this were turned loose on the streets of London.

mistress, covering her face with kisses and poking her nose into the coat pocket that so often had contained sweets for her". Peggy remained at the theatre, where she became a well-fed favourite and Gladys was able to visit her whenever she wanted.

But such stories did little to staunch the tide of dogs being let go each New Year. By the end of the 1920s huge numbers of dogs were being either abandoned or handed in to vets or charities around the country. In December 1928, it was estimated that 250,000 dogs were about to be turned out on to the streets of London. In the run-up to the year end, the Home was inundated with letters from people asking for help with their dog licences.

In response it organized a special fund for licences. That year it raised the princely sum of £23 7s 6d, which included 7s 6d – enough for one licence – collected by children from a Torquay secondary school: they had raised the money by charging for admission to their Christmas play. The Home dipped into its own pocket and paid for 176 licences, worth more than £51. But it was the tip of the iceberg. By the mid-thirties, it was paying for three times as many licences. In 1932, for instance, it funded 543. But the scale of the task was getting too much: "The requests for assistance in this direction are becoming each year more numerous, doubtless in a large measure due to unemployment," the Committee reported that year. For the first time the Home reached out to other charities.

Help was at hand in the shape of two, both formed in 1928. The National Dog Week Movement opened its first branch in the UK. Part of an international organization, the charity offered financial aid to animal welfare groups. Far more significant, however, was the Tailwaggers Club, formed by a Captain H. E. Hobbs in the City of London. The Tailwaggers ran its own magazine and

ABOVE Desperate children peer underneath the Home's gates to catch a glimpse of their pets.

struck a deal with the *Daily Mirror* to publicize its activities. Life membership of the club cost just half a crown, in return for which owners got a metal disc on a chain with their dog's name engraved on it. It had soon signed up seventy thousand members.

The club set up a scheme whereby members could save during the year to buy licences. The impact was immediate. Between 1926 and 1930 the number of dogs arriving at Battersea fell significantly. Between 1928, the year the Tailwaggers began, and 1929, the number of dogs received from all sources, including the police, was

25,220, down by 1,771. In 1930, it had fallen even further, by 3,320 on the previous year.

In 1931 a veteran of the 1 January story at the Home reported that only seventy-three dogs were brought in on New Year's Day. By 1934 the Home was reporting that "with very few exceptions all dog licences are now being dealt with by a central organization". The Home continued to help people buy their licences for many years to come.

In 1936, the Home suffered a significant setback when it found itself without a royal patron for the first time in half a century. Since Queen Victoria had become the Home's titular head in 1885, both of her successors had supported the institution. Edward VII had agreed to take up the role immediately when he came to the throne in 1901 and his son, George V, had done the same, remaining patron for twenty-six years. When his own son succeeded him, in January 1936, the Home was confident that Edward VIII would continue the tradition. From the outset, however, the King seemed to relish breaking with the past, regularly ignoring royal protocol. He was also uninterested in many of the charities that his father had supported during his reign.

In May the Committee wrote to him, explaining the Home's traditional link with Buckingham Palace and asking whether he would be "graciously pleased to continue this favour".

The King's reply was a bitter disappointment. The Keeper of the Privy Purse wrote back in June 1936,

BELOW Schemes to help people buy dog licences helped reduce the number of dogs arriving at Battersea at the end of the 1920s.

> The King convened a Committee and instructed it to make a drastic cut in his commitments

explaining that "owing to the necessity for restricting the number of Institutions and Associations to which The King gives his Patronage, His Majesty regrets that it is not possible to extend this privilege to the Dogs' Home Battersea". The decision clearly caught the Home off guard. One friend of the Home wrote to soften the blow, revealing to a Committee member "between ourselves the King convened a Committee and instructed it to make a drastic cut in his commitments".

But there was a clear feeling that damage had been done. In another letter, a Committee member admitted that "having enjoyed Royal Patronage

ABOVE Unlike dogs, cats didn't require licences, yet they continued to be abandoned in large numbers throughout the early decades of the twentieth century.

continuously for more than 50 years, its withdrawal would give the impression that the Home had fallen under a cloud and this most useful and deserving institution would be hampered in its good work".

A debate followed as to which members of the Royal Family might be approached as an alternative. The preferred choice was the King's brother, Albert, Duke of York, although some expressed doubts about his availability: "I have come to the conclusion that the Duke of York has been inundated with legacies from his brother for patronage and would be better advised to go for

one of the younger ones," a friend of the Home wrote to Committee member Frank Elliott.

The advice went unheeded, however, and the Duke of York was approached in the autumn. Once more the Home received bad news. On 21 October 1936, a letter arrived from St James's Palace informing the Home that the Duke of York's "list of Patronages is already so full that he feels he must not add to it further . . . His Royal Highness asks me to say how sorry he is to disappoint you in this matter."

The disappointment was deepened when the Home discovered that if it had waited a very different situation might have emerged. The King's relationship with a married American, Wallis Simpson, was already causing consternation in the Government and royal circles. In October 1936, at the same time the Home wrote to the Duke of York, Mrs Simpson was obtaining a rushed divorce in readiness to marry the King. By November the relationship had precipitated a full-scale constitutional crisis and by 10 December the King had been forced to abdicate.

The Duke of York became King George VI and might have been well disposed to picking up his father's reins as patron of the Home. But the Home had approached him once and could not do so again. It would be twenty years before it could once more claim royal patronage. By then Battersea – like the monarchy itself – had been engulfed in events that threatened its very existence.

OPPOSITE Despite newspaper suggestions to the contrary, by the 1920s the majority of Battersea dogs were being successfully rehomed.

FINEST HOUR

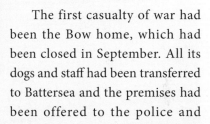

By 1940, THE MOOD AT THE Home – and in the country – was darkening. The advertising in the Annual Report summed up the change. A year earlier, in 1939, the gentlemen's outfitters Isaac Walton & Co. had taken a page to advertise dapper "cruise and tropical" outfits. By 1940 it was offering officers' uniforms and "complete service outfits".

The echoes of twenty-five years earlier were eerily apparent. At the annual general meeting in April 1940 the new chairman, Sir Charles Hardinge, echoed the "it will all be over by Christmas" optimism of 1914. He hoped that "before we have to hold our next Annual Meeting this wretched war will be successfully brought to an end, and those responsible for it will have met their proper deserts". Once more, it was a naïve hope.

The first casualty of war had been the Bow home, which had been closed in September. All its dogs and staff had been transferred to Battersea and the premises had been offered to the police and Auxiliary Fire Service for the "duration of the war". After a few months, however, the AFS had declined to take up the offer. Instead the Home lay empty, watched over by two elderly locals, much to the frustration of the Committee.

As in 1914, almost every able-bodied member of the male staff was called up. Five members of the kennel staff almost immediately left for active service, three with the ill-fated British Expeditionary Force in northern France. Another half-dozen followed in September 1939. The Home agreed to make up their wages if the services didn't match their pay at Battersea with the cash

PREVIOUS PAGE **As the country descended into chaos, Mr Veeney, a long-serving keeper, tried to maintain the same routine.**

"forwarded to their wives weekly". Sometimes the wives kept the Home up to date on the staff's whereabouts, although often the details were vague. One keeper was a bombardier "somewhere in England".

With rationing introduced again, food was in short supply. So, too, was money. As in 1914, there was a "bad falling off" in donations and the slide on the stock market meant investment income was down too. So straitened were the Home's circumstances that the Report's normal plea for funds sounded more heartfelt than usual:

The Committee appeal to the present supporters of the Association for increased and continued help, and beg all their friends to aid them in every possible way, their claim being that they are performing A NECESSARY PUBLIC WORK, as much in the interests of Society as in that of homeless and starving dogs and cats.

ABOVE Up close and personal: a 1940s keeper and a dog show their affection for each other.

With so many members of staff and the Committee in the armed forces, Sir Charles Hardinge decided that the Home would, for the duration of the war, be run by a Wartime Executive Emergency Committee, to meet once a month. The day-to-day running of the Home would be entrusted to Edward Healey-Tutt. A mild-mannered character who wouldn't have looked out of place behind a desk in a bank, he had taken over as secretary in July 1931 and had been a calming influence during a decade of change. His dedication and determination were not to be underestimated, however, as the next six years would prove.

OPPOSITE A dog's best friend: a small dog hitches a ride with a larger pal.

The first glimpse of his unflappable leadership came early on.

When Chamberlain had declared war on Germany, huge numbers of panic-stricken Londoners had turned up at Battersea asking for their pets to be destroyed. It was a dark echo of 1914, only worse this time. With Germany threatening to bomb the capital into submission, many genuinely believed their dogs would be better off dead than alive in a London where the sound of explosions might become the nightly norm. Healey-Tutt spent long, patient hours asking them "not to be in too much hurry to get rid of them". His office was soon full of "grateful letters".

It was easy to lose sight of the fact that the Home was, in many ways, carrying on with business as usual. And as it did so, it was still producing happy endings. In early 1940, it started

getting daily visits from a lady who had lost her dog in Kilburn. One of the keepers, Bert Collett, eventually told her he'd keep an eye open for it to save her making the journey every day. "She gave me a picture and kept in touch with us," he recalled, years afterwards.

Almost eighteen months later, in August 1941, Collett was feeding a little dog that had arrived in the Home three days earlier when he saw a similarity. He retrieved the photograph and recognized the dog immediately. The lady and her pet were soon reunited.

~

The anxieties of those Londoners who had flooded to the Home at the declaration of war eventually proved well founded. By the autumn of 1940, German planes were buzzing in the night sky above the Home. The city's Air Raid Protection (ARP) wardens had advised dog and cat owners to keep their pets indoors during raids. If they were small animals and any injuries were minor, it was the owners' responsibility to get the cat or dog to the network of casualty "clearing stations" the ARP had set up at stables, vets' surgeries, the RSPCA and other charity clinics. Battersea was on the list of approved locations.

Early on, the ARP's animal committee tried to persuade the Committee to allow them to use the Home as their headquarters. The ARP had also wanted to set up a new independent system for collecting dogs in an area from Rotherhithe to Clapham. The plan was dismissed by the Home as "fantastic", with "no chance of its operating in practice". Besides, the Home had a contract with

OPPOSITE **Many Londoners panicked and abandoned their dogs when Chamberlain declared war on Germany.**

ABOVE **Business as usual: despite the bombs, Battersea continued to offer homes to lost and stray dogs.**

the Metropolitan Police, who would continue to bring dogs to it.

As the Blitz got under way, the Home was deluged by animals that had been orphaned when their homes had been hit. The distressed barks and howls of several hundred dogs were often lost against the sound of air-raid sirens and anti-aircraft fire. The Home itself was in a vulnerable position. Not only was it next to a pair of gasometers and a railway, for the past decade it had had as its neighbour one of London's key power stations.

In 1925, the Government had decided to build a new "national power grid", to supersede the existing network of small power companies,

ABOVE "Stout-hearted spirit": Edward Healey-Tutt, the man who guided Battersea through the Blitz and beyond.

and plans had been drawn up for a series of "super power stations". The first of these was to be built on the Home's doorstep. The fifteen-acre plot had been owned by the Southwark and Vauxhall Waterworks Company. The new London Power Company bought the land and in 1927 drew up plans for a station capable of generating 400,000 kilowatts of electricity. The prospect of a giant power station in the heart of London caused a stream of protests. There were worries that it would be an eyesore and that its pollution would damage everything from the plants and flowers in Battersea Park to the paintings in the Tate Gallery a mile or so down the Thames.

But the protests were batted away. Soon two vast white chimney stacks were climbing into the Battersea sky as the first part of the station took shape. Two more would follow. The towers

of Battersea Power Station were soon luring the *Luftwaffe* to drop their payloads. Bombs rained down on the surrounding streets almost nightly. It was inevitable that the Home would be hit at some point.

Healey-Tutt and the Committee briefly considered instituting a plan in the event of a delayed-action bomb falling on the site. The advice was that they would have "three to five" minutes to evacuate the entire premises. To empty the kennels in that time was impossible so the plan was abandoned. If a delayed-action device landed, Healey-Tutt and his staff would have to deal with it as best they could.

Healey-Tutt came up with another plan instead. With the Blitz destroying homes and killing people on a nightly basis, many of the capital's children were being evacuated to the countryside. Every day trains filled with youngsters were leaving for Wales, Scotland and the West Country. In November 1940, Healey-Tutt launched a scheme to despatch dogs to homes in the countryside. They were mostly sent to families who had been evacuated from London and had had to abandon or put down their dogs before leaving. All they had to do in return was pay "the dog's railway fare". Healey-Tutt took on an extra member of staff specifically to ferry dogs to London's main railway stations, from which scores were soon carried away from the bombs.

The Home's luck ran out at around 11.45 p.m. on Sunday, 15 September 1940. A bomb exploded in the entrance yard, severely damaging the keeper's lodge, the staff rooms and the offices. Doors were blown off and glass shattered all over the rest of the site, including in the main kennels. In the immediate aftermath of the explosion "many

OPPOSITE Jumping ship: not all dogs enjoyed the basic mode of transport forced upon the Home's residents by the wartime petrol rations.

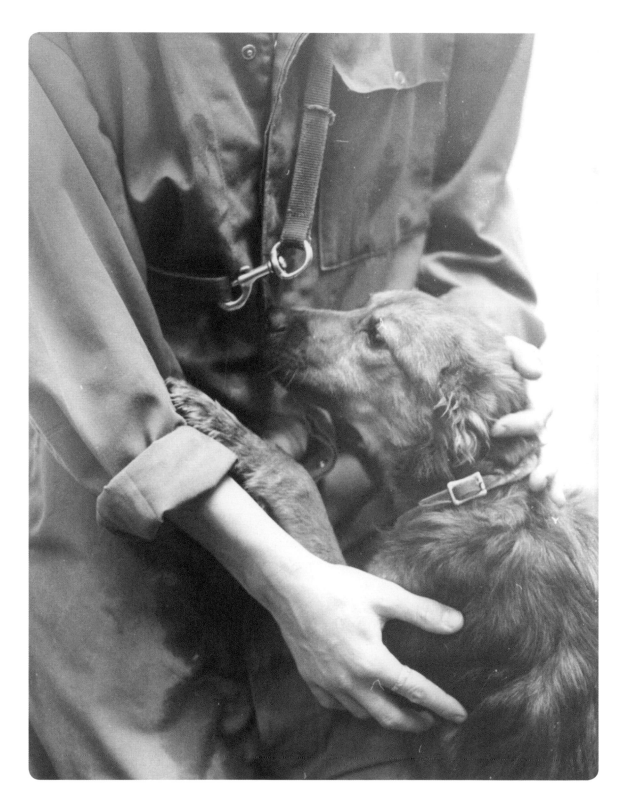

dogs" escaped into the yard where they were eventually rounded up by Healey-Tutt and his two night-watchmen, the only people on the site. Five dogs, however, escaped and ran off into the streets, terrified. They weren't seen again. Healey-Tutt escaped unhurt, as did – miraculously – all of the dogs. A builder was called in the next week to rehang doors, board up broken windows and replace slates on the roof. He took one look at the middle office and the book-keeper's office and decided they were "beyond repair and would have to be condemned".

The repairs were almost immediately undone. On the night of 1 October, another bomb fell and exploded inside the Home. The blast destroyed the shuttering that had been put in to replace the glass blown out in the last explosion. The pattern was repeated for the next six weeks with new explosions as more bombs "undid all that had been done". Healey-Tutt and his skeleton staff remained unhurt.

As if his workload at the Home wasn't heavy enough, Healey-Tutt was also working as a driver for the Auxiliary Fire Service. Two nights a week he was driving around London in one of the AFS's distinctive Green Goddess fire engines, putting out blazes or restoring water supplies. The toll it took on him became apparent in November when a Committee member, a Major Carter, turned up unexpectedly at the Home. He found Healey-Tutt and some of his staff digging a "large hole" in the garden area. The Home had been receiving large numbers of badly injured or dead dogs during the Blitz. Normally they were collected and disposed of by private contractors, Harrison, Barber & Co., but the contractor's premises had been bombed and

OPPOSITE Faithful friends: throughout the 1940s the Home witnessed many an emotional reunion, some involving dogs whose owners had been serving overseas.

> **The repairs were almost immediately undone. On the night of 1 October, another bomb fell and exploded inside the Home**

their drivers hadn't been able to collect any dogs for some time. Healey-Tutt told Major Carter that he was having to bury the carcasses on site.

Carter was shocked by the way Healey-Tutt was living. Because of the stench of the many carcasses that had built up at the Home, he had stopped sleeping in the staff dining room and made a bed in the "paraffin shed" where he was "eating out of tins". On top of this he was now working four nights a week with the AFS, "twice as much as he had undertaken to do". Alarmed, Carter contacted the rest of the Committee, who persuaded the clearly exhausted Healey-Tutt to see his doctor, who told him in no uncertain terms that he had to cut back on his work with the AFS. He also told him to take a rest, which Healey-Tutt said he would when he decided he had the time.

On 16 April 1941 the Home had another lucky escape. A land mine fell on the nearby gasometers. If it had exploded the Home – and probably most of Battersea – would have been destroyed in the resulting blast. But the only damage was to woodwork and what remained of the glass in the Home's windows. This time the builders patched up the windows with sailcloth.

In April 1942, while he was out with the AFS, Healey-Tutt was hit by the blast from an explosion and injured. This time he wasn't given the luxury of choosing when he would take time off to recover. His doctor ordered him to rest so that his wounds could heal and he was taken away to stay with his wife. He would be off for several weeks.

Healey-Tutt's injury was a wake-up call to the Committee. They knew that if the Home was to come through the war intact, they needed their senior officer in one piece. They also knew that when he returned he couldn't continue to sleep in the paraffin shed. They agreed to rent a flat in Richmond for him and his family. They also paid him a public vote of thanks. The chairman, Sir Charles Hardinge, told him how "fortunate it was for the dogs and the subscribers" that a man of his "calibre" was in charge of the Home during this difficult time. He said he "could not speak too highly of the very stout-hearted spirit" he had displayed. The Committee "all hoped that his holiday would give him the rest which he so badly needed".

Just as in the First World War, the number of staff continued to dwindle as every able-bodied man and woman was called up for duty. Some men returned, although often in a worse condition than when they had left. In the autumn of 1943, a keeper called Tyler returned from service with the Commandos: he had been discharged with "duodenal ulcers". Inevitably the average age of those working at the Home rose. Healey-Tutt's main allies were his assistant, Mrs Witherow, and two senior keepers, Mr Ball and Mr Carstairs, who had been transferred from Bow.

If the workload had been lighter than it was during peacetime, the lack of staff might not have been such a problem. Yet the fact was that the Home was taking in as many dogs as it had before the war. Somehow the few staff managed to feed and care for the 145,000 dogs that were to pass through Battersea during the course of the war.

Maintaining supplies was always a challenge and often depended on favours and string-pulling. In many instances, however, the Home was told in no uncertain terms that dogs weren't on the list of priorities.

Petrol supplies were always low and at one point Healey-Tutt had to make a personal plea to a Captain Roberts, sub-district manager at the Albert Bridge Flour Mills headquarters of the Petrol Board. But his request to have the Home's petrol ration maintained at the same level as it had been earlier in the war was rejected immediately. He argued that the Home needed petrol to visit every police station holding dogs. Roberts replied that the stations should be equipped with mobile gas chambers so that dogs could be despatched immediately. Hardly a sympathetic response. Healey-Tutt and his team somehow scrimped and saved enough food and petrol to get by, even though wartime regulations forbade stockpiling. Fortunately he was helped to some extent by the Commissioner of the Metropolitan Police, who agreed to list the Home's drivers under an Essential Works Order.

Food was so scarce that the Home was frequently forced to rely on handouts. At one point the Ministry of Food offered a large amount of "damaged flour". However, the Home refused the offer of a dog-food company that suggested it fed the animals an experimental new product.

Unlike in the First World War, there was no call for dogs to fight on the front lines, which baffled the man behind the 1914–18 Dog Brigade, E. H. Richardson. Major Richardson had started recruiting dogs already, many from Battersea, and was training them again at Shoeburyness. The Germans had trained twice the number of dogs they had in the First World War, with twelve thousand this time. The German High Command

ABOVE Battersea dogs were in demand to help on the Home Front and abroad. This one was an ammunition carrier with the ill-fated British Expeditionary Force.

had ordered all dogs under six years old and measuring between twenty and twenty-eight inches at the shoulder to be handed over to the *Reichswehr*. There were already reports of German Shepherds working successfully as sniffer dogs in the Moselle area. This time Richardson and his recruits weren't called into action on foreign soil.

There was, however, a call for dogs as part of the Home Defence effort. In November 1942, the Auxiliary Territorial Service approached the Home for dogs to do "picket work and to accompany sentries on their night work patrolling ammunition dumps etc". The ATS wanted "the heavier breed of dog" for the work. The Home agreed.

A similar request had come earlier from Flying Officer G. Ricks, who requisitioned a pack of fourteen dogs – seven German Shepherds and seven Airedales – to act as sentries at his Nottingham air base. Ricks obtained an allowance of 2*d* a day to feed the dogs, which also lived on scraps from the mess. A report in March 1940 in the *Nottingham Evening News* revealed that the dogs were "proving very quick to learn their duties". They were being used as sentries at the main entrance to the camp as well as being kept in the most important buildings at night.

The success of the dogs was such that other requests followed, mostly for dogs to help in "picket work". In 1943, for instance, dogs were supplied to the female searchlight team in north London to "protect and guard the site". Later, the War Office bought a large number of dogs from the Home.

ABOVE The RAF were among those who requisitioned Battersea dogs for duty.

~

On 8 May 1945, the news everyone had been anticipating arrived. The Allies had accepted the unconditional surrender of the German forces. Millions turned out in the streets to celebrate VE Day. Healey-Tutt and his staff at the Home staged their own celebrations, although they knew that the hard work would now begin.

Just as the streets of London still bore the scars of war, with bomb craters still in view, so Battersea was a pale shadow of its pre-war self. The bomb damage was still all too apparent. The Committee admitted the Home looked "very shabby". It also conceded that it had been "unable to do very much in the way of repairs other than temporary ones, although a number of broken windows were renewed and replaced by our own carpenter". Applications for money for repairs had been made to the War Damage Commission.

Even if the money had been available, it would have been impossible to maintain the Home as it had been before the war because there still weren't enough staff. At the end of 1945, four members of staff had been demobbed and returned, but several others remained in uniform.

At least the Home in Battersea was still functioning. By contrast, Bow was still out of action. The Home had been forced to rent the premises to any interested parties and its residents now included a herd of pigs owned by an east London branch of the Home Guard.

~

It wasn't until 1946 that the Committee had been able to publish a full Annual Report again. It represented its first opportunity to look back at the remarkable job Healey-Tutt and his team had done during the previous seven years. His stoic, stiff-upper-lip approach, which had seen him and his staff through the Blitz and beyond, remained apparent. The Report's overview of the traumatic times from which it was only now recovering was confined to two brief paragraphs.

During the war years, the number of stray dogs received from the Police and other sources showed no decrease on our pre-war figures and the work of collection continued uninterruptedly in spite of the great shortage of staff and the difficulty experienced by our vans in getting round London and through bombed streets.

In this much bombed area, only a very few dogs escaped at night into the streets when kennel and yard doors were blown open as the result of bombs dropping in the near neighbourhood and in the yard itself but not a single dog was either hurt or killed, although, on one occasion, a number of incendiary bombs fell amongst them in their kennels.

Like the rest of the country, the Home didn't have the luxury of being able to dwell on what was, without doubt, its finest hour. Even if it had wanted to …

By 1948 the War Damage Commission had finally approved some money for the Home to begin rebuilding work. The first allocation was earmarked for the reconstruction of the B Block kennels, which had taken the brunt of the bomb damage. The work was carried out during the summer of 1948. The Commission had also approved another £1,700 or so for more repairs the following year. The work included the reconstruction of B Block. The cattery, which had been abandoned during the war, was put back into working order.

The years that followed the end of the war were characterized by austerity and hardship. The laws of supply and demand took over and with food in short supply the cost of feeding the cats and dogs continued to rise.

ABOVE **Against all the odds, the Home remained open throughout the war. An RAF serviceman brings a dog to Battersea's gates.**

The end of the war presented a perfect opportunity to take stock. The Committee wasted no time in asking a public relations and advertising expert, Frank Goshawk, to turn an outsider's eye on the Home's operations. He walked the site and inspected the finances, and his report, written in December 1945, was enlightening, if a little more adventurous than they'd anticipated.

The good news was that, just as in 1919, demand for dogs had risen at the end of the war. The prices the Home was charging for its dogs were strong, between 7s 6d and £1. "At the moment people are prepared to pay much more for dogs than they were before the War, and, in fact, there is such a demand for dogs from blitzed people coming back to London that there is a greater number of buyers than there are dogs for sale." As a result, the demand for breeding bitches was higher than usual, he added. He said it was "clear that the Home can continue to function".

The bad news, however, was that the Home was in severe need of repair work. Goshawk was of the clear view that they should start "seeking new funds so that real expansion and modernization of the Home can become practical realities". He cited the example of the £17 million the Red Cross had collected during the five and half years of the war. A large chunk had come from the penny collections it had run, which alone had raised more than £4 million. Goshawk wondered whether "some people had got a little tired of Red Cross, Red Cross, Red Cross, and are ready to drop it now the war is over. Before the habit of systematic giving has been entirely lost some of them might be induced to switch their attention to the London Dogs Home at Battersea Park. Who knows?"

He recommended launching an immediate appeal for more money for the Home and a plan to promote its activities. His ideas included erecting more road signs pointing to the Home and large billboards directly outside it, giving the collection vans a more distinctive livery that, "while retaining dignity and avoiding garishness, can be recognized immediately by anybody in the streets". He also proposed lessons in London schools on "the care and handling of pet dogs", producing an annual magazine, called *Dogs' Dinners*, full of entertaining stories written by "eminent people" and forging alliances with pet-food manufacturers, who would become "large scale donors". He also argued that the Home should cater for newspaper editors "on the look-out for strong emotional appeal stories", perhaps make a movie about life at the Home and even go around promoting the Home at music halls with slide shows. He even proposed selling

ABOVE In the aftermath of the war, Battersea's inmates lived in a Home in severe need of repair.

advertising space inside the Home, which he was convinced could generate "quite high charges".

His most controversial idea, however, involved renaming the Home. Like most Londoners, Goshawk had grown up knowing it as Battersea Dogs' Home, but he had heard Committee members refer to it as the London Dogs' Home. He wanted to connect with the nine million people who lived in London at the time and suggested a radical renaming: the London Dogs' Home, Battersea Park. He argued this was less "clumsy" than the Dogs' Home Battersea.

His ideas were, it's fair to say, at least thirty years ahead of their time. The Home would have to pick its way back into peacetime a little more carefully.

OPPOSITE With the war over, families began rebuilding their lives, and some returned to Battersea to find their four-legged companions.

A NEW BROOM

B Y THE BEGINNING OF THE 1950s, Edward Healey-Tutt's health was failing fast. He had for some time been displaying symptoms of Parkinson's disease and had become a shadow of the tireless figure of the war years. The death of his wife had hastened his decline. The Home recognized the debt it owed the man who had – more than any other – guided Battersea through the dark days of the Second World War. The Committee was willing to overlook his occasional lapses and had allowed him to remain as secretary, but by 1953, the Home and Healey-Tutt were forced to face up to the inevitable. Healey-Tutt announced he was retiring to South Africa, where his daughter lived.

The Committee made sure he was given a generous pension and placed a charming portrait of him in the final Annual Report, to which he contributed, in 1954. The Home had had fewer finer servants.

Replacing the quietly heroic wartime secretary was never going to be easy and, in all, seventy or so candidates were interviewed for the post. The choice of his replacement caused an unusually strong reaction within the Home.

The sitting chairman, Sir Charles Hardinge, had led Healey-Tutt's loyal assistant, Mrs Witherow, who had been at the Home for twenty-five years, to believe she would succeed her boss as secretary. The Committee vetoed the appointment, preferring an ex-naval officer, Lieutenant Commander Benjamin Knight. There was, almost certainly, more than a hint of sexism about the decision. Although the Home had been set up by women, Battersea's executive retained all the hallmarks of a gentlemen's club. No female had served in a senior management

PREVIOUS PAGE Normal service resumed: cats and dogs quickly adapted to life in the new, post-war Home.

position or worked as a keeper. More than ninety years on from the Home's establishment, its kennels and yards were still strictly male domains.

Sir Charles and Mrs Witherow were so unhappy at the appointment that, within months, they left the Home, Mrs Witherow taking retirement and the chairman resigning his position. Their objections were entirely understandable. Yet, as it turned out, the Committee had made an astute choice. Benjamin Knight proved to be the ideal leader to steer the Home into the post-war era and its second century. Ironically he would also do more to break down the gender divide than any of his predecessors.

A tall, energetic veteran of the Merchant and the Royal Navy, Knight had been invalided out of the services in 1949, after he had broken his back during the Malta Convoy in 1942. Yet there was little evidence of his infirmity at the Home, where he quickly established himself as one of the most dynamic reformist characters ever to take the reins. As the austerity of the post-war era lifted, he was just what the Home needed.

Knight had been tipped off about the job by the Association of Retired Naval Officers but had been unsure whether it was right for him, especially when he first set foot in Battersea. "It was a grim November day," he recalled, of his initial visit to the Home. "I saw for the first time the grey Home merging into even greyer Battersea surroundings. The smoke-belching power station deposited grit and filth everywhere." He'd found Healey-Tutt's "nice creeper-covered Victorian house" quite cheering. "But a brief look around and our gloom returned with a vengeance," he said.

His reaction was predictable. The Home was a dilapidated and rapidly ageing throwback to another time. Despite the repair work that had been undertaken in the years following the war, the kennels had a dingy, run-down atmosphere and the stone walls meant they were often bitterly cold during the winter months.

Knight was shocked when he inspected the buildings closely. There were "cracks the thickness of my hand", he said later. "I'll give this ten years before it falls down around our ears," he'd said to himself at the time.

Given the number of candidates, Knight had had to wait two months to learn he'd got the job. When he was finally offered and accepted it, he began by refurbishing the kennels with better-insulated false ceilings and walls and replacing the dogs' straw and sawdust beds with hardwood benches. He also improved the smell of the place.

Part of the land next to the Home had been rented to the Perseverance Pig Club. A vast quantity of manure had piled up and the air was thick with flies, especially during hot weather. The stench could be overwhelming, even inside the buildings. Life had become unpleasant for the Home's staff and inmates. Knight went to see the owner of the land who immediately gave the pig keepers notice to quit.

As he set about an ambitious programme of works to modernize the Home, Knight also proved a resilient, resourceful and surprisingly modern manager. When he first arrived, Knight noticed that many of the dogs were malnourished and "Belsen thin". Their diets were still largely the same as they had been during the war years, mainly horse meat and grain.

He cleaned up the kitchens so that "you could cook a human meal here", then started producing more nutritious meals. Knight's menu consisted mainly of a "beef stew, Battersea style", in which up

ABOVE All present and correct: the Battersea staff pose for a group photograph outside the newly-repainted main entrance.

to seventy pounds of beef was left to stew overnight to produce a broth of meat in its own marrowbone jelly. He also introduced special diets of eggs, milk, glucose and fish, to be fed to whelping bitches, puppies and sick animals. "Nobody will ever convince me that good basic food won't achieve better results on badly fed and undernourished creatures – human or animal – than all your drugs," he said.

Knight also pressed for more modern innovations. The Home, inevitably, was steeped in habit and routine, some of it acceptable, some of it not. Knight continued the military-style regimen, insisting his staff lined up for inspection and wore uniform. However, he was determined to update some of the attitudes and practices at the Home. At his prompting, the Committee had, for instance, agreed to begin research into

a quicker, more efficient and humane means of euthanasia. With the approval of the British Veterinary Association, the Home had been recommended an electric cabinet that put the animals to rest almost instantaneously.

His most significant reform was to the restrictive practices that had taken root during the latter years of Healey-Tutt's leadership. Knight had identified a problem with the van drivers and concluded they were "very slack" in going about their daily duties, taking too long to transport dogs from the police stations to the Home. Some dogs were spending six hours in the back of vans, he protested. His arrival coincided with the drivers' claim for a significant increase in their holiday money and the most senior, a man called Hogben, threatened to quit if they didn't get it.

Knight acted immediately and decisively. In September 1955 he gathered all the drivers together one Saturday morning and sacked them. As if this

ABOVE A new fleet of vans was one of the first and most tangible signs of post-war modernization.

wasn't radical enough, his plan for replacing them was revolutionary, with a recruitment drive for "women drivers only". "It seemed to me the one way of making sure the dogs would not be handled badly," he said later.

At first Knight probably regretted the move. The main problem was the fleet of old Bedford Green Goddesses. One was in such a bad state that "women drivers were physically unable to drive it". One had broken her finger trying to manage the unwieldy machine while another had damaged her knee. One woman quit over the condition of the vans.

At one point, Knight took to the wheel of the giant green vans, ferrying dogs from the capital's police stations at the crack of dawn before settling down to a day's work in the office. "The thought of driving one of these lumbering, unfamiliar monsters through the London streets filled me with foreboding," he said. "I remember driving along the bumpy cobbled roads of London's dock area, fearfully aware of the poor dogs every time I misjudged a corner."

Within a fortnight there were three accidents. First a Miss Cox knocked down a pedestrian while driving through Harringay and was prosecuted by the police. Four days later she was involved in an accident with a baker's van. Four days after that another driver, Miss Wise, dented a car in Sutton.

Eventually the Home conceded it needed new vehicles and ordered them. A new garage was also commissioned. Before long the female

OPPOSITE New friends: Battersea's experienced keepers were experts at giving young owners advice on how to manage their new dogs.

recruitment drive was being hailed a significant success. "Gradually, one by one, I got the drivers I wanted, practical, no-nonsense ladies who could drive expertly and handle the dogs gently but firmly," he said, and the Annual Report for 1956 stated, "Many excellent reports concerning both their handling of the vehicles and of the strays they collect have been received and noted." Knight was soon telling anyone who was willing to listen that his new female drivers were superior to their male counterparts – but it would be years before they were paid the same rate as the men.

Knight's new broom swept away other relics of the pre-war era. In 1955 the Committee was finally able to rid itself of the financial millstone that was the Bow branch. The extra accommodation had proven useful when the extended contract for east London was granted to Battersea, but since the war it had ceased to be cost-effective. Its sale removed "a great strain upon the resources of the Association", Knight said. In early 1955 an offer of £15,000 was received from a box company, which pulled out at the last minute. In July an

ABOVE How much is that doggy in the window? In the post-war era, puppies became a cheap – and disposable – commodity.

auction was held, but the highest bid was only £8,500, well below the minimum the Home had set of £10,000.

In September a metal plating company offered £14,000, which was accepted. The money was channelled into modernizing the Home in other ways. The electricity supply system was changed and the garage rebuilt. Slowly but surely a new Home was beginning to take shape.

Knight also suggested that the Home employed a dedicated public relations officer. Four leading PR firms had pitched to handle the Home's business and two – Pritchard Wood and 4D Associates – had been interviewed. The more conservative elements of the Committee won the day, and it had been decided that "there was no need for a Public Relations Officer for the Home, either now or in the future".

Fortunately Knight was a consummate interviewee and enjoyed talking to the press. He played up to his role as the "captain of his ship", referring to the Home's staff as "the lower deck", and called the flat that he and his wife shared above the entrance to the Home "Kennel Number 4".

With his instinctive understanding of the value of publicity, he gave the press a steady flow of uplifting stories about dogs that had been reunited with their owners or found new homes. As ever, there was no shortage, the most popular of which concerned a fox. The cub had been found by a man driving through Canvey Island in Essex. He had spotted a vixen strangled in a barbed-wire fence and the shivering, whimpering form of her cub lying forlornly alongside. The man tried in vain to domesticate the fox so in the end delivered him to Battersea where he was christened Freddy and became an instant star. The keepers fed him a daily diet of milk, bread and fresh, raw meat.

ABOVE Freddy the fox: Battersea's famous resident is handed over to an RAF representative.

News of his presence at the Home delighted the newspapers and soon crowds were coming purely to see its most famous resident. Eventually, however, Knight had a bright idea and contacted No.12 Squadron of the RAF. As an ex-naval officer, he knew their insignia was a fox and asked them if they would be interested in having Freddy as a mascot. They immediately agreed, and Freddy was introduced to the squadron in an elaborate presentation ceremony at their home in Lincolnshire.

On 18 May 1956, Buckingham Palace confirmed that Queen Elizabeth II had agreed to become the Home's patron. After the twenty-year break, the sovereign was once more its most important supporter. The chairman had written to Buckingham Palace only a week earlier, explaining that "my Committee have, on various occasions, expressed their regret that the Home no longer enjoys Royal Patronage". He didn't mention Edward VIII's brief and troubled reign but said he understood why the Queen's father had "found it necessary to restrict the number of Institutions and Associations to which he extended this privilege". He went on to point out that the Home was "financially sound" and "claims to be doing useful public work. My Committee earnestly hope, therefore, that Her Majesty the Queen might be graciously pleased to restore this favour."

A reply came within days: the Queen had accepted the invitation.

LOVE ME,
LOVE MY DOG?

Oɴ 3 Ocᴛᴏʙᴇʀ 1960 ᴀ sᴍᴀʟʟ group of staff, Committee members and invited guests gathered in the yard to witness the unveiling of the latest gift to the Home. The donation was from an unlikely-sounding source: the Metropolitan Drinking Fountain and Cattle Trough Association had commissioned a specially designed drinking fountain to be used by humans and dogs at the Home. The Duke of Portland was on hand to do the honours.

Far more significant than the fountain, though, was the plaque he unveiled at the same time. It marked the hundredth anniversary of the opening of the original home in Hollingsworth Street, Holloway, on 2 October 1860. Just as a century earlier, the event elicited only mild interest in the press, but that was no cause for disappointment. A

few newspapers had already visited the Home during the year to talk to staff about the landmark, including *The Times*, which had printed a lengthy article in January. "The Thunderer" had, of course, done its level best to kill off the Home at birth, and its 1860 leader, in which it had mocked Mary Tealby and her colleagues, had set the tone until Charles Dickens presented his more sympathetic opinion.

A hundred years later the newspaper's view was very different: "By general consent the service that the home provides is invaluable. The existence of such an institution in which all London's stray dogs can be properly looked after until claimed, sold to new owners, or (in the case of old and incurably diseased animals) destroyed, has been of advantage to the people of the capital," its correspondent wrote, then went further, recognizing the quintessential

"Englishness" of Battersea and the remarkably resilient relationship it represented:

> It is in many ways the embodiment of the Englishman's notorious tendency towards animals. Indeed, the founding of the home at time when the popular view of dogs as a rabies-carrying nuisance largely outweighed their status as honoured friends of man had much to do with consolidating the tradition expressed in the dictum: "Love me, love my dog."

Other aspects of life at the Home echoed the previous century, not least the Committee's attitude to women. That year's Annual Report condescendingly pointed out that "Our four women drivers have also contributed much towards the Home by their high standard of driving."

If there was one area of the Home's business affairs that presented a stark contrast to the early days, it was its balance sheet. At the end of 1960, it showed that the Home was sitting on investments and savings in excess of £300,000, earmarked for a new building programme that would take the Home into its second century.

Nevertheless, there were still those who were convinced sinister secrets lurked behind the doors of the Home. The most common was, as Knight put it, the "far too widespread misconception that all dogs received in the Home, if unclaimed by their owners, are destroyed, whether they be fit and healthy or not". The truth was that far fewer dogs than ever were being destroyed. By 1960, of the 10,963 dogs brought into that year, 6,777 were either restored to their owners or found new homes over time, with many more

kept alive as "yard dogs". But that did not stop the insinuations.

The other myth that had endured surrounded the Home and vivisection. Occasionally the Home had to fight fire with fire to defend itself. In January 1961 the *Daily Mail* ran a story about a dog that had escaped from a medical laboratory after being "infected by food poisoning germs". Alongside the article, the paper had run a more general story on vivisection in which it claimed that seven thousand dogs a year were being used for animal research carried out under licence from the Home Office. "Hundreds of them come from Battersea Dogs Home," the report read. "In the Metropolitan area alone the police sent 10,309 dogs to the Battersea home. Many of them were claimed. But animals not claimed within seven days are likely to be sent to laboratories or institutions carrying out cancer research and experiments on the effects of drugs." The allegation was so outrageous that the Home had no option but to issue an immediate writ for libel.

The case was heard at the High Court in October that year. The Home's defence remained as it had for decades: that for it to send dogs to research establishments was contrary not just to its own rules but to the Dogs Act of 1906, which provided that "No Dog … shall be given or sold for the purpose of vivisection." Mr Justice Hilbery ruled in favour of the Home and ordered the *Daily Mail* to pay "substantial damages" as well as the Home's costs.

Clearly, some felt there was no smoke without fire. Within a year, the Home was launching another libel action, this time against an author, Lady Lloyd Packer, who had suggested the same thing in a novel. "The whole purpose of their work is to take care of the dogs in their charge as humanely and kindly as possible and to endeavour to find a home for as many as possible," the Home's counsel David

ABOVE Surveying the scene: a new arrival checks out the Battersea landscape.

Hirst told Mr Justice Havers. "They have never in all their history sold a single dog for the purposes of vivisection." Again the courts found in favour of the Home, this time ordering not only the payment of damages, but that every copy of the book carry a correction or "erratum" slip.

The consistent attacks were far from welcome, but the money that successful libel actions brought was a different matter.

~

The Home continued to rely on its subscribers. They could be as colourful and unpredictable as the canine and feline inmates. One cold November morning, Benjamin Knight found himself standing outside a row of terraced houses on the edge of Windsor in Berkshire. As he recounted later: "I had had to answer a lot of strange requests on behalf of the world's busiest refuge for strays, but staring around at my unlikely-looking surroundings, I couldn't help wondering if, on that occasion, I wouldn't have been better off back in my office."

He was responding to an intriguing letter he'd received days earlier. It read simply: "If a representative would like to call on me, he will hear something to the Home's advantage." When he knocked on the cottage door, he was "ushered into a postage-stamp living room by an elderly lady. She told me she used to live in Battersea, opposite the Home, and knew the difficulty we faced," he recalled later. She handed Knight a "large, damp and dusty parcel". When he turned it over, out fell a mass of pound notes. "And so in that darkened little room I sat and counted out the oddest donation we'd ever had – three hundred one-pound notes, old, much used and slightly damp. Notes obviously carefully saved over the years."

As it turned out, the lady's husband had owned a number of cottages. She had saved part of the rental income over the years with the intention of giving it to the Home. Knight only discovered this when the lady came to the opening of a new kennel some time later. She arrived clutching a damp envelope containing another bundle of notes.

~

In late June 1968, a bedraggled Poodle arrived at the Home with a scribbled note attached to its neck. It read:

To whom it may concern: Would you please look after our dog Kim. We live in a council flat, and the Caretaker has told us to get rid of dog Kim, as we are not allowed to have a dog. My Mum is ill over it and she is frightened to put it out. You see we have not got a Daddy. But our Mum is very good to us, only our Mum is very old – 45 – and always ill, and loves our dog. We are 11 years old and 7 years old. Kim is nine years old and a very good house dog. We all love him.

PS: If we could have our own house we could keep him. Please don't have him put to sleep. Love – Louise and Jimmy.

The dog had been found wandering the streets in one of the better parts of upmarket Hampstead, north London. It turned out the authors of the letter, siblings Louise and Jimmy McGill, had let their dog loose there in the hope that he would end up living with "some rich lady". Instead he had been picked up by a police officer and transferred to Battersea.

By now the Home's long-standing resistance to having a dedicated public relations service had finally been overcome. For the past four years, the media element had been supplied by the Central News Service, which was paid two hundred pounds a year to distribute positive stories to the national press and immediately sensed a good opportunity.

When the poignant letter was released the following day, the reaction was immediate – and remarkable. Fleet Street suddenly went into overdrive first to locate the children, and then to reunite them with their beloved Poodle. The *Evening Standard* found them: they lived within a mile of the Home in a tower block in Battersea. It turned out the story was even more emotive than originally thought, as Louise was suffering from what her mother, Sophia, described as a "nervous complaint". She had bought the dog, even though she knew she was breaking the council's rules, to help her daughter. "Kim was the best medicine Louise ever had," she told the *Daily Express* when its reporter visited her. "But since he went her condition has deteriorated rapidly."

Unsurprisingly, the local council, Wandsworth, were soon back-pedalling. "It was a bit hard on the little girl, we do admit, but we have to stick to the regulations," an official said, and added that they were already looking into relocating the family. "There seem to be exceptional circumstances in this case and we will do what we can to help."

That wasn't good enough for the newspapers. A day later, the *Sun* had extracted a promise from

the housing department, who were actively "trying to find a house where the McGill family can live with their dog".

It took two months to arrange, but in late September the McGills were rehoused and Kim returned to them. A phalanx of photographers was on hand to record the touching scene as Kim, Louise and Jimmy were reunited.

The story proved useful to the Home in several ways. On the simplest level it was further proof, if any was needed, that the power of stories involving children and animals remained as strong as ever. It also reinforced, once more, how hard Battersea was willing to work to reunite owners with their dogs, contrary to the opinion of the hardened minority who still believed the bulk of its inmates were simply put to sleep.

On a deeper, social level, the story of Kim and the McGills illustrated a significant change that the Home had already picked up on. Britain in the 1960s had become a wealthier, more mobile and more acquisitive society. The 1950s consumer boom of the United States had crossed the Atlantic. With the explosion of social housing and tower blocks, in particular, hundreds of thousands of people were moving into cities to live in council flats like those that had housed the McGills, many of which had rules prohibiting dogs. The changing face of Britain was subtly shifting the way in which the country treated its dogs. Again Battersea was clearing up the mess.

The impact of the move into high-rise accommodation and faceless estates was plain to see. Reports of dog packs roaming large council estates were commonplace. In 1968, on one estate in Harold Hill, Essex, police had to intervene to

OPPOSITE Two's company: a pair of new arrivals nestle in the experienced arms of a Battersea superintendent.

ABOVE All dressed up: the Home's vans were decked out to celebrate one hundred years of service.

round up dogs that had been terrifying mothers with young children. The dogs were being turned out of the flats in which they lived when their owners went to work in the morning and left to roam. "Throughout the day they are our worry," a policeman told the *Havering Express* that September. "They are kicked out of the house in the morning. And at night a whistle brings them in again. Sometimes the dogs are left to fend for themselves when owners go on holiday."

Similarly, on the Fieldway estate in Croydon, south London, the local MP had fielded complaints about roaming packs of dogs being "a real problem to children". The police had spotted the trend too, in October that year, citing "34 road accidents

on the estate this year which were known to have been caused by dogs". It was still the police's responsibility to round up dogs that were a danger to society. As a result, the numbers arriving at the Home were on the increase.

With more and more dogs now roaming the streets, there were calls for Parliament to intervene by raising the cost of a dog licence for the first time since 1878, from 7s 6d to £2. In November, Lord Aylwin made an impassioned speech on the matter to the House of Lords. He produced figures indicating that of the 4,750,000 dogs in Britain only 2,750,000 were licensed. With two million unlicensed dogs wandering the streets, he called for the new £2 fee to pay for dog wardens to help the police and tougher penalties for licence dodgers. Aylwin suggested the higher licence fee would put "£5 million a year into the kitties of local authorities".

Opposing, Lord Ferrers said people simply wouldn't pay it. "If there are people evading the licence when it is 7s 6d how many more will evade it when it rises to £2? There would only be more stray dogs."

Controversially, the contraceptive pill had just been introduced for women. The Earl of Arran suggested a "contraceptive pill" for dogs. "I don't believe the most fervent religionists would object to that," he said. "There are far too many cats and dogs born."

The call for a rise in the licence fee provoked a huge response, with opinion divided wildly, even among the country's leading animal and dog charities. The RSPCA generally supported the new fee on the grounds that it would "reduce the number of unwanted dogs". The National Canine Defence League was "wholly opposed to the idea". The only change it supported was the introduction of a licence for puppies from eight weeks rather than the then eight months. The British Union for the Abolition of Vivisection suggested dogs that had been sterilized be exempt from the fee and that dogs known to be capable of breeding be charged a higher amount. The Kennel Club proposed that the licence fee should be abolished altogether.

As the debate raged, Benjamin Knight entered the fray, giving a series of interviews. His view was that the licence fee should be increased to £5 per year. "Of course old age pensioners, guide dogs for the blind and those sort of people would have to be given concessions," he told *Dog's Life* in December. His view was a personal one, "not fully authorized by my Committee because I have not discussed it with them," he admitted. "But both our veterinary surgeon and I … would dearly love to see licences increased to such an extent that inoculation of dogs could be paid for

out of the licences. If you were here, you would give almost anything to bring in some law to get dogs inoculated."

His words generated plenty of publicity, but made little impact on the law. The proposal to raise the licence fee quickly fizzled out in Parliament. It would be two decades before it saw the light of day again.

There were other clues that dog ownership was entering a new, darker era. Continuing a long-standing tradition, Knight had struck a "gentlemen's agreement" with the Prisoners' Property Office to look after the dogs of men and women detained at Her Majesty's pleasure. "They pay us four shillings a day for every dog they send to us," he explained.

There had been a steady, but small, succession of dogs. In August 1965, for instance, a good-natured black mongrel called Beauty had arrived at the Home. She had spent six months there while her owner stood trial for murder. When he was sentenced to life imprisonment, Beauty was offered for sale and quickly bought by a couple in Kent.

Another dog had been kennelled at Battersea for two years. In April 1969, however, Knight and his staff were asked to care for a pack of fourteen Doberman Pinschers. The dogs belonged to the owner of a security company who had been sent to Brixton Prison for non-payment of rates. The arrival of the highly aggressive dogs placed

> The call for a rise in the licence fee provoked a huge response, with opinion divided wildly, even among the country's leading animal and dog charities

ABOVE The police remained the Home's main source of strays. Here a helpful policeman coaxes a dog over the threshold.

an immediate strain on the Home's resources, as they had to be kennelled separately from the rest of the canine population. They also required more food than the 4s-a-day allowance could provide. "We have to hold them until the owner is released from prison. There is nothing we can do…" Knight lamented to the papers "… and there is no guarantee that we will be reimbursed for a bill which may run into hundreds of pounds."

There would have been a time when his reassuring words would, at least, have earned the gratitude of the owner whose dogs were being protected. But the only contact the Dobermans' owner had made had been through his solicitor.

"The owner has threatened to sue us if any of the dogs die," a glum-faced Knight told the press.

If final evidence of the depressing shift in public attitudes towards pets was needed then it came at the very end of the decade, during the Christmas and New Year holidays of 1969. The number of dogs and cats being abandoned in the run-up to and after Christmas had been rising steadily for years. It was the manner in which puppies and kittens were disposed of now that shocked the Home – and animal lovers across the country.

In late December 1969, a wave of stories appeared. In Redditch, Worcestershire, two kittens were rescued from a burning tip where their owner had dumped them. The RSPCA reported a huge rise in the number of puppies found beside the nation's roads. "Dumping is on the increase. With more and more families having cars, this heartless type of offence is growing all the time," its press officer, Tom Richardson, said. Most distressing of all, a woman from Birmingham had appeared at her local RSPCA centre demanding they euthanize the puppy she'd been given because it had "chewed her child's Christmas present".

The figures Knight released at the end of the year bore out the evidence elsewhere. In what one newspaper called "a heartbreaking record", during Christmas week, 576 strays were admitted to the Home, an average of just over eighty dogs a day. Knight was sure that the rise was down to simple economics – and simpler human nature. People were now so obsessed with spending money on themselves they no longer wanted to spend anything on their dogs, he said.

The figures provoked a powerful reaction, once more stoking the fires of the debate on dog licensing. Fleet Street's most famous columnist at the time, the *Daily Express*'s Jean Rook, wrote a seething column:

What sort of human leaves a pup to die, alone and unwanted, after its little Christmas Day of joy in the morning? We do. Hundreds of us do. An apparently normal, home-loving Birmingham housewife did. We must be stopped. Legally.

Don't count on heart-stabbing pictures to flay our shame into our thick skins. Expose us in the eyes of the Joneses whose spaniel is fourteen and still going strong and hit us where it really hurts – in our wallets.

An opinion piece in the most popular dog magazine, *Dog's Life*, struck the most resonant note. The headline read "The Shame of the Sixties".

The last decade has been one of records and achievements. Sir Francis Chichester sailed the world single-handed, the Americans set foot on the moon and England won the World Cup. As the final days of 1969 were running out quietly, Commander Benjamin Knight, Secretary of the Dogs' Home, Battersea announced yet another record, one of which we should be thoroughly ashamed.

Commander Knight suspects that the reason for this all-time high is the increase in Christmas costs, with the subsequent prevalent attitude of "let's get rid of the dog and spend more on ourselves". The tragedy is that he is probably right.

The column went on to argue that we were no longer "a nation of dog lovers":

We could easily have sat back over the festive season, reflecting on the past ten years and congratulated ourselves on a decade of canine achievement. Instead we have given Commander Knight the unpleasant task of upsetting the apple cart.

Money cannot be all that tight when London stores report the biggest ever spending spree. One seldom has to make sacrifices in order to keep a dog. Most of us seem able to afford refrigerators, washing machines, television sets and cars, but somehow we are unable to afford a dog, and so many only realize this after acquiring one.

As the seventies are born, there is nothing anyone can do to make Commander Knight eat his words. The damage is already done. But what we can do is take jolly good care that he never has the opportunity to claim such a diabolical record again. Let the seventies see the end to dogs tied in sacks being dumped in rivers, tied to car bumpers or being abandoned on motorways or streets. Let's get together and conspire to ease Commander Knight and all the other dog-home officials into honourable retirement, let's turn No. 4 Battersea Park Road into a Boarding Kennels, or a Bingo Hall. What about it?

It was, of course, the kind of clarion cry that had been made regularly over the past 110 years. And it would have about as much impact as the rest …

THE CHANGING
OF THE GUARD

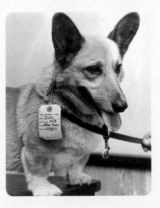

ON 22 JUNE 1970 THE DUCHESS of Beaufort opened the latest and most modern kennel in the Home's history. Work on the block, to be named after the Duchess, had begun the previous year, in April. It consisted of five blocks. Block G contained thirty-five isolation kennels for dogs with acute infections, a clinic and a dispensary as well as an outpatients' waiting room. Blocks B, C, D and E were made up of whelping kennels, capable of holding eight bitches, an ancillary stores and kitchen area, kennels for eighty-six dogs and a cattery for up to thirty cats. The accommodation was luxurious with under-floor heating thermostatically controlled to keep the temperature at 50° Fahrenheit, 140-watt infra-red lamps, fibre-glass dog beds and cat cubicles. The cost of the entire building was £58,000.

By now the Home had its own dedicated public relations officer, Olive Dawes. She issued detailed planning specifications to the press. The papers dutifully reported that the kennels averaged four foot by six by nine high, and had high mesh fronts to which were attached the names of donors. One read, "Mr and Mrs H. Brookarsh. In memory of Bobby." The new Beaufort block meant that more animals could be given their own individual spaces and better veterinary treatment.

The opening generated a lot of publicity, most of it positive, although there were some who considered it a disgrace that the Home had to expand. "The £58,000 Heartbreak", was how *Dog's Life* referred to the new block. "In 1969, more than 11,000 dogs were painlessly destroyed at Battersea and the so-called dog-loving public of Britain pulled the switch. All over the country animal welfare societies are facing the same difficulties and experiencing the same heartbreaks. If Britain cannot do better than that, it's a pretty poor show," said the magazine, continuing its theme of six months earlier. It had a point.

The Home was now taking in on average around forty dogs a day. The new kennel blocks were holding three hundred on average. It wasn't cheap either. The cost of keeping a dog was now around £3 15s a week.

Another of the Home's rising costs was giving the greatest cause for concern, though. One hundred years on from its move to Battersea, it faced a new and entirely unfamiliar problem. Benjamin Knight summed it up at a meeting in February 1972 when he addressed the thorny problem of "obtaining suitable men for employment". He revealed that he had been forced to dismiss a "higher than usual" number of male staff members during the past months. "Drunkenness, drugs and appallingly bad time-keeping being the major reasons. In all cases these were very young men," he explained.

It wasn't a problem unique to the Home. The days when the Home or, indeed, any employer could expect lifelong service from dedicated men like James Pavitt were drawing to an end. Wages at the Home were now modest in comparison to

BELOW A crowd waits expectantly for the official opening of the new Beaufort kennel block in June 1970.

ABOVE A few moments later, the Duchess of Beaufort opens the kennels and clinic named in her honour.

those offered by other manual jobs, and with the cost of living in London rising fast, young people were being forced to look elsewhere for work. As Knight put it, the drain was being "aggravated by young keeper staff marrying and moving to new towns to obtain living accommodation".

Knight had taken the unusual step of advertising for trainees, with notices in well-read newspapers like the *Daily Mirror*. It didn't work. "Advertising for Keeper staff at the rate of £22 or £24 per week had failed miserably," he admitted. He had even enlisted the help of local unemployment exchanges but this, too, had produced "completely unsuitable staff or no staff at all". The combination of long hours, physically and emotionally draining work and low wages was too much for the new recruits. None stayed longer than six months.

So it was that Knight made what was, at the time, a historic decision. With building work once more under way on the site, he asked "whether to alter the Whelping Kennels to accommodate eight female staff". Women had, of course, been driving Battersea's vans since the start of the 1950s. Back in the 1930s too, Hackbridge had employed a team of

highly skilled kennelmaids. Throughout its history, however, Battersea's yards had been a male bastion. As recently as 1968, newspapers still routinely wrote that "Kennelmaids are not employed because the maintenance work is often far too heavy for them to do." That was about to change.

The Committee approved the move, expressly stating that "the Secretary, when employing such staff, should employ them at the same rate for the job as was being paid to male staff".

The first wave of female kennel staff at Battersea was soon arriving, led by Janice Compton. They entered a male-dominated world, an environment that was part animal sanctuary, part army barracks. "It was run like a military operation," remembered June Haynes. "The men all wore grey uniforms, with a grey cap. They all took great pride in their appearance. They wore a shirt and tie and polished their shoes. They even used to have inspections to make sure they were up to scratch."

The weekly routine was equally regimented. The kennel block was still organized into seven spaces, labelled Monday to Sunday. "The system was the same as it had been for more than fifty years," remembered Haynes. "The van drivers would leave at six a.m. and wouldn't be back until eleven thirty a.m. often with fifty dogs. New arrivals were put in pens arranged according to the day of the week on which they arrived. They would stay there for exactly seven days and then we'd move them elsewhere and replace them with the next week's intake."

The scale of the operation shocked Haynes most. "I couldn't believe how big it was when I arrived. At the time it was just block after block of kennels. Each block had thirty pens facing each other with a gulley running down the middle," she recalled.

The rules of the Home were also a throwback to an earlier age. The keeper's lodge, where the

ABOVE Head keeper Fred Hearne, one of Battersea's longest-serving staff members, says hello to a young new arrival.

keepers would take their tea and lunch breaks, was male only. The kennelmaids were given their own cramped changing rooms and quarters. "The keeper's lodge was then the men's tea room. We could only go in there at the weekends.

"The men were a bunch of characters, though. There was an old chap called Charlie Henderson. He always used to say that he saw a strange lady in purple wandering O Block in the small hours of the night. He always reckoned it was Mary Tealby's ghost," Haynes remembered. "They all taught me a great deal, although many were set in their ways and weren't going to change."

The women knew their only hope of establishing themselves at the Home was to be professional at all times. "The most unpleasant

thing was making the feed. The cook would cut up huge chunks of ox cheek and boil it in giant metal vats and then mix with cereal biscuit. It stank."

The arrival of the first kennelmaids wasn't welcomed by many of the male keepers. "They thought women were too soft-hearted," said Haynes. She was accused of being sentimental early on when she fell foul of the head keeper, Fred Hearne, and Colonel H. J. Sweeney MC, another military man who had taken over from Commander Knight, initially as general manager and secretary but, from 1976, as the Home's first director general. "I remember I had a big row with Fred Hearne. There was a cross-bred mongrel that I'd become quite fond of and I came in one morning to find that it was gone. When I challenged Fred he said he was going down with distemper and had

OPPOSITE Plans afoot: a pair of dogs gives the plans for new kennels their seal of approval.

been put to sleep. Afterwards Colonel Sweeney gave me a ticking off. He made it quite clear that I should not have spoken to Fred in that way. Fred was a great character. He had polio when he was young and used to walk with a limp. Fred was a caring person. He was just doing his job."

The only dogs that were never the subject of debate were the yard dogs. The tradition of having a yard dog dated all the way back to Pavitt and later Charlie Peace's guard-dog. In the mid-1970s, the kings of the kennels were a German Shepherd called Tramp and another dog, Racoon. "At one time we had five yard dogs. One girl, called Dot, had a dog called Tina. She produced fourteen puppies which kept her very busy," Haynes recalled.

June had a yard dog of her own, a black Labrador cross called Blackie. "I came in for quite a lot of stick from the male keepers because of him. He could jump out of the pens and he jumped in with a bitch that was in season once, which wasn't very well received," Haynes said. "I got really close to Blackie and one day when I was off work he disappeared from Battersea. He was eventually found and taken in by Fulham Police. I lived in Fulham and he had headed in that direction. He was an amazing dog. He broke my heart when he died. His back legs went."

The women's arrival caused a stir among the men and had an immediate impact. By September 1973 Knight was recommending permanent changes to the structure within the Home. He proposed that there should now be "at least ten or more Kennelmaids and five drivers". In comparison, the male staff would be just "six keepers and seven or eight kennelmen". The head kennelmaid would also take over responsibility for the pharmacy and clinic. Perhaps most significantly, the female staff would move into the large new mess room and the kennelmen to the old kennelmaids' room.

ABOVE Paula Carver, one of the Home's van drivers, welcomes a new intake of puppies.

By May 1974, when Knight had to make his official report to the annual general meeting, it was clear that the changing of the guard was under way. He was delighted to report that the staffing crisis of a few years earlier was now over. "Morale amongst the kennel staff remains high and turnover has been reduced," he told the Committee. "This has been chiefly due to the policy of recruiting kennelmaids who are staying for satisfactorily long periods." The benefits were obvious and immediate, he said. "Stability among the staff leads to greater efficiency and better animal welfare."

The introduction of kennelmaids was one of Benjamin Knight's final major contributions to the Home. He retired in October 1974 after being with the Home for more than twenty years. His farewell Committee meeting in September was an emotional affair. Lord Cottesloe, the chairman, paid a heartfelt tribute. "Those who could look back would be astonished at the change which had taken place over the last twenty years," he said. "Commander Knight, himself, could look back with a great sense of pride." As a gesture of their appreciation the Home gave him his car as a leaving present.

Knight had written a speech but was too upset to read it. It was printed in the minutes nevertheless:

My Lord, Ladies & Gentlemen,
During twenty years' service, the wind of change has blown strongly o'er the Dogs' Home Battersea. My wife and I have enjoyed the cups we've had – certainly some were bitter, but to quote the wine connoisseurs, fruity, inclined to be flinty, improves upon being matured, but becomes crusty with age, keep cool and drink slowly.

Though comparisons may well be odious, the Home has, in recent years, become more respected, locally, nationally and internationally, and quite quietly, but very definitely, now leads the world in many aspects of its work.

My wife and I wish our successors the very best of courage, tenacity – and happiness Thank you all.

Knight was made a vice-president of the Home in recognition of his work. As general manager and secretary, he was replaced by another ex-military man, a former Royal Green Jacket, Colonel H. J. Sweeney, MC. His title would, in May 1976, be changed to the simpler "director general". Sweeney's belief in regimental discipline was, if anything,

BELOW Room for one in the front: a Battersea driver tries to persuade a stray to take refuge in her van.

even stronger than Knight's. "In many ways it is similar to managing a battalion," he said, soon after arriving. "I carry out inspections every day, but instead of five hundred odd men beside their bunks, it's dogs in their kennels." But he didn't attempt to undo the work that Knight had begun. The days when Battersea was a male-dominated world were drawing to a close.

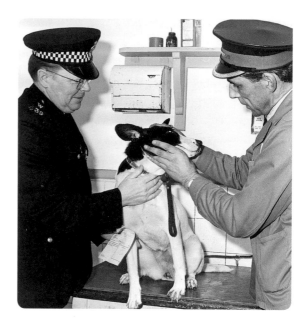

ABOVE Aided by the policeman who delivered it, Fred Hearne gives a new admission a thorough check.

As ever there was no shortage of heart-warming – and humorous – stories at the Home. The Home milked them for every column inch. In June 1976 the entertainer Tommy Steele turned up at Battersea, accompanied by his distraught seven-year-old daughter Emma. The Steele family's much-loved Yorkshire Terrier, Tramp, had disappeared from their home half a dozen miles away in Richmond-upon-Thames three days earlier. They had feared the worst and come to Battersea as a last resort. Within minutes they had been reunited with their pet, which, it turned out, had been collected and brought in by Richmond Police two days earlier. "He is only a tatty scruff. We call him Tramp because he always looks as though he needs a wash," Steele told the *Daily Mirror* afterwards, as he and Emma happily provided the Home with some good publicity. "But Emma was ever so upset. She imagined he'd been kidnapped or run over."

A few months later, in early 1977, another story captured the papers' interest. The wealthy Sheikh Sultan Al Dhari visited the Home in search of a dog but, rather than choosing one of the pedigrees in residence, he fell for a five-month-old white mongrel called Margaret. "He wanted a white dog for some reason," one of his puzzled aides said.

The Home's staff weren't able to tell the sheikh much about Margaret, who had been left outside

the Battersea gates a week or so earlier and had eaten the cardboard identification label that had been tied around her neck. The manner in which she left the Home could not have presented much more of a contrast to her arrival. She departed in the back of a limousine with a promise from the sheikh's chauffeur of a diet of lamb and chicken. "She'll certainly live well if the sheikh is anything to go by," Jim O'Brien told the newspapers.

The *Daily Mail* christened Margaret "The Mongrel That Turned Into a Mogul".

Battersea was going through one of the biggest and fastest periods of expansion in its history. It didn't have much choice. With dogs being kept in bigger, better kennels, any sudden upturn in admissions was bound to create a shortage of space.

Fortunately, the British Railways Property Department had suggested that the Home might like to buy a 4,100-square-foot piece of land adjoining the railway arches. The sale was completed, at a price of £1,400, in 1971. Almost immediately, the biggest and most ambitious building programme the Home had yet seen got under way.

Paying for it wasn't easy. With donations down and the value of its investments falling because of the grim economic climate at the time, the Home had been forced to run a special auction appeal. Somehow it had raised the cash needed and on 16 October 1975, watched by 450 guests, Princess Alice, the Duchess of Gloucester, cut a length of ribbon to open the new building that had been named in her honour.

The Gloucester block boasted 456 modern kennels, a new cattery, a pharmacy, stores and brand new staff quarters. It was the new jewel in the Home's crown, but it was far from the end of the expansion. Ever since the sale of the Hackbridge kennels in 1934, there had been voices lobbying for a new country Home. Battersea was now a highly professional, well-equipped centre but it was felt a second Home would provide more space and a gentler atmosphere for convalescing dogs. It was also seen as a potential money-spinner, with the possibility of lucrative quarantine and boarding kennels, which would be paid for by dog owners. While the reconstruction of the Battersea Home was in progress, there had been little opportunity – or money – to look for a suitable site. With the ambitious new building works now successfully complete, the Committee turned its attention to finding an out-of-town property to complement the work going on in the city.

In 1979, a suitable prospect finally appeared. The Bell Mead Kennels at Old Windsor, in Berkshire, had a long-standing reputation as a

> **Bell Mead had continued to grow and by the end of the 1970s was a highly respected kennelmaid training school turning out up to twenty-four qualified maids a year**

high-quality dogs' home. Coincidentally it dated back to the period when Hackbridge had closed, the mid-1930s. Jane Trefusis Forbes had established the kennels in Haslemere, Surrey, and had used the premises to train kennelmaids for other dogs' homes around the world. She had been forced to give up when war broke out as the kennels were incompatible with her job as head of the Women's Royal Air Force.

The kennels had been taken over by a Mrs Miles, who moved the business to its present home in Old Windsor. She and Trefusis Forbes had remained partners, however, working together to – among other things – breed the famous Dandie Dinmont Terrier.

Bell Mead had continued to grow and by the end of the 1970s was a highly respected kennelmaid training school turning out up to twenty-four qualified maids a year. It also boasted enough comfortable kennels and catteries for more than two hundred boarders.

The purchase of Bell Mead worked well for both organizations. The Bell Mead trainees were soon spending two days a week learning the ropes at Battersea, in particular how to groom and trim dogs with long, unkempt or matted coats. In return, long-stay dogs from Battersea were sent to Old Windsor to enjoy the calm of the countryside.

CHAPTER EIGHTEEN

A THROWAWAY
SOCIETY

On 13 September 1983, the reception office took delivery of a light brown mongrel that had been found wandering the streets of Hackney, in east London, the previous day. After the dog had been given a quick grooming and checked by a vet, the manager, Major Eric Stones, and his staff placed a board around his neck and led him out to meet a small group of reporters and photographers gathered in the yard. The board simply read: "No. 2,500,000". With a broad grin, Major Stones told the reporters the dog's name was Lucky.

The Home was becoming more and more adept at manipulating the media. The two-and-a-half-millionth dog to pass through Battersea's gates, Lucky's rather plaintive features stared out from the pages of most of the following morning's papers along with a story highlighting the memorable statistic he had set. Most reported that he would be put on sale for £10 if his owner hadn't turned up by the end of the standard seven-day waiting period.

Naturally the Home's phone lines were flooded with calls from people wanting to adopt him. None was successful. Six days later, Lucky was back in the public eye, this time at the centre of an even more upbeat tale. According to the Home, his owners, the Anderson family from Sunbury in Surrey, had turned up on the day before Lucky's seven days were up. They had correctly identified him as the dog they had lost six weeks earlier. His real name was Scamp.

If there was a whiff of artifice about the story, nobody was much interested in exposing it. Battersea's popularity in the public imagination was as high as it had ever been. Opportunities like

PREVIOUS PAGE A dog called Lucky: the two-and-a-half-millionth canine admission to Battersea.

Lucky were too good to be missed, particularly in the face of the negative news that surrounded the subject of dog ownership in general.

Since its earliest days, Battersea had been a barometer of the public's attitude to dogs. For all the sentimental feeling that flowed the Home's way when it went public with stories like Lucky's, the reality was that dogs were being treated as badly as they had been in living memory.

Admission figures were always prone to vary from year to year, but since the 1960s the number of abandoned and stray dogs arriving at the Home had been increasing. During the 1980s, the numbers were rising sharply again. The types of dogs that had passed through the Home's portals were always changing too. The most recent fad among dog owners had produced steep rises in the number of Bull Terriers, Dobermans and Rottweilers arriving. The more deep-rooted change, however, seemed to reflect a shift in social values. It was a continuation of the slide that had begun in the late 1960s.

The director general, Colonel Tony Hare, who had succeeded Sweeney, picked up where Benjamin Knight had left off in 1969 and wondered whether the increasing number of discarded puppies was a symptom of a deep-seated malaise, "a manifestation of a throwaway society". Interestingly, he also wondered, publicly, whether the Home was contributing to the situation. It was almost, he said, doing too good a job at presenting a positive, happy front.

How much do the public – and even our members – really know of the misery of the cruelty, starvation and neglect our staff are accustomed to handle every day? They are kept in the dark because we do our work too well. How many people know that at midnight every Metropolitan Police Station will make a Dog Report to Scotland Yard, and that at 6 a.m. every morning Scotland Yard will send us a telexed list of stations with dogs waiting to be handed into our care? Within an hour our five ambulances will be on the road: by lunchtime when the fleet returns, Battersea's resident population will have increased by between 30 and 50 sick and frightened animals.

Hare was voicing, in the Annual Report, a concern that had always niggled away at the Home – and would continue to do so for years to come: whether its job was serve or to educate the public. The answer, of course, was both.

There were – as always – plans to build yet more new kennels to cope with the rising numbers: "But the problem will not be solved simply by building bigger and better kennels; left to themselves strays will produce more strays, so too will household pets," Hare said.

His anxiety was heightened because the dog licence had, finally, been abolished in 1987. By the time it was phased out only half of dog owners were believed to be bothering to obtain one. The revenue generated by the licence – now 37.5 pence – didn't justify an enforcement programme. Politicians had a raft of ideas to control dog ownership, from environmental laws to punish owners who allowed their dogs to foul parks and pavements to legislation to control dangerous breeds. But they were both some way off being introduced. Hare and the Home favoured a national dog register, linked to a nationwide sterilization programme, instead. "We count as an achievement the fact that we perform nearly a thousand sterilization operations every year," Hare said. To treat the 1.5 million dogs

ABOVE A kennelmaid shows an arrival around the new Bell Mead kennels.

within the greater London area "would require four vets working full time 365 days of the year".

Hare's strong language reflected a subtle change in the Home's approach to its work. For the first time in its recent history, it was no longer willing simply to sit back and absorb the changes that society delivered to its doorstep. When it faced an unprecedented surge in numbers arriving before Christmas, it expressed its disgust openly. "It's amazing how many people come in with a dog on a lead and say 'I just found it.' The number of people coming in like that has literally quadrupled in the past two weeks," the Home's then spokesman Stephen Danos said. The surge had left the Home as close to capacity as it had ever been, with 780 dogs crammed into the 460 kennels. "We don't have the room. We cannot continue to accept strays without question," Danos added.

Once more the Home was not prepared to be the public's punchbag. Hare took the unprecedented step of talking about destroying dogs. "The number of dogs we are currently getting is reaching crisis proportions and immediate steps have had to be taken to cope with this callous disregard for the welfare of what we laughingly call man's best friend," he announced. "In the past we would spend a lot of time, money and space nursing sick dogs back to health. Now we are having to ask ourselves: 'Is it worth it?'" It was, of course, public posturing on his part. For the Home, it never had been or would be a question of whether it was worth it. But his mood reflected the natural sense of anger the Home felt at what seemed to be the dog-owning public's decline.

He made an astute comparison with the Victorian era, routinely categorized as cruel and barbaric in comparison to the modern day: "There

were far fewer strays then. An awful lot of kids would bring dogs in on 31 December because they could not afford the half-crown licence fee," Danos said. "These days dogs, often pregnant or with litters, are found in dustbins or lay-bys or just abandoned near here."

≈

In 1984 a pair of new occupants had moved into the flat on the upper floor of Battersea's entrance building. Bill and Ruth Wadman Taylor were unique in more ways than one. Both were qualified vets, making them the first medical professionals to live on the site. More significantly, Bill had also been appointed manager of the Home. It was the first time someone had combined both jobs. The arrival of the Wadman Taylors marked the beginning of another new era, one in which their modernizing influence would play a central role.

ABOVE A home for all: every breed of dog has found its way to Battersea. Here volunteers pose with a group of Greyhounds that found their way to the Home.

As they settled into the Home, much was as the Wadman Taylors had expected. Predictably they were dealing with a range of illnesses and conditions, from kennel cough and distemper to broken bones. "We never refuse a dog so we import disease every day," Bill Wadman Taylor told a visiting reporter, soon after he and his wife had taken the reins.

The Wadman Taylors also knew that they would at first have to work in conditions that were very different from a normal veterinary practice. Sickly dogs were placed in G Block with its isolation units, clinic and dispensary. The Home still didn't have a surgery.

Bill Wadman Taylor had begun pressing the Committee to prioritize a properly equipped modern surgery in the next phase of building work. In the meantime, he and Ruth wasted little time in bringing in a range of new treatments and approaches. "She introduced more homeopathic dog treatments," recalled June Haynes.

Their most significant innovation, however, was to introduce a new and more humane method of euthanasia. Soon after their arrival the Wadman Taylors began to use lethal injections for sick, old and highly dangerous dogs.

The change wasn't welcomed by everyone. "When injections were first introduced the keepers didn't like it. They thought it was a stupid idea," said Haynes. "They also didn't like the idea it was being taken over by Royal Animal Nursing Auxiliary nurses. They were coming in more and more then to deliver treatments and to administer injections. Before then the keepers dealt with the vets who came in for a couple of hours a day."

Some aspects of life at Battersea caught the Wadman Taylors by surprise. Bill had been under the impression that the Home's canine inmates were predominantly what he called "Battersea terriers", playful, intelligent mongrels. He was amazed at the stream of pedigree dogs flooding in, from Poodles and Old English Sheepdogs to Shih Tzus and Skye Terriers.

The other great surprise was the behaviour of the people who visited the Home. By the mid-1980s Battersea was receiving more than eighty thousand a year. More dogs were being rehomed than at any time in the Home's history, partly because, with prices between £15 for a mongrel and £50 for a large pedigree breed, Battersea dogs represented exceptional value for money. Invariably demand far outstripped supply.

At weekends, the Wadman Taylors would often look out from the flat to see queues forming outside the Home two hours before the doors opened to the public at nine thirty. When the gates were opened there would often be a mini-stampede into the kennels containing those dogs that had spent more than a week at the Home and were now officially for sale.

The biggest headache for the Home was families arguing over who had seen a dog first. Bill Wadman Taylor witnessed a "scrimmage" on more than one occasion. Often families would leave a member standing by the cage of a dog they'd chosen while another would go off to find a keeper. Before the family member had returned, however, a keeper would arrive with another interested party, who would be given priority.

Of far greater concern to Bill, though, was the quality of the people who were taking dogs home. He introduced a much more stringent "vetting" procedure for prospective owners. "We have to be very, very careful. We will not sell a dog for breeding purposes or to become a guard-dog or for resale," he explained. "So for a start we ask each potential buyer to fill in a lengthy application form. Then, if we have any doubts about suitability, we ask if they would mind a visit from our inspector so that he can judge for himself whether their home is suitable for the dog.

"I try to preach responsible petmanship and it is beginning to get through. We plead with people not to buy on impulse or to give puppies to children as Christmas presents," he said.

The Wadman Taylors wasted little time in making their mark on the Home. As well as pressing for a new surgery and new accommodation at Battersea, they joined the chorus of voices calling for another satellite Home.

In August 1985, within a year or so of the Wadman Taylors' arrival, an impressive surgery was ready for occupation. As well as an examination room, it had an air-conditioned operating theatre and an X-ray machine. The new surgery transformed the Home. For the first time, cats and dogs could be given a complete medical examination before they were allowed to leave the Home. Even more significantly, the Royal College of Veterinary Surgeons approved the Home as an accredited training centre for veterinary nurses.

The Wadman Taylors had soon admitted two trainees to help them run the surgery. For the first time in its history, the Home had a functioning animal hospital under its roof. The modernization work the Wadman Taylors had instigated was widely hailed as a breakthrough. The changes had come at a cost, though. In the summer of 1985 the Home's then treasurer, C. J. Jay, wrote a rather pessimistic memo: "It is my duty to draw to the attention of members of the Committee my increasing concern at the potentially serious financial situation arising from the escalating costs of running the Home."

The Home had seen its operating expenditure shoot up by 15 per cent to £758,676 in the previous year, 1984. The first four months of 1985 had seen another increase, with the cost of drugs and disinfectants, wages and accommodating boarders at Bell Mead the biggest rise. Plans for celebration of the 125th anniversary of the Home's founding were also draining resources. What was really worrying, though, was that as costs were rising income was falling. In the first four months of 1985, legacies had been £167,191 compared to £223,890 in the same period the previous year. "The above facts speak for themselves," Jay wrote. "I believe therefore that the Committee should exercise great caution for the foreseeable future in allowing further increases in expenditure."

Jay recommended staff increases now be kept to "the absolute minimum" while further building projects "be held in abeyance for some years". He was also worried about changes at the Metropolitan Police, which might produce a reduction in the number of dogs arriving at the Home. As the police paid the Home for each dog they took in, this would mean decreased income. "In summary, I believe that a period of consolidation is now necessary to allow the Home to absorb the many changes that have taken place over the last three or four years," he wrote.

~

In December 1985, almost exactly a hundred years after Queen Victoria had offered her first donation, another letter arrived at the Home bearing the royal coat of arms. The letter explained that Queen Elizabeth II had heard of the new kennels at Bell Mead, Old Windsor. She planned to be at Windsor Castle the following April and wondered whether it would be convenient to visit them on Monday, 28 April.

Despite its long links with the Royal Family, no reigning monarch had ever visited Battersea or one of its satellite homes. The Home accepted the invitation in an instant, then immediately settled into a blind panic that would last for the next four months.

Since Bell Mead had been acquired five years earlier, workmen had been slowly redeveloping and extending the site. The most important addition was a block of twenty-four state-of-the-art individual kennels. They were to have under-floor and infra-red heating in each living space. Unfortunately all that existed at the end of December were a few holes in the ground.

With the Queen due to visit in four months' time, the contractors were told to speed up the work so that the block would be ready by April. It wasn't quite that simple.

Unfortunately, 1986 began with one of the coldest spells in years and progress was slow. Even

ABOVE This handsome stray, here wearing his party hat, was christened Scamp by the Battersea kennelmaids.

worse, March and April brought torrential rain, which caused the builders huge problems. Concrete wouldn't set and wheelbarrows were getting stuck in the mud. As the Queen's visit drew nearer, the panic intensified.

In February, the Committee had been told that to get the building finished on time the contractors would need to put in more overtime "with a consequent increase in costs". The memo they had received from the treasurer the previous summer was still fresh in their minds. Some members were unhappy at paying more to the builders and suggested that "the Queen would not object to opening unfinished kennels". Others, however, felt that it was a "unique occasion and everything should be done to make it successful". They agreed to pay the extra overtime and to save money by trimming the guest list "as much as possible".

By the weekend of 26 and 27 April every available pair of hands was enlisted to try to finish the work. On the Sunday evening, a team of painters worked through the night using flashlights to see their handiwork. When dawn broke on 28 April, the new block was ready for inspection and its official opening.

Liveried vans from Battersea had been driven over to Windsor for the day and lined the yard ready for inspection. Crowds gathered as the Queen toured the kennels, taking her time to look at all the sick, pregnant and long-stay dogs that were living there. She was then introduced to the kennelmaids before meeting members of the Committee and a few invited guests, including the dog artist Julie Brenan, who presented her with a portrait.

~

The Home had always been a magnet for celebrities. Charles Dickens had provided its first and most potent endorsement. Ellen Terry and Hayden Coffin had done their bit, as had Lupino Lane and Gracie Fields in later eras. By the 1980s, however, Britain was entering a new cultural era, one in which the power of celebrity would become ever more potent. The Home had always had its well-known supporters. Now they became one of its most valuable assets.

One of the very first to offer help was the novelist Jilly Cooper. In 1981, she wrote a piece for the junior members' magazine about one of her rescue dogs, Fortnum.

> Fortnum had a very sad start in life. A gang of cruel boys thought it would be fun to kill a little stray puppy, so they wound a piece of wire round its neck, and hung it from a tree. Fortunately they were discovered by a kind man who cut little Fortnum down and nursed him back to life. Fortnum was then given to a woman who didn't like dogs very much, and who went out to work every day, leaving him alone in the house for hours on end.
>
> Because he was so lonely, he used to howl and chew up her things, which made her very cross. In the end she decided to take him to Battersea Dogs' Home to see if they could find him another owner. Fortunately I met him on his way.
>
> He was a little brown terrier with a sad black-ringed eyes. He has grown into a wonderful dog. But because he had such a terrible start to his life, he is still very insecure and howls if I go out even for half an hour, thinking I'm not coming back.

Cooper was one of the first to explain the pleasures – and pains – of owning a rescue dog but she was followed by others. No one had been more supportive than Katie Boyle, the former television presenter best known as the host of the *Eurovision Song Contest*. She had been an active fundraiser and Committee member for many years. Boyle had adopted her own Battersea dogs and – continuing the tradition of the Committee members of the Victorian era – retold the stories surrounding them with relish whenever she could.

She'd discovered one, Charley Girl, in the middle of London on a "bitterly cold" day in February 1986. "It was a Saturday and, with a friend, I was waiting for the lights to change so I could drive across a very busy road," she explained. "Suddenly we saw a scruffy little dog on the opposite side of the dual carriageway, and to our horror she was making her way straight into the traffic."

Boyle's companion screamed at her to stop the car, which she did. The pair then proceeded to run into the middle of the road where the terrified stray was weaving its way through the traffic. Eventually they made it across and found the dog. "By now the petrified pooch must have realized we were on her side because she crouched by a hedge and let us get hold of her," Boyle said. "She had on a scruffy collar – no name tag, of course – and somehow the three of us got back to my car, and, under the curious gaze of my own four pooches, we laid her on the back seat amongst them."

Boyle took the dog to a police station and it eventually reached Battersea. It turned out that the dog had been to the Home twice before. Boyle made sure this was her last visit. The dog, which she christened Charley Girl, had clearly endured a grim existence. "What an eventful and bewildering life she must have had. Somewhere

ABOVE Waiting in line: a queue of potential owners stand patiently outside the Home's main entrance.

along the line her teeth had been cruelly filed down so her bite would be blunt."

Boyle added Charley Girl to her collection, which already included two other Battersea rescue dogs, Bizzie and Baba. "I called her Charley because she looked like a boy. I only discovered my mistake a couple of days later when I gave her a bath! But then I didn't want to give her yet another problem so she just became Charley Girl," she said, in an article for the junior members' magazine in 1987.

Three years later another well-known personality collected a rescue dog from Battersea. Elton John was going through a particularly difficult time in his life and openly credited his first

Battersea dog, Thomas, with helping him overcome his difficulties. "I love rescue dogs, especially as they seem to really know they've been rescued and love you for it. They give you so much back and it's great to be able to offer them a secure and permanent home," he explained. He went on to take in many more rescue dogs from the Home.

CHAPTER NINETEEN

GROWING PAINS

ON THE EVENING OF 2 FEBRUARY 1990, the Home's senior staff gathered with invited guests and a large contingent of press at the headquarters of Coutts Bank on the Strand in central London. The location offered a clue as to the purpose of the evening. Along with Prince Michael of Kent, the chairman of the management committee, Tom Field-Fisher, announced the biggest public appeal in the Home's history. The Home needed to raise £2 million because, as Field-Fisher told the press, "our accommodation is overcrowded so additional space is vital".

Legacies and financial donations had continued to disappoint during the latter part of the 1980s. There had been one rather bizarre offer, from Lord Avebury, a Liberal peer, who in January 1987 announced that he was trying to get his will changed so that his corpse would be left to the Home: "I can understand the Dogs' Home might not want to be lumbered with my body so I'm considering offering them an inducement – a financial bequest – if they will agree to feed it to the dogs," he told the *Evening News*. A recent convert to Buddhism, Avebury said his request was an attempt to help the environment. "I don't want to waste heat and energy by being cremated," he said. His request fell foul of his solicitor, who refused to amend the will on "aesthetic and cultural" grounds.

With the exception of an anonymous donor from Switzerland, who had recently given the Home £140,000, the levels of money being left to Battersea were down. With running costs now at more than £1.5 million a year, and its guaranteed income restricted to the £250,000 a year it was getting from the Metropolitan Police, the Home simply had to appeal to the public at large.

Field-Fisher and his staff knew that to raise the £2 million they now needed would require some creative fundraising. They drew their inspiration from the Home's foundress. When she was establishing the Home, Mary Tealby had tempted donors by offering them governorships for five pounds. Now, 130 years on, Field-Fisher and his colleagues came up with an equally imaginative incentive scheme. Donors making a gift of £10,000 would have a kennel named after them. Smaller amounts of between £5,000 and £1,250 would earn a commemorative plaque in the donor's name.

The most novel scheme gave friends of the Home a chance to "buy" bricks in the new building. Field-Fisher reckoned that if all 37,000 or so were sold this idea alone would raise almost a million pounds. Fortunately the money was soon coming in. Indeed, £37,000 had been raised before the official announcement of the appeal.

The plan was for a three-storey building with enough space for 250 dogs. The aim was that each dog would have its own modern and easily maintained kennel. The kennels were to be spread across the upper two floors. The ground floor was to contain a garage for the vans as well as holding kennels, a mortuary and an incinerator. The building had been designed by the Devereux Partnership and was a more pleasing-looking building than most that had been built on the site in the past 120 years, with the notable exception of Clough Williams-Ellis's cattery, now known as Whittington Lodge. "We have tried to put some architecture into it," Tim McGee told *The Times*.

The Times, once the Home's nemesis, was now its most supportive voice in the press. It carried a four-page special report on the appeal and the work already under way at Battersea, which its headline described as a "Lasting symbol of humanity – and neglect".

In an interview with the paper, Tom Field-Fisher echoed the sentiments expressed down the years by his predecessors. The latest statistics indicated that 15 per cent of dogs were being reclaimed by their owners. "These are not proud statistics," he said. "This may be offensive to people in a country that likes to believe itself a nation of dog lovers but it is true none the less."

There was disagreement on some aspects of the plans that had been drawn up by Devereux. Bill Wadman Taylor was against having a three-storey building, arguing that it was impractical. Most people, however, felt the Home should squeeze the maximum possible amount of accommodation from the development. As many kennels as possible would be fitted into the upper two storeys while the addition of even more kennels on the ground floor wasn't ruled out in the future.

In May 1989, the Committee met to award the contract. Six construction companies had tendered, submitting bids from £2.375 million to £2.147 million. The Committee went with the lowest bidder, Neilcott Construction, who had also bid to finish the job in the shortest period – fifty weeks.

~

Around two thirty p.m. on Wednesday, 27 February 1991, a fleet of limousines swept over Albert Bridge, past the gates to Battersea Park, on to Battersea Park Road and in through the gates to the Home. The entire staff had gathered in the main courtyard. They watched as the motorcade pulled in and the Queen emerged to cheers from a group of invited schoolchildren.

It was a significant moment in the Home's history. Almost 120 years after Battersea had opened its doors south of the river, a reigning monarch had come to visit for the first time. Buckingham Palace had written to the Home agreeing to the visit in November 1990. The Queen would open the ambitious new block, to be named the Tealby Building in honour of the Home's foundress. A Committee had been at work organizing the visit ever since.

Work on the new building had progressed slowly so, just as when Bell Mead had received a royal visit six years earlier, the next few months became a race against time. In December a senior Committee member reported that he was "very dissatisfied with the overall works" and, in particular, the kennelling. Stephen Danos, the Home's spokesman and public relations consultant, was asked to "put some pressure on the architects to explain the lack of progress".

By the New Year things were looking marginally more promising. There was "some likelihood" of the new kennels opening by late January although mid-February was "a more likely target date". The blame game began with the architects blaming the staff – and specifically the Wadman Taylors – for asking for too many "infrastructure services". The Wadman Taylors blamed it on "other issues which had been the responsibility of the architect".

By the week of the royal visit, the panic levels were dropping. The second floor of the building

BELOW Historic visitor: the Queen becomes the first monarch to visit Battersea on a drizzly day in February, 1991.

223

would be ready for occupation on 20 February. Its kennels were full as the Queen began her tour seven days later.

The Queen had agreed to spend an hour at the Home and wanted to speak to as many people as possible, so she had asked to see only a small number of dogs in their kennels before being shown around the rest of the Home's facilities. The Home's long-serving superintendent Fred Hearne and the chairman Tom Field-Fisher conducted the guest around the new block and its state-of-the-art accommodation.

The Queen certainly wouldn't have detected anything untoward as she toured the Home. Afterwards Buckingham Palace let the Home know that Her Majesty had been "most impressed by everything she saw". Her visit ended with the Home presenting the Queen with some knitted jerseys for her grandchildren. With a final wave, and to a chorus of cheers, she headed back across Albert Bridge to Buckingham Palace on time at three thirty p.m.

The celebration continued well after the royal visit had ended. It was such a high point in the Home's history that commemorative mugs were given to each member of staff. The staff were also invited to a reception to mark the event, at which two hundred guests were also present.

It should have been the beginning of a memorable year for the Home. As it turned out, it marked the start of a sequence of events that everyone at the Home would want to forget. The Queen might have called it Battersea's *annus horribilis*. Instead Colonel Hare simply referred to it as a "traumatic" twelve months.

The Home's most immediate headache lay with its staffing. At the end of 1990 Bill and Ruth Wadman Taylor had announced their plan to retire. After eighteen years of service they were moving out of their home on the site at the end of April.

Replacing them was not straightforward as they'd performed more than one role at the Home. A New Zealander, Josephine Henderson, was chosen to replace Bill Wadman Taylor as manager. She didn't want to live on site and was given an allowance to find a flat within a half-hour's journey of Battersea. Finding a long-term vet to replace Ruth Wadman Taylor proved problematic. Again, candidates were reluctant to live on the site. As a temporary measure, the veterinary work was handed over to a local group practice, the Ark.

Part of the problem lay in the fact that the surgery was badly in need of modernizing again. In May 1991, a report concluded that "much of the equipment in the clinic" was "obsolete,

ABOVE Warm arm of the law: the former Commissioner of the Metropolitan Police, Sir Peter Imbert, with a Battersea dog.

broken, dilapidated or unsafe". The Committee was warned that "a phased replacement programme" was necessary "if the Home is to maintain proper standards of animal care and continue as an Approved Training Establishment for Veterinary Nurses". Its members immediately agreed to spend £12,000 on new equipment, including an anaesthetic machine, sterilization equipment, orthopaedic instruments and a modern operating table.

More worrying noises were coming from the new Tealby Building. The first rumblings about the quality of the kennelling had come early on. The keepers quickly noticed that the dogs were barking incessantly and sleeping poorly. In one of their regular reports the veterinary team voiced their concern that "all dogs are hyperactive". In May the manager reported that there was a feeling the design of the new kennels was "causing stress in the dogs".

An investigation was ordered and outside experts were called in to look at the layout and size of the kennels. On 12 June there were grim faces all around as the Committee heard that the kennels "should not be used until they had been redesigned". It was decided to close the Tealby Building to the public from 26 June. The Committee stressed the need to make the right changes and recommended that "it would be prudent to consult widely before coming to any conclusions on any design changes".

As if that wasn't enough, another dark cloud had drifted on to the Home's horizon in the shape of a new piece of legislation, the Dangerous Dogs Act. The Home had always reflected shifting trends in dog ownership and had noticed a sudden rise in the popularity of aggressive "fighting breeds" in recent years. In 1985 the Home had taken in seventeen Pit Bull Terriers and Rottweilers. In 1990 they had taken in more than 350.

The trend had had a dramatic and worrying impact. A series of incidents in which Pit Bulls or other fighting dogs had attacked, maimed and even killed members of the public, particularly children, had been seized on by the press. The result was a hastily assembled piece of legislation that came into force in 1991. The Dangerous Dogs Act, for the first time, made it illegal to own certain breeds and cross-breeds, specifically Pit Bull Terriers and three specialist breeds, the Japanese Tosa, Dogo Argentino and Fila Brasileiro. Only those granted specific exemption by a court could own any of these "Specially Controlled Dogs" and those granted that right had to keep them muzzled and on a leash in public. They also had to register the animals on a list of Exempted Dogs and were required to neuter, tattoo and implant the dogs with microchips. The Act also banned the breeding, sale and exchange of these dogs.

The Act had an immediate impact, with hundreds of dogs being confiscated or voluntarily handed in for destruction. As so often in the past, Battersea bore the brunt. Early in the year the Metropolitan Police had been in contact asking the Home "to help deal with dangerous dogs (particularly pit bull terriers) brought into police stations by owners for destruction". The Home had been reluctant but the police sent a deputation to make their case to the Committee. The Home agreed, but with specific conditions. Stray Pit Bull Terriers would be treated as normal under the agreement with the police. However, the Home wouldn't deal with dogs that were required as evidence for criminal offences by their owners. Most importantly, the Home would "reserve the right to refuse to accept a dangerous dog if it was deemed to be too dangerous to move by the Home's drivers".

Later, the Home also agreed to take in Pit Bulls brought by their owners, and to destroy dogs immediately with a magistrate's destruction order. But it also agreed to rehome Pit Bulls if the police were satisfied that the person had a "Notice of Keeping a Specially Controlled Dog". Such instances were rare indeed. During July 1991 the Home admitted thirty-seven Pit Bull Terriers, most of which were housed in separation units on O Block and the isolation rooms in the new Tealby Building.

The Home's insurance brokers revealed staff weren't covered in the unlikely event they were prosecuted under the new Dangerous Dogs Act while handling banned dogs. The new policy was considerably more expensive. The Home also had to introduce a £500 panic alarm to protect the three-member teams required to handle dangerous dogs.

The impact on the staff was noticeable. The TV presenter Katie Boyle had been an active member of the Home and the Committee for many years. She was a tireless campaigner and helper, organizing fundraising events and fashion shows, making practical suggestions such as the introduction of disinfected mats to stop infections spreading. She would even help clean out the vans if staff were short in supply. It meant that she had her ear to the ground at the Home and was soon picking up on the unhappiness of the staff and was sent a copy of an anonymous letter from those worried at what was happening.

The usual summer surge of dogs meant that the second floor accommodation in the new Tealby Building had to be used during July. It was perhaps no coincidence that five members of staff left during that month, an unusually high number. Once again the vets reported that they feared the accommodation in Tealby was so poor it might be causing "possible psychological damage" in dogs after they were rehomed.

Work to come up with a new, improved design was going ahead as fast as possible. Three reports were

commissioned and it was agreed that the size of the pens had to be significantly increased. There should also be a separate sleeping and exercise area in each one. It was felt, too, that pen sizes should vary.

Eventually a new design was approved. It would cost £400,000 to revise the accommodation and the work took more than a year to complete. It was not until the autumn of 1992 that a new, efficient and comfortable kennel complex was finally completed.

Not all was unremitting gloom. Far from it. The Home's finances were in impressive good health. In 1991 Battersea's investments were worth £11 million and were producing an income of £800,000 a year, which was expected to rise to £1 million a year. It was receiving legacies at the rate of between £150,000 and £200,000 a month.

Equally encouragingly, there had been a 10 per cent drop in the overall number of dogs received by the Home. That year 16,000 had been taken in, compared to 18,000 the previous year. "There may be some indication that the public may be beginning to take more care of their pets," Tom Field-Fisher said. The Home, of course, had a plentiful supply of stories to help continue that trend in the right direction.

Some were uplifting, as in the case of Kim, a heroic little mongrel, or "cross-breed", as people were now required to call mixed-breed dogs. Kim had left the Home a couple of years earlier, placed with a Mrs Clark in London. One evening during Easter in 1991, Mrs Clark opened her door to two strangers, one of whom, a woman, complained that she was feeling sick. Before Mrs Clark knew it the woman had rushed into the house and run upstairs to the bathroom. Her male accomplice had

OPPOSITE The President of the Home, Prince Michael of Kent, gets to know a puppy. He is also modelling a Battersea tie!

pushed his way in at the same time, threatening Mrs Clark. Before the pair could inflict any harm on the terrified pensioner, Kim appeared in the hallway and threatened the man, snapping and lunging at him. Frightened by the dog, the man and woman fled the house. Mrs Clark discovered that the woman had rummaged through her possessions upstairs but hadn't taken anything. She was convinced that Kim had saved her from being robbed and attacked, perhaps even worse, and nominated her for an award. She was on hand a few months later when Kim received the Pet of the Year prize and the new PRO Dogs' Gold Medal Award the following year.

For every happy ending there was always a horror story. There were times when the staff must have wondered whether they were in the 1890s, rather than the 1990s. In December 1992, a Shih Tzu arrived at the Home via the police in a disoriented state. It had been found on a London street being forced to drink whisky by "two young louts", who were "falling about with mirth watching the dog reeling about". At the Home, an examination revealed not just that the dog was drunk but that it was addicted to alcohol.

Weeks of careful monitoring saw the dog weaned off its dependency and it was eventually placed in a good home through a Shih Tzu breed society. It was christened Johnnie Walker, a warm-hearted joke at its unfortunate past.

Around the same time another dog, a tan and white cross-breed called Pearl, arrived at the Home having been almost garrotted by a thin wire that had been placed around her neck. Pearl was extremely nervous and hid under tables whenever she was approached by vets. It took many months of careful and gentle persuasion to get her to trust humans once more. By now the Home had a much more sophisticated rehoming operation. Pearl's

behaviour was monitored by the new Assessment Panel before she was allowed to leave for a new home. Even then great care had to be taken to ensure that she went to a home where a choke-type collar would never be put around her neck.

~

In 1995 the bulldozers returned to the site. This time the thirty-year-old Beaufort Buildings were being demolished. With its eye now always half trained on the publicity angle, the Home asked June Haynes, its longest-serving employee, to take the levers of the bulldozer as it began dismantling the old brickwork. Thanks to the substantial money it was now receiving from supporters, the Home was taking a step into the new millennium five years early.

The most impressive and modern building the Home had yet seen was now taking shape. Costing £6 million and located next to Whittington Lodge, it was, primarily, intended for dogs and cats ready for rehoming, and would increase the capacity of the Home to 650 dogs, 800 during peak periods. The sweeping steel, glass and brick building would also feature a large new reception and interviewing area, and even a shop.

The lessons of the Tealby Building had been learned and the design this time had been painstakingly researched and planned. Six different firms of architects were asked to submit designs to include kennels that were as bright, airy and "customer friendly" as possible. Director general Duncan Green chipped in with one design element – a canine WC that allowed staff to sweep dog mess into a hidden sewage pipe that could then be flushed efficiently.

The work caused huge disruption. For eighteen months or so the Home was overrun with lorries, heavy plant and workmen. It meant that the vast majority of the Home's staff and inmates had to emigrate. Vet Shaun Opperman and his team had to move to a temporary surgery nearby on Battersea Park Road. Many of the dogs had to be taken out to Bell Mead and extra accommodation was rented at Cambridge Kennels, Moor Lane, almost hidden under the shadow of the M25 near Staines.

To make sure the work progressed on time a special sub-committee met fortnightly to monitor progress. They did a sterling job. The building work was completed on target in the late autumn of 1996, a remarkably fast turnaround. Dogs and cats were being admitted to the new accommodation, named the Kent Building in honour of the Home's president, Prince Michael of Kent, by October 1996. This time the teething troubles were minimal.

The way the Home's staff had coped during the building project was testimony to their patience and professionalism. Experience played its part too. The new building was also, more than anything else, testimony to the enduring affection the British public felt for Battersea. Unlike in 1990 when Tealby had been built, the Home hadn't needed to make a public appeal for funds to develop the biggest building project in its history. It had been entirely funded from its own resources.

In 1996, the Home received a staggering £4.565 million in legacies, a record and a massive increase on the previous year's £2.862 million. It must have seemed that it couldn't become more popular with the public. But it could …

BELOW Prince Michael addresses the audience at the opening of the Kent Building, and a canine resident looks on.

CHAPTER TWENTY

PRIME TIME

The opening of the Kent building was supposed to eliminate the problem of overcrowding within Battersea, but within eighteen months of its opening, the number of dogs in the Home was once again at a critical level: 674 dogs were crammed in – an unhealthy number.

In April 1996, Shaun Opperman reported to the Committee that an outbreak of kennel cough had been worsened by the overcrowding. In April he said, "There appears to be a clear correlation between the number of dogs in the Home at any one time and the incidence of infectious disease, particularly kennel cough and its complications." The reasons were cross-infection caused by closer contact between dogs, an increase in stress leading to decreased resistance, decreased air space and mixing of new arrivals with long-stay dogs.

Opperman reckoned that 500 to 550 was a "comfortable" number of dogs; at 600 it began to get overcrowded with a corresponding increase in disease. Beyond 650 it became "very difficult to control and contain the kennel cough". He said there was an urgent need to provide "purpose-built treatment kennels in the Home", especially as intake figures were on the rise that year.

In June 1998, it was decided to stop public boarding at Bell Mead from 1 July. Those who had booked places there would be redirected to another kennel, Forest Glade in Chinnor, which had been prepared for the overflow. The resultant space was all to be given to Battersea dogs.

It was also agreed to look around London and the M25 area for kennels with capacity for a hundred dogs and cats "which could ultimately become satellites for rehoming". In all, around twenty different kennels were looked at. Initially the preferred choice was in Enfield. In December 1998 the Home made an offer of £650,000, which was not accepted. Other kennels in Chinnor, Blindley Heath and Betchworth in Surrey were considered. Eventually the director general found the ideal location. The Foxcroft Kennels were within earshot of the famous Brands Hatch racing circuit and had been built by a retired builder with a love for dogs. The kennels had much going for them, not least that director general Duncan Green reckoned it would only take three weeks to prepare the place for accommodation, a real selling point given the overcrowding at Battersea. The only drawback was the "winding access route". An offer of £572,500 was made and accepted in March 1999.

~

The Home continued to be a magnet for celebrities, even if some arrived at the Home determined not to be recognized. In the late 1990s, when the Oscar-winning actor Kevin Spacey travelled to Battersea to be interviewed with a view to rehoming a dog, he displayed no airs and graces. Jade Hall, the rehoming staff member interviewing him, didn't recognize him, even when he gave his profession as "actor". All she noticed during his interview was that he had a lifelong love of dogs, a responsible attitude to pet ownership and that his manners were as immaculate as his suit.

It was only when one of the senior staff, Mel Wareham, saw his name on the standard application form that anyone realized who he was. Spacey left without fanfare, a happy black mongrel in tow.

Other famous visitors were more visible presences, however. The *Big Brother* television presenter Davina McCall spent a week coming back and forth to the Home weighing up the strays before choosing a Rottweiler called Rosie. When Geri Halliwell came to select her dog she arrived in the company of George Michael and a camera crew filming a reality TV series. Halliwell was eventually paired with a Shih Tzu called Harry, which became the former Spice Girl's constant – and much indulged – companion. The publicity both adoptions generated for the Home was gratefully received, but fleeting.

In 1997, however, the BBC offered the Home and its staff more lasting publicity. In effect, they wanted to make Battersea and its colourful canine, feline and human inmates celebrities in their own right. It began when producer Bob Long contacted the Home, asking permission to film a documentary charting its day-to-day life. Initially, Stephen Danos was told that the series would consist of thirty twenty-five-minute fly-on-the-wall programmes.

The request divided opinion wildly at the Home. The television schedules were filled at the time with so-called "docu-soap" series set in locations as diverse as luxury cruise liners and airports. Animals were a popular staple within the genre, with shows such as *Animal Hospital* and *Pet Rescue* particularly popular. Bell Mead had featured in a few short films on *Pet Rescue*.

The BBC's idea was for a much more significant series than this. The entire series would be filmed at Battersea and Bell Mead and was intended to give viewers a detailed and revealing insight into the work that went on at the Home. There was no doubt it offered huge publicity potential, but some on the Committee wondered whether the Home was a suitable subject for popular mainstream

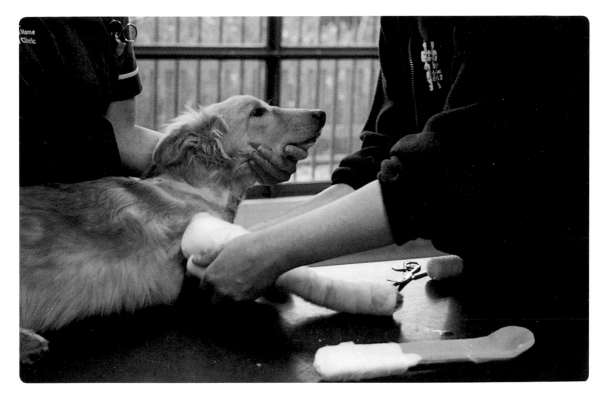

ABOVE As a broken bone is bandaged, this typical scene in the Battersea clinic is captured on film as part of the BBC TV series.

television while others were concerned about whether there was "sufficient drama to fill a thirty-programme series"; maybe there were "too many animal programmes already and yet another would be boring to the detriment of the Home's work". Most importantly, there may have been anxieties that the cameras would concentrate on the "bad" aspects of life at the Home, in particular the negative aspects of dog ownership that Battersea inevitably encountered, cases of "cruelty, abuse and neglect which we see daily and do not wish to be reminded of".

Bob Long and his co-producer, Steve Sklair, were invited to give the Committee a briefing. By this time there was also talk of a book to accompany the series, to be published by BBC Books. Long reassured the Committee that the stories would be positive: "This is daytime television – we want stories about the animals being cared for, maybe reunited with their owners or going to new homes," he told the meeting.

"Daytime television cannot be shocking," Sklair said. "It is watched by the full gamut, from young children to grandparents. In other words we don't want sensation, we just want to show people what you do." The BBC also promised to give the Home full editorial control.

When Long and Sklair had left there was a lengthy debate. When it came to a vote, however, all members of the Committee were in favour. Only the chairman, the Earl of Buchan, reserved judgement.

In March 1998, a small number of BBC staff began arriving at the Home. They were given space in some old offices within a disused warehouse that was, at the time, being used for agility training.

ABOVE The BBC crew films a dog being exercised in the shadow of the railway arches.

The pre-production process took two months and by May and June of that year filming was under way. The camera and sound crews blended into the life of the Home by wearing the staff's distinctive blue sweatshirts with the Battersea logo. Inevitably, some of the newcomers forged such strong bonds with the dogs they filmed that they ended up rehoming them.

Filming also took place at Bell Mead and, in particular, at the new home at Brands Hatch. The cameras captured the new wing of the Home taking shape as fencing was put up, dog runs laid out, electronic gates installed and new steps built, leading up the steep slope to the main building.

The BBC was there, too, on 26 October when the new extension of the Home officially opened its gates and received an immediate surprise in the shape of a stray cat that had been found locally. Within two weeks Brands Hatch had rehomed fifty cats, including the first-day arrival, as well as 150 dogs.

The thirty-minute show was initially a weekday programme and was first broadcast in December. The BBC was so pleased with the viewing figures that it was soon being repeated on a prime-time evening slot. According to the director general, it was the first time this had happened. Audiences were spectacularly good, peaking at around seven million.

The work that the series featured had, of course, been going on for almost 140 years. To the outside world, however, it was an eye-opening experience, one that was laced with humour and emotion. The series concentrated on explaining the day-to-day reality of life at the world's most famous animal sanctuary. As it did so, it transformed some of the staff into celebrities.

The Home's longest-serving van driver, Pauline Martignetti, featured in one episode: she was seen travelling hundreds of miles through London and around the M25 collecting dogs from police stations. Pauline, who by then had been with the Home for twenty-one years, revealed that one of the keys to her job lay in her body language: "I try to put myself in the dog's position. If I were locked up in a foreign jail and had no idea what anyone was saying to me, I wouldn't want some aggressive person coming at me with a big stick. But if someone came in with the right body language, the right attitude and talked to me in the right tone – even if it was double Dutch – then I'd know they were being kind and I'd be more likely to respond," she said.

She also revealed the most eventful moment of her time as a driver – when her van was stolen with eight dogs on board. It had been a Saturday morning and she had been filling up with petrol when it happened. A man jumped into the driver's seat and drove off in the direction of Vauxhall. Pauline had jumped into a two-seater sports car, explained who she was and instructed its driver to follow the van. "We tore along the Embankment towards Vauxhall like a scene from *Starsky and Hutch*," she said. As the van tried to corner Lambeth Bridge roundabout, the driver lost control. To Pauline's horror the vehicle toppled over. A Jack Russell dashed out, never to be recovered, but the other seven dogs were still inside and in one piece. "As far as they were concerned I was the driver responsible. And they all looked at me, as if to say: 'Was that *really* necessary?'"

Battersea's rehoming staff were seen at work. Again, the public had little idea of the stress, strain and frequent danger involved in this seemingly straightforward job. The days when people could turn up and simply walk away with a Battersea dog on the say-so of a friendly keeper were long gone. The Home's system for ensuring that its dogs and cats were only handed over to the most suitable households had become more and more stringent over the years. By the late 1990s, prospective owners were having to go through a long and detailed interview, checks with local authorities and other outside agencies and even, occasionally, home visits before they were allowed to leave with a Battersea dog or cat.

Most prospective owners understand and support this policy, but some do not. In the book accompanying the TV series, a group of rehomers shared some of their nightmarish experiences in dealing with the Home's less desirable visitors. "When I was interviewed to be a rehomer, we talked about dealing with someone who really pushed it and got very nasty," Jade Hall recalled. "I was asked if I'd give in and let them have a dog, and I said: 'No way. I'm not scared of anybody. I'd never let them wangle me into a corner and force me to do something I felt was wrong.' A couple of days after I started rehoming, three huge brothers came in wanting a German Shepherd. They didn't give much away and I guessed they had something to hide."

Jade eventually got the men to admit they had another dog. When she asked whether it would be able to come in to meet its potential new housemate, they confessed it was chained up in their father's garage and wasn't going anywhere.

When she refused to let them have a dog, "They were so gob-smacked that little me could stand there and say, 'No. You're not having a dog,' that they didn't argue. I just opened the door and they walked out."

Another rehomer, Paul Wilkins, had once been confronted by two giant men. When he insisted that they would require a home visit before they were given permission to take a dog, they became agitated. "One of them pushed a stick in my face and told me he was going to wrap it round my head," he said. Wilkins was able to get out of the interview room and call the police. "The whole experience scared me, because I honestly felt it wouldn't have taken much more for the men to have beaten me up."

May Whammond described how a drunken woman had become violent: "She grabbed me by the jumper and pinned me up against the wall." The woman, who had come in search of her lost dog, eventually calmed down but Whammond still had to take her round the entire Home before she would believe her dog wasn't on the premises. "She even accused me of hiding it and I had to insist that she went along all the aisles looking in every kennel to put her mind at rest."

The job had been even more perilous after the introduction of the Dangerous Dogs Act in 1991. Jackie Donaghy told of how she often had to deal with people coming to reclaim the Pit Bulls that had been confiscated by the police and sent to Battersea. "I got a phone call from Battersea Police warning me that a bloke whose Pit Bull we were holding had a record of all sorts of serious offences, including grievous bodily harm and arson. They assured me he wouldn't come to the Home because he knew his dog was illegal. But he did," she recalled. "He had tattoos and scars and broken teeth, and he said he wanted his dog back and he wasn't going to pay anything for it, and if he didn't get it, he was going to burn the place down."

Donaghy was well used to looking after herself but "I was really scared of him and felt like crying. I rang the police and three of them arrived, one in a bulletproof jacket. When he had gone, I couldn't believe how much I was shaking," she said. "We were all so worried that for the next few days we had the police on stand-by in case he carried out his threat to torch the Home."

Predictably, of course, it was the animals who generated the strongest response in the huge TV audiences. Viewers were particularly taken by a Lurcher called Urcher, one of the Home's longest-staying residents, who was now an example of how even the least promising dogs can be rehomed. Urcher had arrived at the Home in February 1985, a skeletal, flea- and mange-infested shell of a dog. He had been found by police on a travellers' site. Urcher was a reasonably well-behaved dog but he was withdrawn and didn't attract the interest of visitors. As can occasionally happen, the longer he stayed at the Home the more difficult he found it to tolerate the company of other dogs. He became aggressive towards them, so much so that staff decided he was not suitable for rehoming.

After thirteen months at the Home, however, it was decided to put him out to be fostered by a member of staff, Michelle Ritter. She had spent six months carefully easing Urcher back into the world. For most of that time he was aggressive towards other dogs and had to be kept on a very tight lead when out walking. Shortly before Christmas 1992, Urcher was attacked by a Staffordshire Bull Terrier, leaving him with physical – and psychological – scars that took a long time to heal. The Home's longest-serving resident withdrew even further into himself and staff began to despair that anyone would ever be willing to give him a home.

Urcher had been at the Home for eighteen months when the Home fielded a call from *Pet Rescue*. They were looking for a dog that might be suitable for an appeal. Urcher seemed the perfect candidate and was put forward.

The response was phenomenal, with 350 offers of a home within hours. Eventually Urcher went to live with Joe and Jane Belasco in Colchester. He settled into life with them and their other Lurcher, Bella, and put all his troubles behind him. The BBC programme showed how well he had done.

ABOVE Feeling the pinch: a cat is filmed receiving an injection in the clinic.

The impact on the Home was as immediate as it was dramatic. It was also surprising. Predictably there was a surge in calls. A special phone system had been installed to cope with the influx of enquiries expected to follow each transmission and it was soon being utilized. Often there were five hundred calls immediately after the programme was aired. There was also a significant rise in the number of visitors to both Battersea and Bell Mead. At the beginning of 1998 the normal visitor numbers over a weekend were between fifteen hundred and two thousand. No sooner had the programme begun than the figure had jumped to three thousand. Staff numbers had been increased in anticipation but even this wasn't enough to cope with the extra demand for dogs. Almost immediately staff were having to work ten-hour days over weekends. At one point Battersea had to close on

Thursday purely to catch up with the paperwork and to prepare the dogs for the next weekend rush. It was all worth it: as a result of the series more dogs were found homes, with, at one point, the Home rehoming nineteen dogs and ten cats in one day.

Even more spectacular was the impact on fundraising. Donations in December 1998 came to more than £43,000, a record and almost twice the figure of £24,000 in the previous December. During the first two months of 1999, as the series audience continued to grow, the Home received more than £1 million in legacies, which the finance sub-committee described as "extraordinary".

There were more surprising aspects to the series' impact. The number of dogs being handed into the Home by the public increased by around five dogs a day and, for the first time, was greater than the combined total of dogs received from the police and dog wardens.

Perhaps the most powerful and valuable effect that the series had, though, was one of perception. People began to understand that Battersea was a place where lost dogs were regularly found by their owners. They also, finally, accepted that dogs were not routinely destroyed after seven days. The greatest myth attached to the Home had finally been laid to rest. For that alone, the experiment of letting in the cameras had been worthwhile.

The success of the programme was such that a second series was soon being considered. The chairman suggested taking soundings from other companies who "could offer the Home money to do a series … Not to consider this could be regarded as not being prudent," he said. In the end, it was agreed that, having done so well with the first, the Home should accept a second series with the BBC. In the spring of 1999, the second series was given the go-ahead, with filming to begin in the summer.

The BBC was so pleased with the reception of the series that it gave the Home's staff £700 for a Christmas party. As a mark of appreciation for all the extra work they had done to make the show and its aftermath a success, every member of staff received a bonus of £100.

~

In the autumn of 1999, the Home capitalized further on its new profile by relaunching and renaming its official quarterly magazine, *Paws*. It had been publishing a variety of magazines for a decade and more. During the 1980s an annual junior members' magazine had been sent to all young subscribers. In 1994, Stephen Danos had overseen the first edition of the Home's official newspaper. It had been produced on a shoestring so was pretty unsophisticated. It was printed on poor-quality paper and contained, along with a series of

> **People began to understand that Battersea was a place where lost dogs were regularly found by their owners**

news reports, a curious "novelized" version of Sarah Major and Mary Tealby's momentous encounter with the stray in Canonbury Square in 1860, written by the new manager, Duncan Green.

What it lacked in polish, however, it more than made up for in commercial potential. The newspaper was filled with advertising, featuring ads from dog-food manufacturers and others. It paved the way for a magazine, called the *Dogs Home, Battersea*, which had now evolved into *Paws*. A thirty-six-page, high-quality glossy publication, *Paws* was a much more professional and accomplished piece of work. It featured news, interviews, advice and short stories on recent successes, as well as portraits of long-term Battersea residents most in need of a new home.

The first edition told the story of Viva, a black and tan mongrel who had been rehomed after more than three years at Battersea. The cover of the first edition carried a portrait of the BBC series' presenter, Shauna Lowry. It also featured practical tips and advice from the Home's expert vets and behaviourists.

The launch of *Paws* symbolized the breadth and sophistication of the public relations and marketing operation the Home was running. It now held an annual reunion in neighbouring Battersea Park, attracting hundreds of former residents and their

OPPOSITE Dolly, a mongrel who won many admirers during her stay at the Home, gazes at the camera.

owners who came to share their experiences. Its growing number of communications and event-management staff gave it a presence at public events from the Lord Mayor's Show to Gay Pride, and major canine events from Crufts to Discovering Dogs. It had even launched a Battersea credit card, in conjunction with Mastercard, which allowed users to donate a share of each transaction to the Home.

Nothing connected with the audience as well as a good story, however, and there were still plenty of those. Battersea dogs had always been popular as working dogs, with many continuing the tradition of Airedale Jack by joining the military. Since 1993 or so, the Home had forged a close relationship with the Defence Animal Centre at Melton Mowbray, in Leicestershire, providing a steady flow of dogs to be placed with the army, navy, air force or security services.

After graduating from the DAC, Battersea dogs had served in locations from Northern Ireland to Bosnia and the Falklands. They had also been given roles as sniffers and security guards at Heathrow, Gatwick and other airports.

For some dogs, it had been a life-saving move. In 1999, a German Shepherd, Jake, had been giving staff major headaches at the Home with his boisterous behaviour. Unsuited to life in the kennels, he had begun nipping staff and confronting other dogs and was facing a bleak future until head behaviourist Jackie Donaghy took him to the DAC. There, he was assessed and trained as a patrol dog. He was eventually given a posting to Germany where the military life suited him perfectly.

The Home's cats were equally sought after. In the summer of 1998 Battersea had been contacted by the new Globe Theatre, a few miles east along the south bank of the Thames. The management had arrived at the theatre one morning to discover its wooden stage overrun by mice. Their request was simple: did Battersea have any cats that might help to alleviate the problem?

Enter stage left two tabbies, christened Portia and Brutus by the Shakespearean staff. The pair quickly fitted into life at the theatre, lying around minding their own business during daytime rehearsals and evening performances, then patrolling the theatre by night. The delighted management was soon reporting mission accomplished. Portia and Brutus were cast in long-term roles at the Globe.

They weren't the only mousers hired from the Home that year. Dr Johnson's House, a museum in Gough Square, also contacted the Home for a cat to deal with its mice. Johnson was, apparently, a cat lover, feeding his favourite pet Hodge on oysters. The Battersea cat was named after another of Johnson's pets, Lily, about whom he wrote in 1738. She quickly proved a popular attraction at the museum, not just by keeping the mice at bay but by providing brides married at Dr Johnson's House with a lucky black cat for the photographs on their big day.

But with the growth of the Internet, there was also the potential to connect Battersea and its message with the entire world. All it needed was the right story, which appeared in 2004.

Ever since the Home had moved to Battersea in 1871, staff had talked of the site being haunted. Keepers and kennelmaids alike had sworn they had seen the spectral figure of a lady in Victorian dress, walking beneath the railway arches or in the corridors of the kennels. Some believed it was the ghost of Mary Tealby. Such talk had always been dismissed as fanciful nonsense.

In the autumn of 2004, however, there seemed to be no other explanation for the curious events that were unfolding in one of the kennel blocks each night. How else were up to nine dogs managing to get out of their pens and into the block's kitchen to help themselves to treats when the staff had left?

The mystery had first surfaced in September. Staff had been arriving in the kennel block each morning to find it looking like a bomb site. The scene was, according to one staff member, "a complete mess with dogs and food everywhere". On each occasion a few dogs were out of their cages. One was a Lurcher called Red.

In an attempt to discover what was happening the Home asked a film company to set up a closed-circuit television camera in the block. After a few nights, the real culprit was revealed. It wasn't Mary Tealby but Red.

Red had been brought into the Home in June that year with his brother, Lucky. Malnourished and badly cared for, he had been little more than fur, skin and bone when he had arrived. After a few months, however, he had been restored to good health and was ready to reveal that he was an exceptionally clever dog. The staff were amazed when they reviewed the footage. Red had clearly spent the past few months observing the staff opening and closing the powerful, spring-loaded catch on his door.

Within fifteen minutes of the day staff leaving the kennels, Red had slipped his long, narrow muzzle through the bars of his cage and used his needle-like teeth as prongs to flick the spring-loaded catch open. Not only that: having strolled out to freedom himself, he had then walked along the corridor repeating the same trick for a select few of his kennelmates, in particular, Bear, a white German Shepherd, Joel, a former racing Greyhound, and a Golden Retriever cross called Barney.

In an attempt to curtail his nocturnal activities, staff immediately put an extra lock on Red's door.

They also released the footage of the resourceful dog to the press. "As Red was so thin when he came in, we think it was his desire for food that spurred him on," one of the Home's publicists, Liz Emeny, told the press. "He was obviously getting very good at this as it was happening within fifteen minutes of the day staff leaving at five p.m."

In the age of the Internet, the grainy footage of the dog orchestrating the great escape soon became an online sensation, drawing huge audiences on sites like the BBC and later YouTube. It also helped generate a huge interest in Red, who was soon on his way to a new home in St Albans.

It wasn't long before he was up to his old tricks again. Two days later Cristina, his new owner, left him for the first time when she popped out for ten minutes to get a pint of milk. But when she returned she found her door locked. She had to stand, stranded in the cold and wet, for four hours while she waited for a locksmith to let her back into her house. When she discovered scratches on the door handle, she immediately suspected Red and – with the help of the *Daily Mail* – set up a camera. Sure enough, Red was captured on film locking her out.

Within minutes of his mistress leaving he would stand on his hind legs, bring his mouth level with a latch next to the door handle, then use his teeth to grip and push down the latch. "I might end up having to get a more secure lock," she said. "But I am not really angry because he is very playful and a great character. I didn't think I'd get Red because the dogs' home had so many enquiries about him, so I feel really lucky."

CHAPTER TWENTY-ONE

A TWENTY-FIRST-CENTURY HOME

THE AUTHOR ALDOUS HUXLEY was a notable dog lover. "To his dog every man is Napoleon; hence the constant popularity of dogs," he once – rather wisely – wrote. He also wrote something rather wise about history: "The charm of history and its enigmatic lesson consist in the fact that, from age to age, nothing changes and yet everything is completely different."

That principle certainly applied at Battersea. Even as a new millennium began the Home remained the same mixture of the old and the new, the familiar and the unfamiliar. Battersea continued to receive elderly, infirm and very sick dogs, so nothing had changed there, but in the new veterinary clinic much was different.

The Home's senior vet, Shaun Opperman, had arrived in 1991 as a locum and intended staying for "two to three weeks". In 2009 he was still there, overseeing facilities and veterinary services that bore no resemblance to those he'd begun to work with eighteen years earlier: "When I arrived the clinic was very basic, little more than a corridor with a few rooms, really. The only operating theatre was six feet square, not much bigger than a broom cupboard." Also when he began he was the only vet and was assisted by eight nurses. By 2009 there were five vets and twenty-five nurses.

The types of problems he has to deal with have remained broadly the same, but he and his team can now do much more to heal and prevent illness: "Veterinary science has moved on. Given that we know so little about the animals that come in to us, diagnostic work is very important so that we can provide owners with as much information

PREVIOUS PAGE "Whatever comes through the door":
a stray cat enjoys life, and human interaction, in the
Battersea cattery.

as possible about their new pet. For example, radiography and ultrasound are techniques which we use routinely to shed more light on heart problems in cats and dogs. We have such a large throughput here with two hundred or more animals coming in every week. Sometimes it feels like a conveyor-belt. We operate every day here and at Windsor, doing fifteen to twenty surgical operations a day. Of course, there is a lot of neutering to do, but we also perform a lot of other soft-tissue surgery, minor orthopaedics and seemingly endless dentals. Kennel cough is a particular challenge for us and our intensive-care areas are usually full."

The hardest part of the job remains taking the decision to put a dog or cat to sleep. That, too, hasn't changed in 150 years. "To our credit, Battersea has always taken in whatever comes through the door, whatever the condition of that animal. We will always do what we can to find a home for an animal but sometimes you are left with little choice. If you have an old dog with heart disease or severe arthritis, or a cat with kidney failure, then you have a responsibility to that animal," said Opperman. "If we didn't take them in, then what would happen to them? Euthanasia isn't something that you ever really get used to but it is a responsibility that comes with the job."

There is good news, though: "In the time that I have been here, one of the more obvious changes is that we rehome many more older dogs now than we used to. Perhaps that's a reflection of society. People's circumstances may be less certain now and they may not want the responsibility of a pet for ten to fifteen years," said Opperman. "Personally, I like the older ones – they seem to have more character.

Also, for some elderly owners, having a dog whose lifespan will mirror their own is an attraction."

Sickly dogs and cats remain only part of the picture, of course. Lost, abandoned, abused and homeless animals still arrive at the Home in their hundreds week in, week out. Another major difference now is that the chance of an owner being reunited with their lost pet is immeasurably better than it was fifty, twenty or even ten years ago. The Home's Lost Dogs and Cats Line was first established on 17 July 2000. The service uses a special database that collates details of registered animals with reports of lost and found cats and dogs from and around the Greater London area. Its growth has been remarkable. By 2007, more than three thousand dogs and cats a year were being reunited with their owners, and the team at the Home still regularly handles more than eighteen thousand lost and found reports each year.

No case illustrates the remarkable power of the scheme better than one dealt with by the service in November of that year. Lyn O'Byrne had been separated from her much-loved Lurcher, Rhia, in January 2001, when she had been living in Kent. An opportunistic thief had walked into Lyn's then veterinary surgery and calmly left with the dog. The theft had left Lyn distraught. She had done all she could to find Rhia, but with no luck.

Despite this, when she had moved to Brighouse in Yorkshire six years later Lyn had dutifully changed the details on the national microchip database that records the personal contact details of all dog owners. That autumn, Rhia somehow arrived at Battersea, though where she had been for six years remains a complete mystery. Among the routine checks carried out on all dogs, a member of staff scanned the microchip she found in Rhia's neck. It was then left to a member of the Lost and Found team to telephone an astonished Lyn with

ABOVE Cattersea: in 2005 the Home finally became known as the Battersea Dogs & Cats Home, despite admitting cats for the past century.

the news. Lyn and Rhia's reunion was among the happier scenes that Battersea has witnessed.

As ever, of course, there were other less positive developments. Perhaps the most striking and far-reaching change within the Home during the first decade of the new century has been the breed profile of the dogs now arriving at its reception desk. The breeds that found their way into Battersea's kennels had always been subject to change but since the 1990s the Home has witnessed a rapid rise in the number of bull breeds and so-called "status dogs". For much of the first hundred years, "mongrels" dominated the inventory. By 1973, when the Home first started listing the dogs received by breed, the ten most common, in descending order, were "Alsatians, Labradors,

Collies (all types), Poodles, Jack Russell (type), Greyhounds, Beagles, Boxers, Spaniels (all types) and Corgis".

Twenty years later, in 1993, that list was still headed by German Shepherds. But the third most common breed hadn't figured on the list two decades earlier, the Staffordshire Bull Terrier, 355 of which had been brought in that year. A decade later the Staffie had become by far the most common dog at the Home and at present the breed makes up more than 40 per cent of the Home's canine residents.

The Staffie has a long and distinguished history: it was first bred in the 1850s when a bulldog was crossed with an English white terrier, and its friendly, curious and courageous nature has made it a hugely popular pet. But it has fallen victim to its own success. During the 1990s back-street breeders began selling Staffies to all comers – many of whom

245

proved unsuitable owners, later abandoning them. The Staffie has also become a status dog among young people drawn to its macho image. This has created a vicious circle in which naturally friendly and sociable Staffies are developing behavioural problems and being increasingly abandoned as a result.

It is, in many ways, an echo of the Home's early days. "It conjures up the Dickensian image of Bill Sykes and Bullseye. Society has not progressed very far at all if you consider the way status dogs and fighting dogs are now so common in some areas of the country," said Scott Craddock, the Home's director of customer services.

Nothing has changed, yet everything is different. In particular, the Home is no longer content to sit back and watch society treat its dogs as status symbols to be discarded at whim. In the past it had simply built more kennels to accommodate the rising numbers. Now it prefers to engage in an attempt to change or challenge attitudes. "We mop up all the time, we are like the A and E service for London's dog and cat population. Every day we have to take hard decisions – and it's a heavy responsibility but it has to be done," said Craddock. "We could build endless kennels as the demand is almost infinite. But in the long term that is not the answer. We have to tackle the root causes of the problem if we are to continue to provide this vital service."

Battersea has, of course, always had its outspoken voices, from John Colam to Benjamin Knight. But they tended to speak as individuals rather than on behalf of the organization. Despite being better placed than most, Battersea had remained a quiet, almost passive voice in the animal welfare community, preferring to keep its own counsel. As the new decade progressed, this finally began to change.

The shift was summed up in 2009, when Battersea laid out a "strategic plan" for the next four years. The plan stated that, up until that time, Battersea had not seen itself as a campaigning organization and had taken a low-key media approach but that in the future the Home was to "become more proactive and use its position to speak out about, and influence, policy and debate on the issues that most affect it and the animals that come into its care".

By 2009 this policy was already in evidence, with staff talking more widely to the media about issues; from the rising numbers of Staffies and other "status dogs" to the fundamentals of good pet ownership and the benefits of rehoming rescue dogs and cats. In that year, Battersea took part in over thirty dog shows and local community events, and the Education Unit gave over 160 talks and presentations to schools and youth groups. The demand for information continues to grow, but the results are paying dividends.

For instance, in 2009 Battersea has increased the numbers of Staffordshire Bull Terriers being successfully rehomed. "We challenge the perception that these dogs should be branded as 'demon dogs'. " said Laura Jenkins, the Home's head of animal welfare. "And so far we have found that people are willing to listen. You do see changes in people's attitudes and their general willingness to consider a rescue dog. We've seen a twenty-one per cent increase in our rehoming figures in the past year, and that means that many of the dogs being rehomed are Staffies. We are also seeing more and more people coming back to get a second rescue dog and, in many cases, that means second Staffies."

OPPOSITE "An infinite demand": even as the twenty-first century began, Battersea was still overwhelmed by the number of arrivals, including this dog named Kane.

The usual suspects: five dogs obediently pose for the camera, including (left to right) Benji, Jonah, Milo, Blue and Rocky.

And yet, as always, the Home cannot control the way society – and its laws – change. For the ordinary dog owner, life had undoubtedly become more demanding and tightly regulated. During the first decade of the new millennium, the Animal Welfare Act placed a greater duty of care on pet owners, and the revised Clean Neighbourhoods and Environment Act has given local councils the right to restrict dog owners from using public parks and spaces. As a result, the popularity of keeping cats rather than dogs has risen – hence the Home's decision in July 2005 to change its official name to Battersea Dogs & Cats Home.

For the Home, however, by far the more significant piece of legislation was the Clean Neighbourhoods and Environment Act, which came into force on Sunday, 6 April 2008. It was

then that the police relinquished their duty to receive stray dogs, thus ending more than a century of tradition.

The police had pressed to be relieved of the responsibility for many years. Constables up and down the country had long complained that having to keep noisy and sometimes aggressive dogs inside police stations was a drain on resources. With the post-war rise in dog ownership the job had become more of a burden and the red tape involved had become overwhelming. In the run-up to the abolition of the dog licence in 1987, serious consideration had been given to forming a national Dog Warden Service, but this had come to nothing.

Instead the responsibility was passed on to local authorities. In 1990 the Environmental Protection Act required every authority to appoint an officer to deal with stray dogs and be in a position to "seize stray dogs where practicable". Slowly some local authorities had created kennelling services of their own and, by 1993, were taking in 130,000 strays a year.

So it was that the Home's morning collection runs focused on visits to the few council kennels that existed rather than the hundred-plus police stations that had previously accepted stray dogs. Some boroughs were better equipped to deal with the new landscape than others. So, perhaps unsurprisingly, the 2008 legislation saw an immediate increase in the number of dogs arriving at Battersea, with a thousand more brought in during the first year after its adoption than in the previous twelve months.

ABOVE Blue, a "super-intelligent" Border Collie who was adopted by a member of staff, ponders the daily crossword.

As so often in the past, Battersea was expected to deal directly with the operational consequences of this new legislation. The irony was that it was having to do so during the deepest recession in a generation, and in an environment when it needed to modernize and develop its services at a rate unprecedented in its history.

Innovations and new practices were being brought in on an almost daily basis, from a new cat-fostering scheme to an online rehoming application system, from a new cattery at Old Windsor to brand new facilities for both cats and dogs at Brands Hatch. There were even plans for another Home outside London, to be opened by "the end of 2013". The familiar office building at the entrance to the Home was flattened to be replaced by a more modern and spacious cattery. Yet donations and legacies were dropping off as the Home increasingly found itself competing for funds with other, newer, animal-welfare charities.

The irony wasn't lost on Howard Bridges, who took over as interim chief executive in the autumn of 2009. As the Home's former director of estates, Bridges knew better than anyone the commercial value of the Home's three sites. For the London site, plans to re-develop the adjoining Battersea Power Station into a luxurious retail and residential development would, in the coming years, inflate that value yet further. "If this place didn't exist, if this site had been turned into a supermarket or become another upmarket residential development, what would happen to these dogs and cats? I don't think people have ever given it a thought. It's assumed that Battersea will naturally and automatically continue to do what it does, what it has done for the past hundred and fifty years," said Bridges.

He was, of course, expressing a sentiment that had been voiced regularly ever since the move south of the river in 1871. It was a reality that had been best summed up at the start of the new century, in 2000, by the then chairman, the Earl of Buchan: "If only people would understand what is involved when they take on an animal, we could reduce the number of strays and unwanted dogs and cats ending up here. One day, I'd like to get a call from the Home to say we have an empty house, instead of a full one, but I don't think that will ever happen while we have people out there who simply do not realize the obligations of dog and cat owners.

"It worries me that in the twenty-first century we are still dealing with cruelty to animals. When the Home was first founded there was bull- and bear-baiting in this country, and London's streets teemed with homeless dogs and cats. Have we really advanced that much since then?"

The answer – of course – was yes and no. Nothing had changed, and yet everything was different.

~

A century and a half later, nothing remains of the refuge Mary Tealby opened in the dark, damp stables on Hollingsworth Street in October 1860. Neither the mews, nor indeed the street, are still there. Her old home, at 20 Victoria Road, is no longer standing either, having been demolished by a German bomb during the Blitz. Today the site of the original Home for Lost and Starving Dogs stands in the middle of an Islington council park on a piece of ground that now – rather aptly – is home to an inner city farm.

But if Mary Tealby's ghost really did return to walk the yards, railway arches and corridors of the modern Home a few miles to the south in Battersea, she would find that while much

had changed there was still much that was comfortingly familiar.

She would no doubt be amazed at the sheer scale and complexity of today's operation – not just one Home but three, supported by a large workforce and more than three hundred dedicated volunteers with an annual budget of around £13 million – still funded almost entirely by public donations. She would also marvel at the work of the on-site veterinary and behaviour teams, who work tirelessly to reshape animals' lives and to offer the best possible chance of finding permanent new homes. She would nod approvingly at the way the modern staff welcome each arrival with the same care and compassion that her original keeper, James Pavitt, showed, and she would certainly take great pride in the fact that more than five thousand dogs and cats are successfully rehomed every year, their lives changed for the better by the support and care they receive from the Battersea staff and volunteers.

However, she would also shake her head with anger and disbelief at the appalling treatment owners still mete out to the most underprivileged and abused dogs, and now cats. And she would almost certainly show her frustration at how the Home is still nearly always full to capacity.

Most of all she would recognize that the Home is still dedicated to the same simple principles that she, Edward Bates, Sarah Major and the rest of the original Committee enshrined when they sat down in the autumn of 1860. Its mission statement is still: "to do whatever it takes to make sure we never turn away a dog or cat that needs our help."

The work she began continues. As does the remarkable story of Battersea Dogs & Cats Home …

OPPOSITE Battersea's cats and dogs are often cared for by the many volunteers who give up their time at the Home.

ABOVE A quiet reminder: Angus.

ACKNOWLEDGEMENTS

RESEARCHING AND WRITING THIS BOOK WAS A HUGELY ENJOYABLE EXPERIENCE AND FOR THAT MY primary thanks must go to the staff at Battersea. In all I spent almost two years rummaging through the assorted boxes, books, ledgers, cuttings collections, minutes and files that constitute the Home's archives. It was a time of change within the Home's management, but the warmth of the welcome and the help I received never wavered.

In particular I would like to thank both the Home's former and present head of communications, Helen Dexter and her successor Claire Filby, both of whom were this book's most generous supporters. I would also like to thank the current chief executive, Howard Bridges, and his predecessor, Jan Barlow, for their encouragement and input. Many other members of staff helped me along the way but I would like to express my particular gratitude to the following: Helen Mirko, Charlotte Fiander, Siobhan Wakely, Claire Palmer, Alison Russell, Rachel Tooby, Kate Ward, Amy Watson, Scott Craddock, Laura Jenkins, Micky Swift, Shaun Opperman, Kirsty Walker, Lucinda Lighting and June Haynes. Apologies to anyone I have overlooked.

My publishers, Transworld, also underwent some changes during the book's journey from embryonic idea to finished manuscript. I must first thank its former publishing director, Francesca Liversidge, for asking me to do the job in the first place. While I was terribly sad to see Francesca leave Transworld, I was delighted to be given the opportunity to work with the brilliant Sally Gaminara. She lived up to her five-star reputation and provided all the support and encouragement I needed to cross the finishing line. Kate Tolley was equally brilliant in her editorial role, particularly in helping me sift through the Home's mass of photographs and other visual material. I would also like to thank copy editor Hazel Orme for her excellent work in ironing out the manuscript and designer Bobby Birchall. Thanks, too, as ever, to my agent Mary Pachnos and my wife Cilene and children Gabriella and Thomas.

A huge vote of thanks must also go to Antoinette Sutton for her genealogical research into the life of the mysterious Mary Tealby. It is a huge injustice that the founder of the Home is one of the least celebrated women of the Victorian era. Without Mrs Tealby, Battersea wouldn't exist. Without Toni's relentless and inventive detective work, this would have been a much diminished book.

Perhaps fittingly, my final thanks must go to a dog, a regular at the Battersea offices named Angus, a rather elderly Collie whose acquaintance I made during my visits to the Home. Each time I took up residence in the office which served as my most regular bolthole, Angus would pad in and lie down at my feet. He would remain there, impassive yet happy to snooze – and sometimes snore – the day away. On more than one occasion I had to clamber over his inanimate form to leave my desk.

On the very rare occasion when I lost sight of why Battersea remains such an important and unique establishment, even in the twenty-first century, Angus reminded me.

Since the Home first opened its doors in 1860, millions of vulnerable dogs and cats have been able to call this place their home. It is a truly remarkable institution, which deserves its place in the nation's affections and the continued support of animal lovers everywhere.

INDEX

TRANSWORLD PUBLISHERS
61–63 Uxbridge Road, London W5 5SA
A Random House Group Company
www.rbooks.co.uk

First published in Great Britain in 2010 by Bantam Press
an imprint of Transworld Publishers

A CIP catalogue record for this book
is available from the British Library.

ISBN 9780593059678

Addresses for Random House Group Ltd companies outside the UK
can be found at: www.randomhouse.co.uk
The Random House Group Ltd Reg. No. 954009

The Random House Group Limited supports the Forest Stewardship
Council (FSC), the leading international forest-certification organization. All our
titles that are printed on Greenpeace-approved FSC-certified paper carry the FSC logo.
Our paper procurement policy can be found at
www.rbooks.co.uk/environment

Designed by Bobby Birchall, Bobby&Co
Typeset in Minion Pro
Printed and bound in Great Britain by Butler Tanner & Dennis Ltd.

2 4 6 8 10 9 7 5 3 1

As a charity that receives no central government funding and relies almost entirely on donations from members
of the public, Battersea Dogs & Cats Home is constantly looking for ways to raise money or generate income
that will allow it to continue its work.

There are many ways in which you can help. If you would like to donate to Battersea Dogs & Cats Home,
or to find out more about any of the Home's fundraising schemes, please visit the website:
www.battersea.org.uk/get_involved/index.html
Alternatively you can text 'Home' to 70123 to make a direct donation. Thank you.